Why do singers sing in the way they do? Why, for example, is western classical singing so different from pop singing? How is it that Freddie Mercury and Montserrat Caballé could sing together? These are the kinds of questions which John Potter, a singer of international repute and himself the master of many styles, poses in this fascinating book, which is effectively a history of singing style. He finds the reasons to be primarily ideological rather than specifically musical. His book identifies particular historical 'moments of change' in singing technique and style, and relates these to a three-stage theory of style based on the relationship of singing to text. There is a substantial section on meaning in singing, and a discussion of how the transmission of meaning is enabled or inhibited by different varieties of style or technique.

VOCAL AUTHORITY

Richard, I guess most
of this is your fault ...
but thanks anyway!

John P

VOCAL
AUTHORITY

Singing style and ideology

JOHN POTTER

CAMBRIDGE
UNIVERSITY PRESS

PUBLISHED BY THE PRESS SYNDICATE OF THE UNIVERSITY OF CAMBRIDGE
The Pitt Building, Trumpington Street, Cambridge CB2 1RP, United Kingdom

CAMBRIDGE UNIVERSITY PRESS
The Edinburgh Building, Cambridge CB2 2RU, United Kingdom
40 West 20th Street, New York, NY 10011–4211, USA
10 Stamford Road, Oakleigh, Melbourne 3166, Australia

First published 1998

Printed in the United Kingdom at the University Press, Cambridge

Typeset in Baskerville 11/12½ pt [CE]

A catalogue record for this book is available from the British Library

Library of Congress cataloguing in publication data
Potter, John, tenor.
Vocal authority: singing style and ideology / John Potter.
p. cm.
Includes bibliographical references and index.
ISBN 0 521 56356 9 (hardback)
1. Singing – Interpretation (Phrasing, dynamics, etc.)
2. Singing – Instruction and study.
3. Vocal music – History and criticism.
I. Title.
MT892.P68   1998
783'.043 – dc21 97–11031 CIP MN

ISBN 0 521 56356 9 hardback

for
A. G. POTTER
(1918–1988)

Contents

Preface

This book is an attempt to shed some light on why singers are more likely to sing in certain styles than others; it is about how singing styles evolve, change and relate to each other. It began life as a PhD thesis, which I researched while working as a singer. Like many so-called products of the English choral tradition, I first began to sing at about the age of seven, when I joined my local church choir at the insistence of my father, who happened to be the organist. A small amount of talent and a lot of parental vision enabled me eventually to get a place at the choir school of King's College, Cambridge just as the Boris Ord era was giving way to that of David Willcocks. The daily round of practices and services in that glorious fifteenth-century chapel leaves an ineradicable mark on the children privileged to sing in it, and when I moved on at the age of fourteen it seemed the most natural thing to want to return to one of the Oxford or Cambridge colleges as an undergraduate to carry on where I had left off. In the mid-sixties, therefore, with a newly acquired tenor voice, I found myself having singing lessons in order to attempt the necessary choral scholarship. At about the same time as I started this rather serious business, I became caught up in something entirely other: the almost visceral excitement that was the sixties pop scene. Like thousands of other teenagers, I started a band to play rhythm and blues, and became fascinated both by the music itself and the question of 'authenticity' in blues performance. Teenage bands of that era had an almost religious respect for Muddy Waters, Howlin' Wolf and a host of other more obscure singers, yet we still assumed the right to make their songs our own and would happily compare our versions with the 'originals' and with those of other bands.

Naturally enough, or unnaturally enough as it seemed to me then, I had to sing in one way to get a choral scholarship and quite another when fronting my band. Although the musics were very different from each other, I could see no musical reasons why two utterly incompatible modes of singing were required. I was not a very good blues singer, and I put it down to the fact that my 'classical' training inhibited my blues delivery. Even forming the words in a natural manner seemed to be hugely difficult. And anyway, how could I, by then a thoroughly middle-class English boy, hope to imitate these American accents with any integrity? At least the Beatles had decent regional accents. My career as a pop singer did not last long (though I later did some session singing for well-known seventies bands), and I went on to become a 'classical' singer, seemingly the only possibility that my background allowed.

The question of why classical singing is so different from pop singing has gnawed at me ever since, and during the seventies and eighties it became even more pressing when conventional attitudes to singing began to be questioned by the early music phenomenon and the exploration of avant-garde vocal techniques which paralleled it (and had actually been going on for several decades). I found myself again involved in a plurality of singings ranging from the conventional variety that I had been taught through to the more esoteric styles that some of us were trying to rediscover or invent. Curiosity (research is too dignified a term for it) led me to look at Renaissance and baroque singing treatises with the idea of finding out whether or not pop and classical singing may once have been the same thing, that there had perhaps been a time when singing was simply singing, and singers did not have to make these socio-musical distinctions. The more I delved, the more complicated the question became, and I eventually formalised my search into a PhD thesis with the Open University while still continuing to make the music itself as a career. I still sing, and I still engage in a kind of critical dialogue with my chosen profession, so this book should be read as a kind of work-in-progress written against a background of continuing experience.

It soon became became clear to me that if there ever was some sort of primal song it could only have existed in a social context, and that singing styles evolved as sociological circumstances changed. I did not find that I could make specific links between singing and society (although some anthroplogical studies suggest a case for this), but rather that a general ideological process works on the singer in the society in which he or she finds him- or herself. The earliest writings about singing imply the communication of a text, and it is an underlying assumption of this study that whatever else singing may do, if it has an archetypal function it is to enable words to be communicated in a particular way. My main conclusion is that however singing develops, whether the singer is Mick Jagger or Elisabeth Schwarzkopf, stylistic renewal is driven by a need to find more appropriate ways to deliver the text. Exactly what these ways are will depend on the sociological context in which the music is sung. Historically, there have been many moments at which it is possible to identify significant text-related stylistic change. This is often followed (and in the examples I give in this study, always followed) by a period of development during which the style becomes in some way more elaborate or virtuosic, eventually reaching a plateau beyond which further evolution is not possible until another text-related change is triggered.

Because the task at the back of my mind was to explain why singers such as myself have to sing in different ways in different circumstances, my account is inevitably a personal and Anglocentric view of singing in the West. There is a much broader cultural question yet to be tackled, and each chapter implies questions for further research. I have used evidence from non-English sources generally where it pertains to a notional outcome relevant to singers in England today. It would be impossible to write an account of any classical singing tradition, for example, without referring to Italian singing, and the same principle applies to pop music and the USA. The book is not intended to be a comprehensive history of singing (which would need many volumes) but a broadly chronological series of snap-shots of periods where stylistic developments seem to me to be particularly significant. I begin not quite at the very beginning, though as close to it as the surviving evidence will permit, with a brief discussion of that period of antiquity which gave us the word 'classical'. This is followed by chapters on the medieval and baroque periods, in which I look at the nature of singing in secular and sacred contexts before the development of what we would recognise as a modern technique. Exactly how the voice works, and how it came to be used in opera in a very specific way is considered next, and this is followed by a chapter on choral singing. I then turn to popular music, beginning with the earliest recordings which can tell us what the singing actually sounded like. Chapters 6–8, dealing with more recent popular music and alternative varieties of singing

Acknowledgements

I owe a great debt to the many people who have inspired me to sing or encouraged me to write: to my late father, who in many senses started me off on this quest; my fellow members of the long-derailed South Bound Blues Train (and its successors with names too embarrassing to mention); Edred Wright, for stimulating my interest in 'serious' singing; Ward Swingle, for opening my eyes to the way words really work; Richard Wistreich, the other wing of Red Byrd, for our often-terrifying flights into the vocal unknown, and my Hilliard Ensemble colleagues for occasionally and unwittingly acting as a kind of living laboratory. Thanks also to Richard Middleton at the Open University, whose supervisory sessions were enormously thought-provoking and kept my intellectual spirits up over a very long period. I am grateful to Donald Burrows, who suggested that what I had written might be a book, and to Alan Durant who in coining the phrase 'vocal authority', turned a conceptual ragbag into a useful portmanteau and gave the book its title. I should especially like to thank John Butt, Richard Middleton and Christopher Page whose many perceptive and helpful comments on earlier drafts encouraged me to make the book a good deal more user-friendly than it might otherwise have been. None of this would have been possible without the unstinting support of my wife Penny.

Parts of chapters 6 and 7 have been previously published in *Omega* (Open University Press, 1995) and *Companion to Medieval and Renaissance Music* (ed. Fallows and Knighton, Dent/Oxford University Press, 1992) and are used by permission.

I am grateful to the British Voice Association for permission to reproduce the diagrams on page 97, from D. Howard, 'Quantifiable Aspects of Different Singing Styles' (*Voice 1*, 1992).

Lyric reproduction of 'Birth of the Blues' (lyric by Buddy deSylva and Lew Brown, music by Ray Henderson) is by kind permission of

Redwood Music Ltd. for the territories of the Commonwealth of Nations, Germany, Austria, Switzerland, South Africa and Spain, and by kind permission of Warner Chappell Music Inc. for the rest of the world.

'Rockin' Chair' by Hoagy Carmichael copyright © 1929 by Peer International Corporation. Copyright renewed. International copyright secured. Used by permission.

CHAPTER I

Classical ideology and the pre-history of singing

The human voice is a marker of individual personality: no two voices sound the same. When the speaking voice is extended into song it becomes the supreme articulator of human desires, emotions and aspirations; almost every individual (or group of individuals) has the potential to use this resource in whatever way is appropriate. Every utterance we make, from the first scream or grunt onwards, is conditioned by our own past and that of the society we live in, and most of the time neither singer or listener is conscious of this ideological baggage that we all carry with us. In western society of the late twentieth century there seems to be an infinite number of vocal styles and techniques (a style being the outward sign of a singing variety, a technique the means of its realisation). The relationships between varieties of singing change over time according to the needs of singers and listeners. One variety, that used for what we in the West call classical music, appears to have a uniquely authoritative status relative to all other possible kinds.[1] Its current status (and that of all kinds of singing) is the result of historical processes that have formed and re-formed over many hundreds of years. We all know what we think we mean by the commonsense term 'classical music' and the classical singing that comes with it. What is less easy to grasp is the idea that the concepts that underlie the term are extremely ancient, and although the use of the word 'classical' in connection with music dates only from the nineteenth century, the ideology behind it stretches back to classical antiquity and beyond.

The self-limiting orality of singing, its very existence defined by its transience, means that a historical study of the subject which pre-dates the gramophone era relies not on direct evidence in the medium itself, but on speculation based on written sources. Evidence for singing in pre- and proto-historical times depends on a

tenuous mixture of iconographical archaeology and literary extrapolation, to which may be added the cautious use of ethnomusico-
logical and anthropological studies. The link between speculation
about pre-history and deductions about the earliest historical
evidence is particularly problematic: while anthropological theories
have been developed to account for singing in 'primitive' societies,
little work has been done on how this relates to the earliest
historical references such as the Babylonian fragments.[2] The oldest
surviving musical artefacts are palaeolithic bone whistles, which are
extremely crude compared with the Mesopotamian harps from the
mid third millennnium BC. It is probable that an oral tradition of
thousands of years, to which we shall never have access, occupies
the space between these two varieties of instrument, between the
anthropological theories of Livingston, Richman and others, and
the musicology of the ancient world which essentially began with
Sachs and Wellesz.[3] Compared with the millennia during which
oral traditions apparently flourished, written music has a very short
pedigree.

In most early representations of musical activity (harpists represented on cylinder seals, for example)[4] it is not possible to be certain
whether the player is also singing or speaking. It is only when
notation of some sort appears to coincide with text that we can be
reasonably sure that the text was actually sung. A critical moment
for the study of singing therefore occurs at the point where the
earliest indications of literacy are to be found. This is important not
only for the implications that flow from the idea of a literate culture,
but also because of the light that may be shed on the (presumably)
advanced oral culture that might have preceded it, interacted with
it, and probably continued to co-exist with it. Similar periods of
oral–literary interaction are to be found in Gallo-Roman Europe,
where the legacy of classical texts existed alongside an evolving oral
culture and again in Europe after the invention of the printing press,
which fundamentally altered the definition of literacy. In the late
twentieth century we are in the process of coming to terms with a
plurality of literacies, a consequence of the development of information technology and electronics, one aspect of which is the
legitimisation of Afro-American 'oral' musics as important cultural
forms in a society in which literacy is conventionally thought of as
playing a central cultural role. The earliest periods at which
oral–literary interaction can be analysed are therefore of particular

significance to a sociological study of singing, especially since (as I argue below) this terrain forms the field in which the ideology underlying a number of central concepts in western music first emerges.

It is as well to be clear what is meant by literacy and orality (although different definitions may be seen to apply in different circumstances and periods). There is a misplaced assumption in much twentieth-century writing that oral and literate cultures are mutually exclusive.[5] The earlier writers were bound to what Leo Treitler (1981) has called the 'literary paradigm' where it was assumed that orality was a primitive precursor of literacy. This meant, in musical terms, that research was conducted with the assumption that the function for which notation eventually evolved was somehow inherent in it as its goal at all stages of its development. Anything that did not fit the model was discarded (which in itself illustrates what has become one of the characteristics of literacy: the ability to support reflexive analysis). The bias towards literacy is further compounded by the fact that all academic work is of necessity literate, and the attempts of more recent writers to come to terms with this has occasionally led to considerable irony.[6] As Richard Middleton (1990) has pointed out, a performance is in some sense always 'oral', which precludes the more extreme reductive theories. A further stage in the definition of a purely 'oral' performance is the fact that it exists only for as long as the performance takes. A written piece has a life independent of its performance and can be decontextualised (or rather re-contextualised); purely oral musics are context specific. The performance of oral music is also the means of its transmission, which is then dependent on specific social contexts for its dissemination. Written music is transmitted independently of its performance by a class of scribes who may not actually perform the music at all. What we cannot know (because the surviving sources are few and fragmentary) is how the first notations related to the oral tradition in which they arose.

There has been a good deal of research on early Christian chant which suggests that notation arose in that context for two related reasons: to unify a system of widely varying traditions in order for 'a full and flawless record of the truth'[7] to prevail, both in ritual performance and in the learning process that is the means of transmission. The unitary tradition is of fundamental importance in defining the terrain on which socio-musical relations evolve. The dominance of any one tradition implies an ideological dominance where such variants as there might be become marginalised as the central tradition achieves an accepted legitimacy. This analysis is certainly appropriate to the Frankish empire in which Christian chant notation first appeared, and a similar case may be made for the earliest Greek notations. However, in stating the case for an ideologically determined change we must bear in mind the implications of Treitler's caveat that a new development does not of itself imply a specific series of related developments. The new ideology defines the terrain in which such developments are likely to occur, but a complex and potentially infinite variety of possibilities may be unleashed by such a change. The use of symbols in learning ritual chant must also have had considerable advantages in terms of time, for example, compared with a presumed mixture of mnemonic and formulaic learning that it came to replace. This is a purely practical result, but a further consequence with ideological implications is that in exchange for easier access to the tradition the receiver of it gave up the possibility of adding his own features to it. This pragmatic consideration would in time become embedded in the ideology: it would be impossible to conceive of the music except in terms of what could be written. As Susan Rankin (1984) put it: 'Once notational practice had altered to allow a greater degree of pitch definition by placing notes on a Guidonian stave . . . all melodic repertories had to be notated acording to the same criteria. This is a sophisticated system, not one that would develop into something else.'

Anthropologists and ethnomusicologists have given a great deal of thought to the relationship between music and ritual, and it is in these fields that an idea of the link between oral cultures and written traditions may eventually be discerned. The earliest recognisable (though, as yet, undecipherable) notation occurs in an Assyrian document dated to around 800 BC.[8] It consists of a text, each line of which is preceded by what were for a long time considered to be nonsense syllables. Research carried out on the Samaritan sect during the 1960s and 70s suggested that these syllables may in fact be musical notation. The Samaritans, of which only a few hundred members survive, have been the subject of much attention from philologists, anthropologists and musicologists as the sect appears to have preserved its traditions virtually unchanged for some two and a half thousand years, having been separated from Judaism since some time in the first millennium BC. Evidence of continuity in the Samaritan tradition comes from their similarity to the rituals of Yemenite, Kurdish and Lithuanian Jews, who have been separated from each other since the post-AD 70 diaspora. It is now thought that the Assyrian syllables represent groups of notes, similar versions of which appear in Samaritan neumes. Some of the Samaritan signs are apparently ornamental, having become so when the meaning of the signs (which were supposed to be secret from the layman) failed to be passed on to the following generation.[9] The tradition of secrecy in early notations (similar examples can be found in India, Egypt and Ethiopia) is a curious one. In a culture where the only known use for writing was for recording commercial transactions and what would now be called stock control, it is odd that the meaning of a ritual formulation should be entrusted to this medium, rather than be passed on directly to the intended recipient by word of mouth. A possible answer (which recalls Treitler's warning not to see the final destination inherent in the process) is that musical notation was closer to a magical formula, something that would inform initiates to whom its use was restricted, and intimidate the majority who were outside the priest cult. Its only connection with other cuneiform writings is that both are semiotic systems.

The Mycenean civilisation of the second millennium BC was also literate in that it used a form of writing (Linear B) to record commercial and legal transactions. There is no evidence that the alphabet was used for literary or artistic purposes of any kind, and it subsequently fell into disuse when the civilisation was destroyed around 1200 BC. Evidence that an oral culture flourished during this period is provided in spectacular form, however, by the appearance in the eighth century BC of the 27,000 Greek hexameters that make up the *Iliad*. For a long time Homer was thought to be the father of European literature, who had somehow conjured up out of nowhere one of the longest poems in any language. Thanks to the work of Parry and Lord and their successors it is now generally accepted that the *Iliad* represents not the beginning of a new tradition but the watershed at which an oral poetry was written down.[10] Pre-literate societies are essentially rural and tribal, and the collective memory of tribal society reinforces its cohesiveness. That memory, or mythology, resides in the epics or sagas created by both the poet-singers of ancient Greece and the bards of post-Roman Europe. The singer of such poems was neither composer nor performer in the modern sense. Using a formulaic system the poem would be re-created for each performance, the performer in effect becoming the text in a way that ensured not only its performance but the survival and transmission of the mythology of which it was a part. The subjects of oral epics are typically family loyalty and war, with which all strata of a tribal society can identify, but they were performed by specialists who presumably had to spend many hours at the feet of a master. Thus although the oral epic takes a different form from its written counterpart, there is probably considerable overlapping of social function.

The epic was not the only form of singing known to pre-literate societies (though it is through literacy that we are aware of other varieties). Homer tells of singing associated with drinking and after-dinner entertainment, a context in which the oral formulae of transmission of the epics themselves must have developed, but there are also ritual songs which accompany weddings and funerals, the latter using professional mourners for formalised laments, a custom that still persists in the Aegean today. There is more private music, sung to the *phorminx* (a plucked, harp-like instrument), and early examples of the association of singing, dancing and gymnastic or athletic display so characteristic of Greek culture. It may also be assumed that the worksongs mentioned by later authors were also being sung at this time. Athenaeus, for example, mentions songs sung by flour-grinders, loom-workers, wool-workers, bath atten-dants and reapers, among others.[11] In their pre-written form the Homeric poems would probably have been chanted to the accom-paniment of the *phorminx*, in a heightened form of speech. This flourishing musical tradition gives no hint as to why it was suddenly considered appropriate to inscribe 27,000 lines of Homeric verse. The fact that the *Iliad* and *Odyssey* are at least twice as long as any other known Greek epic might perhaps have been a reason to preserve them, had there been any danger of their disappearing. There is no evidence for this (indeed the tradition seems to have continued, and Parry and Lord's work in the former Yugoslavia suggests that an oral tradition will work within and beside a literary one if the social conditions are appropriate). Lord's own theory is that the application of writing to poetry occurred in eighth-century Greece because a similar phenomenon had happened elsewhere in the East. He observes that the earliest Old Testament books were written down in the ninth century, and that King Sargon II of Assyria had established a library at Nineveh which contained works dating from the second millennium. In this cultural climate the Greeks would tend to emulate their neighbours, to whom they owed many aspects of their culture. While Lord's answer may be valid as far as it goes, his hypothesis begs the question of why the Assyrians, Hebrews, Sumerians and others felt it necessary to commit their oral poetry to a permanent form. I suggested above that a move towards literacy may be associated with a shift in power relations, and the epics appear in written form at about the same time as a change in the relations of production that accompanied the development of the urban socio-economic systems which replaced tribal relations in Hellenic Greece. The minstrel of the oral tradition was, it appears, a free man. This was not the case in Hellenic Greece: Aristotle (*Politics* 1341) forbids education in performance techniques as 'appropriate not to free men, but to menials' in contrast to an earlier period where the gods themselves had indulged in song. It was a time when what Maróthy (1974) calls the bourgeois 'ego' begins to assert itself: an individualism replacing the 'collective' manifestations of earlier society. The military expansion under the Tyrannies (*c.* 650–510) enabled a relatively free peasantry to be replaced by large-scale slave labour, thus releasing freemen 'to emancipate their ruling stratum for the construction of a new civil and intellectual world' (Anderson, 1988, p. 35). The slave mode of production had the practical consequence of enabling an agrarian economy to be successfully run by absentee landowners who lived in the Greek 'polis', a city in which leisure was the only occupation fitting for free men, and which produced an environment in which education, militarism, sport and the arts could be developed for their own sake.

A consequence of the association of work (and therefore specialisation) with vulgarity was the separation in status of the performer and his audience. In such a polarised society (the proportion of slaves to free men at any given time could be as high as two to one) two distinct strata were the norm: a free class of appreciators, consumers of broad education who formed the potential audience, and an understratum of unfree specialists ranging from artisans to gymnasts and musicians. Free men developed the science of music as an academic and philosophical discipline; practical music-making, beyond the minimum necessary for educational purposes, was the province of the unfree. This separation of music into its practical and theoretical aspects was to have important consequences for later European culture, contributing to the idea of a permanent intellectual elite in whom resides the true nature of music, a music whose existence is in the first instance a written one.

A further development towards the musical ideology of the present day was the separation of the performance of music from its transmission. In the 'instant' creativity of the formulaic oral tradition these two aspects were inseparable. The function of epic poetry and the idea of performance adapted to the new system of socio-economic relations. The oral epic continued, but its context changed. The rural courts in which the epics had originally been made as post-prandial entertainment had disappeared. The collective mythology and history still needed to be expressed, and this took the form of the competitive festivals of music and sport in which individual excellence was the main criterion. The socio-economic relations that produce such individualism were encompassed in what Maróthy (1974) describes as the change from tribal relations to those of commodity production. Maróthy perhaps oversimplifies the ideas of commodity and production (or perhaps his argument has lost something in translation) though what he says certainly applies to medieval Europe. As Anderson (1988) points out, the slave economies of the ancient world were not producers in the modern sense of the word, but agrarian economies which could support towns. Nevertheless Maróthy is correct in assuming a fundamental change from a vertically integrated and rural clan society to an urban one in which the elements of horizontal integration required an individualism which would have consequences of its own, one of which was the fact that the musician and his music became commodities available to whoever wished to purchase them. The same social polarisation led to the separate marketing of performer and music: a composer could be a free man, a performer could not.[12] A class of *rhapsodoi* developed for the recitation of the great epics. These were not minstrels in the Homeric sense but orators (without instruments) who performed other people's work. They were specialists: Plato's Ion for example is a *rhapsodos* who performs only Homer, in which he is a consummate expert; he is available for hire when not competing. He is not an oral poet:

ION: . . . good poets say these things as the gods' interpreters.

SOCRATES: And don't you *rhapsodoi* in your turn interpret what the poets say?

ION: That is true too.

SOCRATES: So you are interpreters of interpreters?

ION: Absolutely.   (Plato, *Ion* 535a)

Here we have the divine inspiration of the composer, who is completely differentiated from the performance of his music.

Parallel with this spoken tradition a custom of singing to instrumental accompaniment grew up (perhaps a modification of the Homeric singing tradition) for similar occasions. These singer-poets also sang the works of known composers, as well as works of their own devising. The oral poet re-created his stories on the occasion of each performance; he was not an interpreter of a music but of a society (or, as Lord put it, a seer). The new singer-poets were one stage removed from this cultural heritage: they were a product of their society and they interpreted its music, which had an independent existence beyond the individual performance.

The idea of a separation between composer and performer is a product of literate societies. One of the prerequisites of literacy is the division of mental and physical labour, which is characteristic of successful slave economies (Anderson, 1988, p. 222). The early alphabets had proved their worth in fixing transactions permanently, and in systems of commodity production a second use for the alphabet evolved in which music and literature could be quantified. It is this socio-economic phenomenon more then any other which led to the writing down of Homer's verses, and from which the separation of performance and composition springs. The move to literacy is characterised by a new idea of written text associated with economic success in a stable imperialistic system, in which mythology is only one of many possible themes. This is invariably a male-orientated process: with the notable exception of Sappho, the musical roles of women remain marginalised in the rituals of the temple, worksongs, weddings and funerals. Greek writers, never far from the experience of war, constantly extol the ideal manly virtues of music as opposed to what Pseudo-Plutarch called the 'effeminate twitterings' that they occasionally have to endure.[13]

By the seventh century a singing (as opposed to reciting) tradition had become re-established for the works of Hesiod and the 'lyric' poets, and this became increasingly sophisticated during the next two hundred years. Until the around the fourth or third centuries Ancient Greek was a pitch-inflected language in which the boundaries between speech and song were often blurred and the oratorical and singing modes of delivery appear to have developed as branches of the same art but with different social functions. Oratory was used in the law courts and for political debate, singing for competitive festivals and informal entertainment. The expressive possibilities of pitch inflection were developed to a high degree and later came to be incorporated into Roman and medieval Latin oratory. Pitch does not seem to have been notated but written texts appear to have been sung in one of a number of 'modes', a mode in this context being what we would now call a scale associated with a particular emotive or symbolic state. As composers and their music became more sophisticated they became increasingly criticised by conservative writers, from whom most of our evidence is drawn. The relationship between pitch and emotional expression was further developed in the sixth and fifth centuries. Barker (1987, chapter 7) points to Pindar's wide range of moods and functions, from the stirringly and publicly patriotic to the subtly elegant and private, and to the compositions of Timotheus later in the century, emotional, dramatic and highly ornamented, with an exaggerated poetic diction. Without notation for such works we can only imagine what the effect of such rhetoric must have been.

Aristophanes identifies many types of music including the convivial *skolion*, a sort of catch or round sung before and during dinner, *mele*, which were unison choral songs, and *nomoi*, solo songs with or without accompaniment. The concept of the composer is by now very sophisticated: he is a divinely inspired genius, who frequently achieved fame beyond his own lifetime. He can compose masterworks which increase his status over succeeding generations. In a written medium his songs were capable of analysis, and were therefore suitable for educational purposes, with wider social implications. As Maróthy (1974, p. 150) put it:

A professional artistic activity grows which is in the service of the emergent ruling class. However, its equally important function is to exercise an effect on the masses of the people. The possibility of such an effect lies in the fact that in the behaviour and ideology of various classes and layers, basic common points of agreement can be found.

It is with Plato and Aristotle that the ideological force of musical expressiveness becomes apparent. Plato evolved the idea of *mousike*, music and poetry as a socio-cultural by-product of philosophy. The term, originally implying 'of the muses', gives the modern word 'music'. The Greek word for songs was *nomoi*, which was the same as the word for 'laws'. The etymological relationship has been argued by scholars to suggest various possibilities from the idea of laws having at some point been sung, to a more general ideological connection between singing and control. The question does not seem to have been looked at in the light of Plato's definition of *mousike*, which is specifically an ideological construct (see, for example, *Republic* 397–401b). Historians tracing the development of music as a concept have also tended to ignore the element of social control and censorship inherent in Plato's definition. Plato re-affirms the three *dicta* of Aristophanes that music must be manly and not effeminate, morally uplifting and socially cohesive. He is able to trace the libertarian excesses of democracy to corruption by music. The connection between music and morality is a recurring one among Greek writers. Pseudo-Aristotle (*Problems* XIX, 27) asks 'why is it that what is heard, alone among perceptibles, has moral character?'. Aristotle is more pragmatic but he too observes the vulgarity of public performance and clearly identifies a range of musical modes and rhythms that may or may not be appropriate for his three 'limits to be imposed upon education: moderation, possibility and propriety' (*Politics* 1342b). Unlike Plato he can accept the appropriateness of 'vulgar' music in its place: for vulgar people. For free men music as a liberal art was both a science and a philosophy, to be studied in the abstract, discussed and listened to but not performed unless drunk, or for fun. Both Plato and Aristotle were widely read in classical times and the force of their arguments obviously suggested 'basic common points of agreement' which appealed to many parts of society.

The essence of Hellenic culture was subsequently absorbed by Roman society. The Romans developed a far more advanced slave economy, which was dependent on military conquest for its renewal into succeeding generations. The eventual closing of the Roman borders diminished the supply of slave labour to such an extent that the expanding Germanic tribes were finally able to overrun the overstretched empire whose economy had collapsed. A great deal of Greek literature became Romanised by translation. Beare (1950) remarked that the most obvious single feature of Roman drama is its lack of originality: all surviving Roman comedies, for example, are translations or adaptations of Greek originals. The Roman capacity for cultural renewal in its own image strongly suggests that Roman musicians took over many elements of Greek music in the way that they appropriated the traditions of oratory and rhetoric. Unfortunately only a handful of Greek compositions has survived to the present day, and no authentic Roman ones at all. The traditions of oratory and rhetoric survived and flourished, the transplanting to stress-accented Latin serving to further reinforce the difference between poetry and singing. The young Gaius Caesar is reported by Quintilian (*Institutio oratoria* 1.viii.2 and 1.x.27) as saying 'If you are singing, you sing badly; if you are reading, you sing,' which perhaps suggests that the Romans could find pitch-inflected speech confusing. Quintilian, who believed that 'the art of letters and that of music were once united', also mentions Gaius Gracchus, the leading orator of his age, as needing a musician to stand behind him with a pitch pipe for even the most emotive speeches. Conversely, the pitch-inflections of poetry became less musical and more poetic as the Romans strove to adapt Greek hexameters to Latin. The philosophical and scientific ideals of music, those of the free men, survived largely intact in later post-Roman society as the *quadrivium*.

Despite the somewhat conjectural nature of recent attempts to decipher the few surviving fragments of Greek notation it is clear that in urban societies where music flourished it displayed many of the characteristics which we would recognise today: the idea of an 'art' music which had a high status within the cultural mainstream and which could survive beyond the lifetime of its creator. Although it is not possible to establish the relationship between singing and instrumental music with any certainty, the role of singing as carrier of the word, both in ritual and as the symbolic keeper of cultural inheritance suggests a logocentric function for singing which it has never lost. As far as we know there was no concept of a singing 'technique' in its modern sense: singing was purely a vehicle for *logos* in whatever form was culturally appropriate. Developments after the fall of the Roman empire show evidence of a change in this attitude, towards isolating and encodifying specific parameters (tone colour and pitch, for example) as a means of controlling both current performance and those of future generations, especially in sacred music. The impetus for this came not from the declining classical culture, but in the emerging Romano-German synthesis and in the form of synagogic chant on which the new Christian chanting was based. In historical terms the importance of the Roman period lies in its mediation between Hellenistic classicism and the Judaeo-Christian tradition. The synthesis of these two strands, the one characterised by advanced literacy and the other becoming the religion of the state, ensured the ideological conditions for the development of a religious art music. Sacred (or liturgical) as opposed to purely ritual music is a concept which apparently did not exist before the Christian era. The releasing of sacred music from its strictly liturgical context would eventually have important consequences for the concept of what we know as 'classical' music and its hegemonic status relative to other varieties of music.

CHAPTER 2

The medieval period: religion, literacy and control

Since the Renaissance, historians have been accustomed to period-ising history into a number of compartments which perpetuate the Renaissance view of history, a view which sees an authenticity in ancient culture (especially that of classical Greece and Rome) which is the yardstick by which subsequent 'ages' are measured. So the source of all true intellectual and artistic activity is seen to go underground during the 'middle' ages (which are initiated by a 'dark' age), to be rediscovered in the 'renaissance' of classical ideals. While the invasions of the northern tribes disrupted both the social and economic order, there is relatively little evidence of intellectual hiatus. At the peak of tribal expansion there is a dearth of written material, but this is an indication of the difficulties that any civilisa-tion faces at times of such crises: the *Ordines Romani* of the eighth-century Roman mass are informed by the same ideals as the patristic writers of the fifth century, which is a powerful argument for the continuity of classical ideals. During this period and the later Middle Ages, classical thought became an important ideological foundation to ideas about how singing functioned both in religious music and in secular courts, as notational systems were devised which ensured the primacy and authority of written music. This ideology took firm root in the church, with its unique access to literacy and its significant social position, ensuring a development of what we might loosely call 'art music'. Such evidence as we have (and it is not a great deal) suggests that singing itself probably became more disciplined, and indeed within the church became a discipline. It was very much a word-orientated discipline, and there is no evidence at all of the technical and tonal characteristics of modern singing.

The period from the beginnings of the Christian era to the Edict of Milan in 313 (when Christianity became the established Roman religion) is not an easy one to interpret, not least because of the separate paths taken by the historiography of church and society. Until relatively recently church history has been written by clerics whose main concern was to reinforce the unbroken line of tradition from Jesus to the present day and who have little interest in explaining Christianity in its social or political context.[1] Conversely, historians outside the church have tended to marginalise its influence. The initial spread of the new religion appears to have been largely among artisans and craftsmen, practical people who could presumably see the advantages of an organised religion which combined compassion with common sense. A polytheistic society depends on a number of cults offering different varieties of fulfilment; one may dominate (as in the case of emperor worship) but in the context of many others which come and go and compete for attention. Monotheism demands a different kind of commitment from its followers, who expect it to provide for the totality of their spiritual needs. Disciplined organisation was essential to survival. Judaism offered this kind of experience and had successfully resisted other faiths but was of its nature ultimately self-limiting. In making the consequences of monotheism available to all who would listen, Christianity eventually outgrew its Jewish roots. The idea of a church as a social entity had no precedent in classical society, whose rituals were specific events geared to meeting particular ends and were exclusively in the hands of a priest class that had little contact with the rest of society. The early Christian fathers had devised what was in effect a secular priesthood whose job was to organise the laity, and ensure conformity of belief and ritual within a leadership structure that had no equivalent in its rival religions. By the end of the third century the hierarchy of bishops and priests was firmly established, though small in number, and well- placed to attach itself to the Roman state. Although the reasons for Constantine's conversion can only be speculated upon, it is certainly the case that his empire and the new religion shared similar attitudes to organisation and discipline, a respect for the rule of law, and what Denys Hay (1964, p. 11) succinctly summarised as 'an itch for system'. Once Constantine was persuaded of the merits of conversion the entire bureaucracy which supported the worship of himself as god was available to the church, and it required very little adjustment to fuse the two to form a secular religious state, giving Christianity access to Pierre Bourdieu's 'gentle, invisible form of violence, misrecognised as such, chosen as much as it is submitted to' (J. Thompson, 1984,

p. 43). This symbolic violence is implicit in state power and guaran-
teed the dominance of Christianity as a part of the ruling ideology.

The language of the early church fathers had been varieties of
Greek. Perhaps the most important aspect of the legitimising process
was the availability to the church of Latin, through which could be
established the idea of a universal church owing allegiance to a
Roman centre. It was Latin rather than the older vernaculars that
had been the language of government and the arts under the empire.
Both the vernacularisation of Latin itself and the subsequent development of those discrete vernaculars which would become the
Romance languages are of central importance in ensuring the
continuity of a classical intellectual hegemony. As Helen Waddell
(1968, p. 9) put it in her classic account of the medieval Latin poets,
'there is no beginning, this side the classics, to a history of medieval
Latin . . . To the medieval scholar, with no sense of perspective, but
a strong sense of continuity, Virgil and Cicero are but the upper
reaches of a river that still flows past his door.' In its vernacular form
the language was acceptable to those who might otherwise have
rejected it (and who might have committed their own vernaculars to
written form at a much earlier date). This process of articulating a
passage from one ideology to a new realisation of itself is of vital
importance in the maintenance of the authority of the dominant
culture. It was in the mass conversions of the fourth and fifth
centuries that Latin passed from being the language of an elite of the
previous age to being a *lingua franca* for the new Christian elite. It
saw its greatest flowering in the monasteries, whose relative security
ensured the survival of classical texts.

James McKinnon (1987), in his comprehensive collection of source
material relating to early Christian music-making, identifies four
categories of reference in the literature. There are those concerned
with denouncing pagan musical traditions (especially the use of
instruments), those which accept music as a liberal art, those which
are concerned with liturgical chant, and a body of more general
material using music as a figure of speech. One of the problems of
the early church was the question of how to achieve a balance
between absorbing pagan traditions while maintaining and developing its own identity. Taking over the imperial theocratic infra-
structure enabled it to re-articulate pagan rituals in the form of
Christian equivalents within a decade of the Edict of Milan; thus
martyrs and saints became the occasion for holidays (the word is a

reminder) instead of the heroes of antiquity. This perceived continuity enabled a more profound break with the past to be made in
the concept of liturgy, and more particularly the role of music in it.
Instead of instruments, which implied rhythm, which in its turn
implied the dance of pagan ritual and peasant hearth, the new
church would use only the voice in order to emphasise a moral
stance which would distance it from both Judaism and the devalued
currency of Roman excess:

The tympanum sounds not nor does the cymbal . . . neither are there
drunkards in lawless carousals or in dances . . . Never may we . . . pour the
blood of slain sheep upon the libations of sacrificial bulls . . . but rejoicing
with pure heart and cheerful spirit . . . with propitiatory psalms and chants
beseeming god, we are called upon to hymn thee, immortal and faithful
god, creator of all and understanding all.[2]

The new Christian intellectuals were perhaps also aware of the
strictures placed on the excessive use of instruments by Plato and
Aristotle. Many, including St Augustine, took a neoplatonist route to
Christianity and found it both easy and convenient to identify
current classical thought with that of Christianity. Christian singing
was restrained and disciplined, in marked contrast to the often
hysterical outpourings of the Roman cults. The discipline of monotheism and the confident restraint of a religion grounded in a
message of compassion but which found itself close to the centre of
secular power found expression in a very particular variety of
singing.

There is a continuing argument among historians about the role
played by Jewish music and ritual in the early church. Most of the
debate has evolved round the question of whether or not Jewish
temple or synagogic chants were incorporated into Christian rite.
There is remarkably little evidence either way, but it can be assumed
that the earliest experience of Christian chanting was rooted in
Judaism simply because most of its first adherents were Jews. In
addition to the fundamental idea of monotheism Judaism gave to
Christianity the synagogic custom of the localised meeting place (as
opposed to the witness of sacrifice found in the Jewish temple and
also in the pagan cults), at which the sacred texts are discussed and
interpreted.[3] The texts themselves were those of the Old Testament,
which meant that the 'new' religion was thus able to call on a history
which went back to the beginning of time. There are no early

references to Jewish chant forms in Christian worship, from which it may be deduced that Christians retained the idea of singing (especially in the context of the ritual meal) but eventually preferred to develop forms of their own. Current research recognises two kinds of Christian singing, the monastic and the secular, which were clearly differentiated by the fourth century. The secular rites and chants may well be derived from Jewish tradition, being 'familiar everywhere from the Orient to Gaul, and from North Africa to Milan', as Hucke (1980) put it. In the monasteries the monks appear to have experimented with an evolving liturgy which was further influenced by a tradition of singing psalms and hymns in procession after the Syrian manner, culminating in the full community taking part in the Benedictine rite of the sixth century.

The earliest chants (both Jewish and Christian) were composed and performed according to oral formulae, which must have operated in a similar way to those used in Greek epic poetry. Modern research on chant dates from the Solesmes school of the late nineteenth century which culminated in Peter Wagner's *Einführung in die gregorischen Melodien* (Leipzig, 1911–21). For several generations the literature was heavily indebted to this work, which posited a Jewish origin and assumed the oldest written chant to be from Milan. More recently Leo Treitler (1974) has convincingly applied the Parry–Lord theory to liturgical chant. As with the *Iliad*, our first experiences of chant occur when it is at a high point of development, and we cannot be sure of the origin of specific chants. During a period of more than one thousand years Christian clergy and monks (especially the latter) composed, and performed daily, what John Stevens (1986, p. 3) has rightly called 'the largest and finest monument of melodic art in the European heritage'. It is difficult for us to imagine the extent to which liturgy and music were in many respects one and the same thing. Within each foundation, local versions of thousands of chants were created using the formula system during the centuries of decay and destruction that followed the disintegration of the Roman empire. There are many references to singing as a practical aid to the celebration of the divine office, especially in the monastic foundations that were becoming the intellectual and spiritual heart of the religion. From later sources it can be deduced that the monks were trained in singing from childhood. The length of time that it took to train a monk adequately varied from ten years and upwards, many apparently never mastering the intricacies of the chant to the satisfaction of their teachers. As Isidore of Seville (d. 636) put it: 'unless sounds are remembered by men they perish, for they cannot be written down',[4] and the monks' years of training consisted of little more than a continuous memory exercise (a feat by no means incompatible with current ideas on memory and formula learning). Pope Gregory I (590–604) was credited by later sources with having founded the first monastic singing schools and composing many of the original chants. He was also said to have compiled an antiphonary which unified the many diverse singing traditions that were by then common. It is now thought that history may have attributed these achievements to the wrong Gregory and that the pope whose name was originally associated with chant was in fact Gregory II (715–731). Whichever Gregory it was, his function was that of an administrator who probably saw his task as codifying the liturgy rather than the chant *per se*. He may have founded orphanages with the aim of improving the supply of singing monks but he did not 'compose' chants any more than any other singer of his time would have done. His antiphoners (examples survive) do not contain music, and they would have had to be accompanied by a singing monk familiar with the appropriate formulae in order to be used effectively. It was under Gregory I and his successors that the papacy first became an international force to be reckoned with, however, and it is significant that later Romans wished the chant to be associated with his reputation, and that liturgy and chant were seen to be virtually synonymous.[5]

The administrative and social chaos that followed the northern invasions was brought to a halt in the eighth century by the military expansion of the Franks under Charlemagne. In the thirty years that followed Charles Martel's defeat of the Islamic armies at Poitiers in 733 Charlemagne conquered the entire Christian world west of Byzantium and in 800 proclaimed himself Emperor of the West as part of a 'massive ideological and administrative effort to "recreate" the Imperial System of the old world' (Anderson, 1988, p. 137). If it was military strength that achieved unification it was the church that was instrumental in maintaining it. As part of the imperial need for legitimacy the chant was to be unified and 'authenticated' by recourse to that practised at the papal court, creating a unified, standard version that would link the new empire with the most venerable Christian tradition. This is another vital stage in the process by which the dominant ideology evolved. We have seen how the church was able to legitimise itself by attaching itself to the state; the church was by now sufficiently authentic for the initial positions to be reversed, and the state sought to gain legitimacy by association with the church. This led directly to the development of a new ideological instrument, by which not only the literary texts were written, but notation was devised to encode the musical texts, which would gain new functions and significances. The task of codifying the corpus of chant must have been enormous. Those who inscribed the chants used notation systems that reflected the task as they saw it, namely to capture the essential qualities that characterised each one. Pitch initially formed only a small part of this programme, which 'represented chant as performed, that is, as event rather than as object,' as Treitler (1984) put it. The indications of pitch were sufficient to a singer who already knew a version of the music. The earliest Frankish notation systems were based on punctuation marks similar to those used in classical oratory as guides to pitch inflection. As Hucke (1980) has noted, the earliest chant books must have been for archival purposes as they are too small to be performing copies, and performance must have remained 'oral' in that there were still large areas which would have been of an improvisatory nature. The terminology of notation, and of the science of *musica*, developed along the lines of classical grammar, rhetoric and poetics. Although undoubtedly shaped by pre-existing practice, the concept of quantity used in the gropings towards *musica mensurabilis* depended on the use of the *ordines* of classical poetry.

Perhaps because of the unaffected nature of their singing monks seem often to have been regarded as mere chant-fodder by the intellectual community. Their salvation was at hand, however, as the corpus of chant (each with its appropriate function in the liturgy) became so great that Guido of Arezzo was moved to write that

many clerics and monks of the religious order neglect the psalms, the sacred readings, the nocturnal vigils, and the other works of piety that arouse and lead us on to the everlasting glory, while they apply themselves with unceasing and most foolish effort to the science of singing which they can never master.[6]

The pedagogical possibilities offered by written systems had opened up the prospect that chant might be taught almost instantaneously and in permanent form if pitches could be accurately notated. The excitement in the treatises of Odo of Cluny and Guido of Arezzo when propounding their newly developed pitch-specific notational systems is almost palpable. Monks could now sing 'without a master' music that they had never heard before. This made the monks both more literate and less dependent on their singing masters and must have increased their status. But the new notation meant also a stricter discipline, the elimination of errors and vagaries of interpretation, a new definition of music in terms of what could be written down. The church as the only source of literacy became the only provider of formal education in the Caroline revolution, with the founding of monastic schools whose primary task was to prepare novices in the liturgy. The more academically orientated of these would also be taught the *trivium* (grammar, rhetoric and logic) as well as the *quadrivium* (arithmetic, music, geometry and astronomy). This same set of subjects was taught (without the chant) at the later secular (i.e. non-monastic) cathedral schools (in England, the grammar schools), and in the universities. Learning was primarily by memory: books were extremely expensive, thirty copies of the Gutenberg Bible requiring the slaughter of some five thousand sheep.[7] The significance of rhetoric and oratory in non-literate societies has yet to be fully explored, but it is reasonable to suppose that the educated elite were exposed to 'performances' of literature as a matter of course. Oratory and rhetoric, the performing arts, were the basic tools of education: books were written in order to be read aloud. Preachers, the essential link between the church and the peasantry (who were excluded from the schools, which were for sons of free men only), were orators. One effect of this, through the mediaeval period and beyond, must have been a tendency for the aristocracy and clergy to be perceived as performers, as the only source of high culture, while the peasantry had a passive role, conditioned to receive those performances, which they could ape at certain times of year in the Mystery plays and other vernacular festivals.

The division of education into monastic and secular is reflected in the production of two different sorts of musical treatise, both of which have their origin in the ancient world: the practical, for the use of 'composers' and singers in the monastic schools; and the academic, as taught in the *quadrivium* (the *ars musica*). The earliest treatises also happen to contain some of the earliest examples of music notation: the pedagogical imperative also contributing to the need for notational systems. Unlike Jerome and Augustine who praise the spontaneous and natural in singing, the writers whose texts form the core of the *ars musica* were concerned to pass on the classical notion that singers (*cantores*) were craftsmen ignorant of the true art of the *musicus*, which could exist only in theory. In his *De institutione musicae* Boethius says:

Every art . . . considers reason inherently more honourable than a skill which is practiced by the hand and the labour of an artisan. For it is much better and nobler to know about what someone else fashions than to execute that about which some one else knows. (Bower, 1989, p. 50)

He divides musical knowledge into three parts, two of which, the instrumental and the vocal, are to be 'separated from music', which is the 'skill of judging . . . in reason and speculation'. This is a purely classical formulation dating back to Plato whom Boethius frequently invokes. Music, performance, and singing in particular, were clearly based on ideological premises which had survived many hundreds of years, and which have an echo to this day in simple musical snobbery.

It is relatively easy to suggest ideological/historical interpretations of early Christian music-making based on written sources, but it is of course impossible to have any idea of what the singing may have sounded like. It is possible to look at what might have been the criteria for good singing and to try to establish whether there may have been a differentiation of technique between singing used in the service of the church, and that used outside it. Whatever form it took, it is likely that the singing of the early Christians sounded very similar to that of their Jewish contemporaries. The diaspora which began after the fall of Jerusalem in AD 70 would have meant a movement northwards of Jewish chants at the same time as Christianity began to fill the vacuum left by the collapsing Roman cults (themselves derived from southern Mediterranean and African antecedents). The archaeology of pre-Carolingian Gaul points to the existence of flourishing communities of Greek and oriental merchants (especially Syrians and Egyptians) which survived until they were destroyed by Saracen incursions. Gregory of Tours reports that in 585 King Gontrand entered Orléans to cries of acclamation in Latin, Hebrew and Syriac.[8] The general picture, from a vocal point of view, is of a much closer relationship between north/west modes of singing and those of the south/east. The cultural shift which enabled this did not end when Christianity became the official

Roman religion but was reinforced by the pseudo-classical atmosphere in which learning survived the invasions of the northern tribes, by the northward movement of Christian conversion, and by the renewed contacts with the south/east at the time of the crusades. The attitude of northern Europe to the south (what we would now call the Middle East) became more ambivalent as it gradually acquired its own cultural identity. After the violent rise of Islam many classical manuscripts found their way to the north and were enthusiastically copied by monks who were at the same time supporting the crusades, thus in effect colluding in the destruction of their sources. This circularity was part of a world view that reinforced the idea of a universal known world. There is little reference to the sound of singing, suggesting a basic singing style so universal that no comments on it are to be found. The many commentators who accompanied the crusading armies apparently did not notice anything very different from what they heard at home (though they brought back instruments as souvenirs[9]). There was, as yet, no concept of a stylised way of singing comparable to that which today characterises cathedral choristers (both children and adults). Singing seems to have been praised for its naturalness, as a means of illuminating meanings, rather than a sound as an end in itself. St Jerome (d. 420) says:

Sing to God not with the voice but with the heart; not, after the fashion of tragedians, in smearing the throat with a sweet drug, so that theatrical melodies and songs are heard in the church . . . and though a man be cacophonous if he have good works, he is a sweet singer before God. And let the servant of Christ sing so that he pleases not through his voice, but through the words that he pronounces . . .[10]

The earliest treatises specifically concerned with singing date from much later than the period under consideration, but it is possible that these may throw some light on practices that must have been to some extent traditional. The *Scientia artis musice*[11] of Elias Salomon is a treatise dating from 1274 written by a cleric from the south of France. It is clearly within the mainstream of traditional classical ideology, and contains the theoretical elements of *musica* that are found in earlier works. Salomon also gives indications as to what he found musically and aesthetically acceptable as a choir master. He does not like rough or uncouth singing, but insists that singers should have flexible voices able to produce sufficient (but not too much) volume. There is an indication of a division of voices into those who would sing high and those who would sing low. His comments contrasting church musicians with their secular colleagues are confined to the apparent inability of the latter to master singing in fifths for improvised organum. There is no suggestion that they actually sound different from each other. Writing around 1400, Arnulf de St Ghislain, in his *Tractatulus* on the different sorts of musicians that he has had to deal with, divides singers into those who are untrained and sound like wild animals, those who sing sweetly, well-intentioned teachers, and complete masters of the 'noble art of singing' (Page, 1993a, p. 19). Arnulf suggests that those in the last category take their singing very seriously indeed. Later in the fifteenth century we encounter a more detailed treatise which gives an insight into the training of singers for the chant. This is Conrad von Zabern's *De modo bene cantandi* ('On how to sing well') dating from 1474.[12] Priest, theologian and musical scholar, Conrad matriculated at Heidelberg University, probably in 1412, and became a master and preacher there. He travelled widely in western and southwestern Germany during the early part of the fifteenth century, and seems to have devoted his entire time to the improvement of the singing of chant in religious services. The treatise is the product of a lifetime's work to this end. He wrote in Latin, though the work was subsequently translated into German as *Lere von Koergesanck* and it was undoubtedly well known to his contemporaries. Its importance was considerable and its influence long-lasting. Conrad's precepts even appear in Dowland's translation of Ornithoparcus' *Micrologus* of 1609, attesting to their widespread currency. He talks of 'singing with proper refinement', which he describes as being 'with discrimination and not coarse'. He does not like intrusive *h*s, singing through the nose, or distorted vowel sounds. Many clerics, he says, sing 'as though they had food in their mouths', and he cites the old medieval joke *aremus* – let us plough – rather than *oremus* – let us pray – as evidence of such practices. Vowels should not change during melismas: tone should not be forced, but sweet. High notes should not be excessively loud: amplitude should be even throughout the range of the voice, thereby reducing the chances of straining from singing too loudly too high.

Conrad provides a great deal of information and the entire thrust of his writings suggests an increasingly sophisticated approach to singing, which had probably developed over several generations.

The treatise does not contain evidence of what in the twentieth century would be considered a 'vocal technique', but Conrad clearly has a concept of singing as a performance, and as something quite different from mere vocalising. The key phrase is 'satis urbaniter cantare' – 'to sing with proper refinement'. What Conrad is really saying is that monks should sing in a more delicate way than those who would form their congregation. Much of what he says would be taken for granted as common sense by singers of today – sing together and in tune: basic principles of choral singing. The fact that the treatise achieved such a wide distribution over some one hundred and twenty-five years indicates the great relevance it had for singers. As a printed book, rather than a laboriously copied codex, it must also have been the kind of tool that would reinforce the idea of singing pedagogy: singing was worthy of 'improvement'. It is possible to deduce significant ideas as to what the singers did use by way of technique from what Conrad writes. The tendency to strain on high notes is a natural one among untrained singers of today, and so is the use of an *h* to articulate wordless passages. The latter is evidence of unsupported breathing (as used in speech), using the false vocal cords for articulation rather than the cords themselves which would require more pressure. Such a technique, if we add to it evidence from the next century (for which see below), would probably produce a sound with more of a speech-like quality than we would expect from a modern church singer. The difference perceived by Conrad's contemporaries would be in the intentions of the singers, a realisation that what they were doing should be 'more refined' than was the common practice, more precise and more obviously crafted. A difference, in other words, of style, rather than technique.

Conrad von Zabern's treatise is one of very few works from the Middle Ages that really gives us any insight into what singers may have sounded like, into the criteria which were important in singing. He was a cleric, writing for clerics: it is another three-quarters of a century before we get to the first secular treatise, and we have little idea of what secular music may have sounded like. With Conrad, as the first of what within a relatively short time would become a flood of writers on practical singing, we find evidence of the continuing development of singing as discipline.

The status of singers must have risen with the development of polyphony, as Salomon's remarks suggest. The origins of *organum* (the practice of 'harmonising' a melody at a constant interval) are unknown and references to the practice in its improvised form first occur in the ninth century in the treatises of Hucbald and Reginaldo of Prüm, which give formulae for its performance. Similar practices exist in folk cultures but a folk origin which suggests that fifths may occur instinctively when musically illiterate congregations attempt to sing notes that are too high for them sounds most unlikely, given the preference of many modern congregations for intervals that have little to do with the overtone structure. It is surely more likely that *organum* was a specific construct by clerics well versed in Pythagorean doctrine who saw the possibilities inherent in a mode of singing that would enable them to retain some creative input into what was a very precise discipline with an increasingly long tradition behind it. An accidental mis-hearing of a starting note cannot be ruled out as the initial stimulus for this. The reinforcement of the third harmonic as the result of a particularly esoteric pronunciation or vocalisation could lead to the fifth note of the scale being perceived as the fundamental. I have sometimes found in the course of workshops on extended vocal techniques that the perception of reinforced harmonics is much more acute in children than in adults. One possibility which future researchers into the origins of polyphony might consider is that hyper-hearing among choir boys may have been a significant factor in the evolution of *organum*. Men and boys singing together would in any case produce *organum* at the octave, with a consequently richer overtone structure which would make mis-hearing more likely. There is no evidence as to the status or abilities of the first singers of *organa*. By the twelfth century the rise of Paris under the Capetian kings, and in particular the fame of its university and cathedral, ensure that there is far more written evidence of vocal practices. Given the improvised (though formulaic) nature of *organum* it is not surprising that the singers of extra parts were soloists. The Parisian rubrics, though full of information about the numbers of singers, are rarely entirely clear about who sang what, but there are references to the music for the *Alleluia* being chanted by four singers or sung in *organum* by two.[13] Those who sang the chant sections were known as *tenoristae*, while the polyphony singers were known as *machicoti*. Both these categories were distinct from the ordinary clerics who sang the 'choir' sections of the chant. This hierarchy of singers is further evidence of the increasing isolation of singers from listeners, occurring within the ritual practices of the church.

The same specialist singers were responsible for the development of written secular music. In Paris, for example, Philip the Chancellor wrote secular verses either to existing tunes or newly composed ones, presumably for performance at home or in the hall. There are three possible areas in which secular music would have flourished: the theatre, poetry and folk music. Elements of classical theatre may have survived the fall of the Roman empire despite the antipathy with which it was regarded by the invading northern tribes. The fifth century quotation from St Jerome above is not an isolated reference to 'tragedians'. Isidore of Seville says in his *Etymologiarum*:

The first division of music . . . is the modulation of the voice, is the affair of comedians, tragedians, and choruses and of all who sing. (Strunk, 1981, p. 95)

Like Boethius, Isidore is a commentator who links the ancient world with the Middle Ages and his treatise is a classically orientated academic one, so he may not have had current practices in mind. His audience, however, would at least need an idea of what he was talking about, and the continuous tradition of oratory would imply some experience of drama, with its stylised quasi-musical performance. The Roman *mimus* or actor/entertainer survived in a number of guises, a minstrel in the widest sense of the term. The vernacular sagas and rituals of the Goths, Ostrogoths, Vandals and others undoubtedly drove classical drama out of the mainstream of public consciousness. The survival of Latin as the official language of the religion of the later empire and the increasing dramatisation of the liturgy during the seventh and eighth centuries led to the beginnings of church drama in the ninth century. This expansion of the ritual parameters would again suggest an increasingly formal role for the singers.

In the previous chapter, I discussed the relationship between oral and literary forms of 'poetic' music-making, and pointed to the survival of the oral epic in written form at the same time as other written forms were evolving in ancient Greece. Similar processes can be observed in the period between the end of classical Roman literacy and the emergence of a Gallo-Roman synthesis in the second half of the millennium. The entertainment preferred by the new 'barbarian' aristocracy was that of the saga sung by the *scop* or gleeman. The function of the gleeman was not unlike that of an African *griot*, part historian, part propagandist, wholly entertainer,

accompanying or punctuating his utterances with a primitive instrument and re-composing each song according to a number of
formulae. Both poet and singer (Boethius uses the terms interchangeably), his method is to be found in the later German Minnesingers,
the Provençal troubadours, and the French trouvères. Here is the
seventh-century *Widsith*:

Wherefore I may sing and utter a measure; recite before the company in
the mead hall how the noble were liberal to me in their generosity.

Like the Greek epics, the recitation takes place at court, where the
eponymous minstrel Widsith first needs to establish his credentials.
He, or his assistant, accompanies the tale on a harp:

Her praise was spread through many lands, whenever it befell to me to tell
in song, where under the sky I best knew a gold-adorned queen bestowing
gifts. When Scilling and I with clear voice raised the song before our
victorious lord – loud to the harp the words sounded in harmony – then
many men, proud in mind, of full knowledge, said they had never heard a
better song.

Having told his tale he passes on:

Thus the minstrels of men go wandering, as fate directs, through many
lands; they utter their need, speak the word of thanks; south or north, they
always meet one wise in measures, liberal in gifts, who wishes to exalt his
glory before the warriors, to perform valorous deeds, until light and life fall
in ruin together: he gains praise, he has lofty glory under the heavens.
(Gordon, 1976)

Epic verse had a late flowering between the eleventh and
thirteenth centuries in France. The subject-matter is still the heroic
exploits of a warrior class, but a genre of 'romance' is also to be
found at French courts where more subtle topics are sung. Johannes
de Grocheio (*fl. c.* 1300) mentions a form of song which recalls
battles and deeds of old, which he calls 'Gestual Cantus':

for the elderly, for working citizens and for those of middle station when
they rest from their usual toil, so that, having heard the miseries and
calamities of others they may more easily bear their own, and so that
anyone may undertake his own labour with more alacrity. Therefore this
kind of *cantus* has the power to preserve the whole city. (Page, 1993a, p. 23)

This is surely the old epic, not what evolved as the *lai*, also a poem
on a grand scale possibly of formulaic origin but reworked with the
discipline of literacy. The ideological function is clear.

A similar phenomenon is to be found today in those parts of

Eastern Europe which have managed to resist the total absorption of western music practices. As was touched upon above, the epics from the former Yugoslavia have been particularly well documented in the work of Albert Lord and others. Like the earlier German, English and French epics the Yugoslav songs co-existed with other folk songs and composed music. The earliest Serbian epic transcription actually dates from 1555.[14] The social position of the composer-poets who flourished immediately prior to the first polyphonic music is still the subject of some debate (despite the apparent freedoms of Widsith). They cannot have been serfs, who did not have freedom of movement, and in the case of the Latin songs of the *Carmina Burana* manuscript, for example, there must have been some connection with the church. The *vagantes*, or wandering scholars, seem to have been clerics who failed to obtain permanent positions. The *goliards* would seem to have been men who had left clerical life altogether, while beneath them in status came the *jongleurs*, entertainers who could do anything from juggling to bear training. There are no references extant to differences in the way these singers sang. *Jongleurs* were possibly akin to folk musicians or minstrels and the pejorative references to them are in contrast to what earlier writers suggest of the singing of the peasantry. If art music was not written down it is not surprising that knowledge of the nature of folk music is almost completely speculative. Most modern writers do not risk making the attempt, or suggest that Troubadour song was folk song (which it clearly was not). There are one or two glimpses, however, such as an extensive passage in St John Chrysostom's *Exposition of Psalm XLI*:

Nothing so uplifts the mind . . . as modulated melody and the divine chant composed of number. To such an extent indeed is our nature delighted by chants and songs that even infants at the breast if they be weeping or afflicted are by reason of it lulled to sleep. Nurses . . . singing certain childish songs to them, often cause them to close their eyes . . . travellers also, driving at noon the yoked oxen sing as they do so, lightening by their chants the hardship of the journey. . . Peasants often sing as they tread the grapes in the wine press, gather the vintage, tend the vine and perform their other tasks. Sailors do likewise pulling at the oars. Women too, weaving . . . often sing a single certain melody, sometimes individually, sometimes altogether in concert . . . (Strunk, 1981, pp. 67–8)

An idealistic picture perhaps? 'The golden voiced', as St John Chrysostom was called, would have risked his credibility if his words did not have the ring of truth. The reason that there are so few references to the worksongs and entertainment of the peasantry is perhaps because it was ever so, and taken for granted. St John's account could apply equally well to parts of Europe today, sixteen centuries later (the weavers, particularly, call to mind the waulking songs from Barra). St John makes no distinction, vocally, between any of these folk styles and chant; for him they were all just singing, using a 'natural' vocal technique (in modern terms not a technique at all). This is further reinforced by the *jubilus*, a word literally meaning 'shout' which is found in St Augustine and others, and which became incorporated into the chant, perhaps as an early form of melisma:

Those who sing, whether at the harvest or in the vineyard or in any ardent work, when they have begun to exult with happiness in the words of the songs, turn from the syllables of the words, as though filled with such joy that they cannot express it in words, and pass into a sound of jubilation. (McKinnon, 1987, pp. 156–7)

I have made almost no reference to popular music in the medieval period. There is a wealth of iconographical evidence to suggest plenty of dance music which may have included singing. Common sense suggests that it would probably have been rougher and more exuberant than the more respectful singing to be found in church or at court, but we have no way of knowing this with any certainty. It is also difficult to talk of folk or popular singing in quite the same way as we do today, as the contexts for popular music are very different now. What is almost certain, however, is that singing in taverns and fields was related very much to the speech of the singer. What emerges during this long period from the end of the Roman empire to the beginnings of the Renaissance are not recognisable singing techniques to distinguish 'classical' singing from other sorts, but a reinforcement of an ideological framework that had probably been evolving for many thousands of years in the ancient world. The uncountable numbers of chants that were created to sustain the liturgies of the state religion led to a common perception that singing in church was something special. The association of this universal idea with the power structures of church and government in a society which had inherited Aristotelian and Platonic ideology, formed the basis for the increasing authority of a stylised way of singing.

CHAPTER 3

The Italian baroque revolution

The direction of research into historical singing is inevitably determined by the nature and geographical distribution of the surviving
evidence. This may result in an unbalanced view, especially where
survival or loss is due to chance, but the survival of a body of
evidence may equally well be an indication of the importance that it
had at the time of writing. The texts which have come down to us
from the fourteenth and fifteenth centuries in 'medieval' Germany
and England are relatively few compared to those from 'Renaissance' Italy during the same period. From the seventeenth century
onwards there is useful evidence from a much broader range of
sources and it confirms the seminal nature of Italian ideas on singing
throughout Europe. The ideological continuity from the classical
world through to the medieval period underwent a radical change of
emphasis when, as Anderson (1987, p. 148) put it, 'the Renaissance
discovered itself with a new, intense consciousness of rupture and
loss'. In musical historiography the period from the mid fourteenth
century to the mid sixteenth is conventionally thought of as representing a late flowering of the Middle Ages, a period during which
polyphony evolved towards its ultimate, 'Renaissance' form. Music is
thought to catch up with the Renaissance around 1600 with the
appearance of monody and the attempts to recreate the music of
ancient Greece. Paradoxically this period is seen as the beginning of
the baroque era. This historiographical mismatch is not quite as
illogical as it appears; the ideals of Renaissance humanism strongly
influenced the composition and performance of what is conventionally known as late medieval vocal music, which continued to develop
relatively autonomously, a radical break occurring only when the
possibilities of working within the existing musical forms had been
exhausted.

The subtle metamorphosis of the medieval ideology of classicism

into its humanist form has no obvious starting point and the reasons
for its development are not at all clear. The late medieval Italian city
states were very different from their ancient predecessors, being
centres of urban production supported by sophisticated capitalist
financial structures (as opposed to the slave-based centres of consumption of the ancient world), and were in many ways small-scale
precursors of later European absolutist states (Anderson, 1987). The
elite of the city republics consisted of merchants, manufacturers and
lawyers, and it is among this latter group that the earliest humanist
thinkers are to be found. The more elaborate socio-economic
structures required a more sophisticated legal system which was
enabled by the revival of Roman law. Roman law, like aspects of its
twentieth-century equivalent, depended on the arts of oratory and
rhetoric, especially the latter which is also a branch of literature. It
may be this connection which accounts for the fact that one of the
defining criteria of Renaissance humanism is the primacy of the
word. By the early fifteenth century the bulk of the known corpus of
Latin literature had been recovered and was soon widely dissemi-
nated in print.[1]

Performances of early polyphony were not concerned with the
literal communication of text. The very fact of polyphonic music
works against the idea of transmitting a text to an audience,
especially when monophonic chant was the normative 'literary'
musical form. In the universalist theocratically orientated culture of
the Middle Ages the communicative process was between cleric and
God, not between performer and audience.[2] Polyphony was a
symbolic phenomenon in which many varieties of communication
between God and man can take place simultaneously, to the extent
that each part may sing not only different music but also different
texts which need not even be in the same language. As the
Renaissance progressed the scholastic and symbolic gave way to the
secular and humanistic: words become the means of communication
between man and man. The word-painting found in fifteenth- and
sixteenth-century polyphony is a traditional semantic device that
supports the idea of the text rather than its literal meaning, as it
would come to do in the seventeenth century.

Polyphony was only one branch of secular music, but it was the
province of the literate elite, a fact which ensured the survival of a
considerable amount of it relative to other varieties. There are
tantalising glimpses of song repertoires ranging from street cries to

popular epics of great virtuosity, the existence of which can only be deduced from the incorporation into later music of what are assumed to be archaisms.[3] One of the problems that has bedevilled research into medieval secular music is that the iconographical evidence often does not seem to correspond to the surviving music. There are no surviving medieval works known to be for voice and lute (and very few indications that instruments were used at all), yet there are many illustrations suggesting that this was a popular musical combination, as was self-accompaniment on the vielle (a medieval fiddle). The pictures often show performers without music, which suggests that they may have been either playing from memory, or improvising.[4] There are occasional references to great performers, singer-poets whose entire repertoires have been lost. A relatively late source is Castiglione's manual of court etiquette known as *The Book of the Courtier*, dating from 1516. His references to music are few, but he mentions what we would recognise as folk-singing, and also the musical appreciation that would have been required by one who would lead a courtly life:

In my opinion the most beautiful music is singing well and in reading at sight and in fine style, but even more in singing to the accompaniment of the vielle . . . But especially it is singing recitative with the vielle that seems to me the most delightful, as this gives to the words a wonderful charm and effectiveness.[5]

Castigilione appears to be discussing two kinds of singing: that which is done 'at sight' (and therefore presumably from a score or part) and the self-accompanied 'recitative' which may well be a form of improvisation. Later in the sixteenth century a clearly identifiable school of virtuosi emerges, basing their improvisations on solo versions of polyphonic madrigals, which they accompanied on the lute. The earliest useful evidence comes from Ganassi's *Fontegara* of 1535, an ornamentation handbook for recorder players. His constant reference to singers suggests an existing tradition in which singers were pre-eminent.[6] Ganassi's treatise is only the first in an ever-increasing series of such works which reach a peak of complexity in the publications of Dalla Casa, Bassano and Rogniono towards the end of the century and into the next. These works, solo 'divisions' (jazz-like, embellished variations) on the polyphonic madrigals of earlier generations, testify to the great virtuosity of the performers but they are also an indication of a change that was occurring in the creative balance between composer and performer.

By writing out versions of what had been previously improvised, composers were in effect appropriating an area of creativity that had been the prerogative of the performer. Ironically, the evidence for improvisation contains the seeds of its eventual demise, and what had originally been a spontaneous act of creativity becomes instead a resource for composers and singers to use. The process of capturing improvisation and confining it to a written medium is the same as that which turned Greek oral epic into literature and formulaic chant into manuscripts. As could be predicted from this development, ornamentation becomes the basis for a pedagogy of singing, the implications of which are considered below.

The original function of improvised ornaments was to enhance the idea of the text rather than to clarify the meaning of individual words, and in this sense ornamented solo songs were no different from polyphony. Once the skills needed for the ever more elaborate *passaggi* had become entrenched in pedagogic principles, virtuosity inevitably became an end in itself, completing a process that begins with creative spontaneity which is then brought under control and developed to the point where it is no longer able to support its original function. What follows is what I think of as a decadent phase (a subject I shall return to in the final chapter) in which the style is no longer dynamically evolving. In the context of humanist thought the idea of amplifying the macro-text gave way to illustration of the poetry in a much more detailed and specific way, and on a basic level this could only be accomplished by reducing the number of notes per word. By the early seventeenth century the singing style of lavishly ornamenting an already highly decorated score had outlived its usefulness. Caccini, in the preface to *Le nuove musiche* (1602) says:

It occurred to me to produce a kind of music in which one could almost speak in tones . . . in both madrigals and airs I have always sought to imitate the ideas behind the words, trying to find those notes of greater or lesser affect (depending on the feelings of the texts) and of particular grace. As much as possible I have hidden the art of counterpoint. I have formed chords on the long syllables, avoiding them on the short, and I have observed the same rule in making *passaggi*, although for a bit of decoration I have sometimes used, mainly on short syllables, a few eighth-notes [semi-quavers] for as long as a quarter of one tactus or a half at the most. These are permissible since they pass by quickly and are not *passaggi* but merely an additional bit of grace . . . .And if . . . roulades must still be employed, let it be done according to some rule observed in my works and not either by chance or according to contrapuntal practice.[7]

Caccini says that improvisation (*'passaggi'*) should be kept to a minimum and only applied according to rules which he has devised. In saying this he is informed by the medieval interpretation of classical ideology which concentrates power in the hands of a small theorising elite (as opposed to the craftsman or paid performer); yet in seeking to ensure the primacy of the text at the level of the syllable he is applying humanist principles to text setting in which the music is freed from the need to imitate the text but becomes an extension of it. In order to achieve this he rejects 'Renaissance' counterpoint in favour of a musical line supported by chords. The vertical conception of harmonic as opposed to linear contrapuntal writing was not new (the practice of improvising faux bourdons could produce, in effect, a series of 6/3 chords); what is revolutionary is the new attitude to text-setting and it is this which characterises the *secunda prattica* of Monteverdi and the 'baroque'. Earlier in his preface Caccini refers to Plato ('who declared that music is naught but speech'), whose writings legitimise both medieval and humanist points of view, and confirm a tendency to view music as a pedagogic and disciplinary tool.

Italian ideas spread throughout most of Europe, and some of the most interesting sources of information about Italian singing are contained in the writings of foreigners who studied in Italy or who had Italian teachers. The German composer and theorist, Praetorius, in his *Syntagma musicum* (1619), like many Italian writers, draws a parallel between singers and orators and refers to the works of Caccini and Bovicelli. Mersenne, in *Harmonie universelle* (1636), says of Italian recitative:

As to the Italians, in their recitatives they observe many things of which ours [the French] are deprived, because they represent as much as they can the passions and affections of the soul and spirit as, for example, anger, furore, disdain, rage, the frailties of the heart, and many other passions, with a violence so strange that one would almost say that they are touched by the same emotions they are representing in the song . . . (MacClintock, 1994, p. 173)

This description would certainly have been recognisable to Giustiniani, in whose *Discorso sopra la musica* compiled in the late 1620s he recalled witnessing a performance by the ladies of Ferrara and Mantua some forty years before:

> They moderated or increased their voices, loud or soft, heavy or light . . . now slow, breaking off with sometimes a gentle sigh, now singing long passages legato or detached, now groups, now leaps, now with long trills, now with short . . . accompanied with appropriate facial expressions, glances, gestures . . . They made the words clear in such a way that one could hear even the last syllable of every word. (MacClintock, 1994, p. 29)

The kind of event described here has many of the conditions necessary for what would become opera. Singing in plays was a well-documented tradition, as was the custom of musical interludes (or *intermedii*) between acts, but the insertion of songs into spoken dialogue does not of itself result in music theatre in the integrated sense of opera. The problem was one of realism: how was it possible that an actor could legitimately sing his part without overtaxing the audience's suspension of disbelief? The Renaissance obsession with classical mythology provided part of the answer: mythological characters existed in a different reality and could not be expected to behave in a realistic way. In addition it helped if the characters were actually portraying singers. The first successful proto-opera was probably Poliziano's *Orfeo* in which it is known that the eponymous hero was played by Baccio Ugolini, a priest who accompanied himself on a kind of lyre for some parts of the performance. Poliziano's work is accepted as a major work of literature; no music survives, nor was any probably written, Ugolini being well known for his improvisations, but it is in such pieces that the pre-conditions for opera could flourish.[8] The development of monody and recitative was therefore not the entirely intellectual construct that historians have sometimes claimed it to be. The debate between Peri, Cavalieri and Caccini about the nature of recitative was essential to the fashioning of a truly authentic style but was not its *raison d'être*. It was the coming together of the mythological reality with the histrionic delivery of the chamber style of singing that enabled an operatic form of music theatre to compete in its own right with spoken theatre.

The acceptance of a heightened form of reality for continuously sung music theatre was also aided by the nature of the new singing itself. The descriptions of singers in action give us some idea of what this was like, but there are also important clues in the music. A great deal of early recitative is very close to heightened speech. My own experiments with singers confirm that early recitatives tend to follow (and exaggerate) the natural intonation patterns of spoken Italian. In workshops on early baroque singing I have sometimes presented students with texts from Italian operas previously unknown to them and asked them to improvise recitative in the style of the composer. Invariably the students invent a variety of speech-song which has a pitch contour very close to that of the unseen original. With a grounding in rhetoric and oratory common to performers and listeners alike, the new style won easy acceptance once the necessary components had come together.

The earliest manifestations of what are today known as operas were typically called *favoli in musica*. Initially these were private, courtly events but public opera performances towards the middle of the seventeenth century were grander affairs which brought changes in the nature of patronage and in the attitude of singers towards their performances. The first public opera was *Andromeda* by Ferrari and Manelli, performed in Venice during the Carnival of 1637 at the Teatro San Cassiano. It was public in the sense that the audience paid for seats in a theatre previously used for *commedia* performances, whereas previous operas had been private and by invitation. It was nevertheless still a pursuit of the wealthy: the theatres were bought as investments by aristocratic families with the management and administration entrusted to an *impresario*. The figure of the *impresario* is a crucial one in the devolving of responsibility for high culture performances from the aristocracy to the bourgeoisie and it is from this point that singing begins to become professional in the sense that we now understand the term. Singers now had the possibility to become stars of wide repute.[9]

Later operas were dominated by the castrati. Used in the Eastern church since the twelfth century, castrati did not appear in the Sistine chapel until 1562 (possibly helped by Paul IV's edict of 1555 dismissing and excluding all married men from the chapel). By the time opera was conceived, the castrati were recognised as being singers of phenomenal ability. This was due to the unique physical conditions produced by the act of castration. The effect of removing the testicles before their glandular function had begun resulted in abnormal physical development: a larger, more effeminate body, with the chest often measuring the same from front to back as from side to side. The ossification process of the entire skeleton was delayed, with consequent effect on the larynx, which remained in its pre-pubertal cartilaginous state for much longer and never grew to the size of a normal adult male voice-box.[10] The effect of a much larger chest acting on a much smaller larynx must have given the castrati the wherewithal to accomplish great feats of breath control which have never been matched. It was the legendary achievements of these singers which gave rise to the myth of bel canto. Singing acquired many of the trappings of performance art that it still retains during the present day largely as a result of the careers of these mutilated men.

The spread of new thinking was hastened by the increased production of printed scores. Between 1600 and the 1630s more than two hundred volumes of songs appeared from the Italian presses (Tomlinson, 1986). The peak was reached within the first decade and publication declined rapidly after the economic crisis of 1619–20 which caused a steep rise in the price of wood. Bianconi (1989) suggests that an additional reason for the reduced output may be the change in the pattern of socio-musical relations as musical consumption became polarised between those who performed and those who listened. The printing boom had been led by music for courtly or middle-class domestic performance. Madrigal books, for example, were produced in sets of parts, each print-run needing as many volumes as there were parts plus the necessary title-pages. Production of opera scores, however, virtually ceases after the fourth decade of the century and they circulate in manuscript only. Barthes (1977a), in 'Musica Practica', makes a distinction between music one does and music one listens to, pointing to the fact that up to a certain historical point music is in some sense available to be practised by all. When this point is passed (for Barthes, by Beethoven) relations between composer, performer and audience change, the composer becoming the Romantic genius, the performer becoming interpreter and the mass of people who could do neither of these things becoming listeners. This process undoubtedly begins with a similar change of relations from the co-operative and sociable secular polyphony to the solo song, where communication with one's fellow performers is replaced by communication between performer and audience. The socio-economic conclusions that follow from this support a reduction in the output of printed scores and the further concentration of power in the hands of fewer people towards the end of the century in Italy.

The articulation of socio-musical change is a complex process that occurs at many levels. A direct correspondence between specific musical and socio-economic events is relatively rare. Humanism and the Reformation did not prevent a medieval style of church singing from persisting into and after the sixteenth century, not simply in the musical forms of the *prima prattica* but in a particular style of performance-practice. Italian theorists of the period make a distinction between *cappella* singing – in church choirs – and *camera* singing (what we would now call chamber singing). Vicentino, in his *L'antica musica ridotta alla moderna prattica* says that in church one may sing with full voice with a large number of singers (i.e. more than one to a part, the customary number for madrigal singing) (Uberti, 1981, pp. 491–2). Maffei's letter to the Count of Alta Villa in 1562 says in reference to camera singing that 'you should keep your mouth moderately open, no wider than when you are conversing with friends' (MacClintock, 1994, p. 45). This would produce sounds similar to speech which would be lost in a large church but appropriate for an intimate chamber performance. Zarlino, in 1558, makes a similar distinction:

In churches and public chapels one sings in one manner and in private rooms another; for in churches one sings in full voice . . . and in rooms one sings with a more submissive and suave voice, and without yelling. (Uberti, 1981, p. 493)

He reproves, as Conrad had done before him, those whose vowel sounds make a mockery of the text. The *camera* voice seems to have been an extension of speech into song, as Caccini would later put it. From the accounts of contemporary commentators *cappella* singing came to be considered rather loud and crude (partly for acoustic reasons).[11] The two styles were separate enough for singers to be able to employ either as required, though not without difficulty, apparently: there is one report of a fifteenth-century Italian singer who excused himself as he could not use his *voce di camera* for the moment, having sung in church for so long that he needed a rest.[12]

The conception of singing and its pedagogy continued to evolve. Castrato singing was beyond the reach of ordinary men. These singers, more than any of their predecessors, legitimised their performance as high art, with the implication that other ways of singing were not high art. The refining process which began around the time of Conrad, and continued through *camera* and early opera singing, reached a high point from which it has never been dislodged. A vast number of treatises appeared during the baroque period, all saying broadly the same thing. One of the most widely read was Pier Francesco Tosi's *Opinioni de' cantori antichi e moderni* published in Bologna in 1723. An English translation appeared in 1743 entitled *Observations on the Florid Song,* and a German version with a substantial preface by Johann Agricola was published in 1757. Tosi himself was a castrato and many of his maxims are directed at male sopranos who would retain their unbroken voices, though he is at pains to point out that what he says applies to all voices (despite his obvious dislike of women singers). The reason for the wide distribution of Tosi's work (apart from any economic forces that may have been operating) was the fact that it was comprehensive and summative, capturing the flavour of singing of the period. To modern ears most of what he says (in common with his predecessors) is plain common sense: stand up straight, sing in time, and so on. There are many clues as to taste and style, but the core of the work is an ornamentation handbook. For Tosi and his contemporaries teaching singing was largely a matter of mastering the *bravura* passage-work so characteristic of the music of the time and, like the *passaggi* of two hundred years before, symbolised the decadence of a style that would itself eventually be superseded. There is nothing new in Tosi about breathing, the indispensable foundation of modern technique. The sound he made, for all the trappings of style that accompanied it, cannot have been anything like that of a modern opera singer. Those who were not castrati, especially female sopranos, cannot have sounded very different from pre-Renaissance singers.[13]

England's position as an offshore island meant that there was a greater time-lag before the influence of 'new' thinking permeated local tradition. Politically, England had never followed the same course as mainland Europe. The replacement of the Anglo-Saxon aristocracy with an almost completely new Anglo-Norman elite effectively removed the territorial imperative that was at the root of European development. The growth of naval power jointly with mercantile ventures during the sixteenth century ensured a reasonably stable prosperity for the landed classes at home. The universities of Oxford and Cambridge became great centres of humanism (Erasmus taught at Cambridge) and London was a substantial mercantile city, though its unique status as the one central economic and cultural centre must also have meant a lack of artistic competition compared with that in the Italian city states. There was a flourishing musical tradition in the Middle Ages, with many links to the continent. This was a two-way relationship: the *countenance Angloise*, or tendency to use thirds and sixths as consonances (suggesting an earlier change from Pythagorean to meantone temperament), influenced Dufay and Binchois. There are frustratingly few useful references to singing in medieval England, perhaps the largest number of singers being known only because of a fashion for listing singers' names to provide a motet text. The dislocation and destruction of manuscripts following the dissolution of the monasteries after the 1530s and the further disruption caused by the civil war a century later certainly destroyed an enormous amount of valuable material, but there seems to have been no equivalent of the Italian *improvisatori*. There was a considerable increase in the output of printed sources during the late sixteenth century, however, and these enable us to have some idea at least of what music was sung.

The sixteenth century is often cited as being a time when all sections of society enjoyed most of its music, with popular and 'learned' music co-existing in a way that may not have happened before or since. David Wulstan (1985) paints a vivid picture of Tudor England as a time when there was an 'unselfconscious confluence of popular and learned heritages', when composers incorporated popular tunes into their compositions, when waits and choristers mediated betweeen classes. The former would play at feasts, masques and plays as well as performing their original task of keeping the watch, and choristers would sing in chapel before retiring to the tavern. This is a somewhat idealised picture: although composers borrowed popular tunes, the demands of literacy would ensure that the borrowing was in one direction only. The tendency to idealise the period as a 'Golden Age' has been rightly criticised by Alan Durant (1984) as a much later ideological construct (one that we shall encounter again in considering the myth of bel canto). The Protestant Reformation in England caused a radical re-assessment of ideas of language and text-setting, as it had done in many northern European kingdoms. The criteria applied to music by Cranmer and his colleagues meant that both monophony and polyphony should be in the simplest note against note style and in English as opposed to Latin. For the first time in perhaps a thousand years those in authority in the church wished the broader mass of people to participate in, and fully understand, the liturgy. This was not the

populist movement that it might have been but a return to the
discipline of plainness, devoid of elaboration and ornament.
Whereas in Italy the radicalism of Wert and others in using homo-
phony to set 'realistic' texts is rightly held by musicologists to be a
precursor of the *secunda prattica*, the importance of the English
sixteenth-century attempts at relating singing to speech is often
overlooked. It may be that the ideas of the *secunda prattica* took so
much longer to become established in England than elsewhere in
Europe because, ironically, the English already had experience of
realistic word-setting and were reluctant to explore further in that
direction because of its association with extreme Protestantism,
elements of which continued under Elizabeth at the same time as
more complex music began to flourish again.

The type of singing required for the simpler forms of church
music would surely have been closer to that used for domestic music-
making. The basic precepts of Conrad's treatise of 1474 had found
their way into Andreas Vogelsang's *Musicae activae micrologus* of 1515,
which was translated into English by John Dowland in 1609.
Dowland's writings were intended for aristocratic, courtly consumption and referred both to the professional singers of the royal chapels
and the courtly amateurs for whom much of the madrigal and lute-
song repertoire was composed. Despite the insular qualities of the
English madrigal and the uniqueness of the lute song the English
were aware of musical trends on the continent of Europe, though
new ideas often did not reach the country until they were no longer
new elsewhere. There was something of a fashion for Italianised
English madrigals: Nicholas Yonge's *Musica transalpina* appeared in
1588, with a second volume in 1597 but these are firmly within the
prima prattica. Dowland travelled extensively in Europe but despite
the apparent modernity of his later songs remained unconvinced by
the new style. Italian musicians settled in London, and the English
composers Cooper and Philips made the journey in the opposite
direction. It was this sort of channel which opened the way for
Robert Dowland's *Musicall Banquet*. This contains French, English
and Italian songs, including two by Caccini but with the *continuo*
parts realised in tablature by Robert Dowland for the lute, English
musicians presumably being as yet unfamiliar with the practice of
reading and filling in from bass lines. The Notari manuscript
contains re-arrangements of many Italian composers including
Monteverdi, but this seems to be an isolated piece of avant-garderie.

The next generation of English song writers includes Robert Johnson and the Lawes brothers, who handle bass lines confidently and are totally at home in the new style. The manuscript sources of Johnson's works show evidence of a kind of late English division school, some songs existing in very elaborate versions, and songs which use obviously Italian models. Johnson's *Arm, arm!* is a case in point. It is a battle song, written in the first instance for Beaumont and Fletcher's play *The Mad Lover*, with effects which suggest that the composer may have known Monteverdi's *Tancredi e Clorinda*. By the end of the century, the music of Pelham Humfrey and Henry Purcell shows a similar sophistication to that of their Italian contemporaries such as Carissimi. All of these composers were men of the theatre, for which they composed songs (John Wilson and Robert Johnson both collaborated extensively with Beaumont and Fletcher, for example), but it was the masque that claimed the energies of serious composers. Masques were entertainments in words and music, professionally written and sung but performed with the participation of the courtiers as dancers. Being so closely allied with the court, and in a situation of very limited artistic competition, the masquing tradition inhibited the early growth of opera as an aristocratic pastime. The initial creative stimulus was primarily literary (as was the case with early Italian operas) but the stage machinery, sets and choreography were considered equal in importance to the text, with music having a far less structural role.

This exclusively aristocratic music drama had less effect on the development of true opera than its lower-class equivalent, the jig. Originally a dance form, the jig evolved into a playlet with songs during the Elizabethan period and it is the farce jig in particular that influenced the beginnings of the play-with-music.[14] Under Purcell and the later seventeenth-century composers this would become a sufficiently sophisticated vehicle for some stage works of the period to be considered by some historians as opera. The evolution of opera in England as a music drama with spoken dialogue had consequences that were to make the *genre* very different from its Italian counterpart. When Italian opera did arrive in England with the first performance of Handel's *Rinaldo* in 1711 it was to become an upper-class or higher bourgeois entertainment, largely because of the vernacular dialogue of the play-with-music and its association with what was to become vernacular comic opera.

The popular reaction against Italian opera in the 1740s was partly

chauvinistic but also to do with the increasing complexity of the
music and the remoteness of performers from their audiences, the
change in the sense that Barthes (1977a) might have described it, from
music as activity to music as something performed by someone else.
But in the success of the *Beggar's Opera*, which used well-known tunes
in simple arrangements interspersed between spoken dialogue in the
vernacular, and the rise of the pleasure gardens in which 'art songs'
could be served up in more palatable form, we can see the development of a petit-bourgeois middle-of-the-road audience which is still
with us today. The English vocal style, light in the prevailing taste
and commercially exploitable through sheet music sales, is the fore-
runner of the diluted technique used in light opera, music hall and, in
the twentieth century, musicals. Although singers were by now largely
free from aristocratic patronage and were, in this respect at least,
closer to modern professionals, the definition of a singer was much
looser than we might expect. The spoken dialogue tradition ensured
a good deal of common ground between singers and actors. Mrs
Cibber, Thomas Arne's sister, was a noted actress, yet she sang the
alto part in the first performance of *Messiah*. Handel much admired
Cibber, 'whose voice and manners,' said Burney, 'had softened his
severity for her want of musical knowledge' (Burney, 1988). Singers
were also publicised for their acting ability. Nancy Storace created
the role of Susannah in Mozart's *Le nozze di Figaro* but went on to
become a famous Drury Lane actress. Mrs Arne (Thomas Arne's
wife) 'was deliciously captivating: she knew nothing in singing or in
nature but sweetness and simplicity', as Charles Dibdin (1800) put it.
English singers had no answer to continental virtuosity but could
make a virtue of simplicity. The fact that *Messiah*, the most serious
art-work of its time, could actually benefit from the singing of an
actress is a powerful argument against anything like a modern
technique. A modern English analogy would be perhaps Michael
Crawford playing Albert Herring. The more histrionic delivery,
harking back to oratorical and rhetorical tradition, may account for
the ease with which actors could become singers and vice versa.
Arne's circle certainly contained virtuosic singers (such as his mistress
Miss Brent) as well as actresses. His one attempt to write an 'English'
Italian opera, *Artaxerxes*, met with some public success but as far as
Burney was concerned the project was a total disaster. Burney's
comment says a great deal about the social aspects of operatic style as
well as the flawed nature of Arne's attempt at compromise:

The doctor kept bad company: that is, had written for vulgar singers and hearers too long to be able to comport himself properly at the Opera-house, in the first circle of taste and fashion. He could speak to the girls in the garden very well; but whether through bashfulness, or want of use, he had but little to say to good company. The common play-house and ballad passages, which occurred in almost every air in this opera, made the audience wonder how they got there.[15]

It was not sociologically possible for an English composer to write a successful Italian opera, so close was the relationship between class structure and musical *genre*. Burney perfectly expresses the social attitudes of his time, attitudes that have to a considerable degree remained characteristic of opera audiences in England to the present day. English Italian opera had its own theatres, its own singers (who sang in a language that almost none of the audience understood and who generally adopted Italian stage names regardless of their country of origin) and its own London-based upper-class audience (although Addison does describe in *The Spectator* a brief hybrid period when the main characters sang in Italian and the subsidiary roles in English). In the late nineteenth century the Italian emphasis shifted to encompass any foreign opera given in its original language, a policy that continues at Covent Garden in the late twentieth century. English opera, with its stylistically naïve native singers and music free of plot-impeding virtuosity, was open to everyone (and in the provinces it was the only variety of touring or provincial opera available).

Opera in Italy followed a different sociological course. It has often been assumed that the wide public for opera in Italy is to do with its nationalist associations. Rosselli (1984, pp. 165 ff.) has pointed out that such a view is an oversimplification, with the composers' works likely to be used in support of both revolution and *ancien régime* on different occasions. A more likely explanation is the widespread commercialisation of opera in the second half of the nineteenth century, when many new opera houses were built and the lowest seat prices kept within range of all but the most poor. To this extent the Italian experience has a parallel in the British music hall. It may also be significant that Italians had a preference for rigidly tiered seats in which all sections of society could be accommodated at the appropriate level. This would have been in contrast to the separate buildings favoured by English society.

Can the changes that we can document in Italian singing really be described as revolutionary? What we can see during this period, simply because there is surviving documentation to enable us to make a judgement, is how a singing style develops and changes. If later periods show a similar pattern of evolution it would be possible to derive from this a basic theory of stylistic development, and I shall return to this question in my final chapter. There was undoubtedly a revolutionary change in singing style from what we usually call the Renaissance into the early baroque. How far this was a one-off event, and how far it represents some sort of cyclic pattern will become clearer in the next chapters. It is clear, too, that the basic ingredients of the ideological divide between classical and popular singing were already firmly in place well before the nineteenth century.

CHAPTER 4

The development of the modern voice

It was during the nineteenth century that the social and musical conditions for the development of the modern idea of 'classical' singing came into being, with a well-documented change from the speech-related singing that probably characterised the high status form in earlier periods to a new dedicated form of singing that was radically different from what had gone before. The new singing was underpinned both technically and ideologically by a pedagogy increasingly based on scientific principles. Parallel with this was the tendency to mythologise singing of the past, and it is during this period that we first encounter references to bel canto, as a mythical vocal technique from a previous era. The science, the myth, and the ideologies that framed them both, are still very much a part of many aspects of singing in the present day.

The evidence examined so far suggests that until the nineteenth century there was no precise definition of what singing actually was, but for the aspiring elite singer there was one traditional method of learning the art: he or she would attach him- or herself to a master, who would not necessarily be a practising singer but a musician who had a reputation for sound teaching. This could be as a private pupil or, in the case of Italy, at a private *accademia*, many of which flourished from the late Renaissance onwards. The method of instruction is to be found in the countless treatises published in the eighteenth and nineteenth centuries: empirical, pragmatic methods which revealed the latent talents of the pupil. Much of the evidence for change comes from the more detailed instruction manuals of the nineteenth century and the autobiographical writings of singers. Singing technique became the subject of debate, and successful singers could assure themselves of additional kudos later in their careers by revealing technical aspects that would help to legitimise a subsequent teaching career.

One of the main technical means by which singers acquired their technique had traditionally been the *solfeggio* exercise. This had the twin purposes of teaching sight-reading and giving practice in the *fiorituri* of the time. *Solfeggio* is in essence a virtuoso version of what Odo of Cluny and Guido of Arezzo had used to train their monks: it was a method that had served singers adequately for many hundreds of years. By singing the Guidonian names of each note, sight reading became easier, vowel colour was clearly differentiated and a certain muscular facility was encouraged. Michael Kelly, the celebrated Irish tenor who was to create the roles of Don Curzio and Don Basilio in Mozart's *Le nozze di Figaro* studied for a time in Naples with the castrato Giuseppe Aprile. Aprile, described by Charles Burney in his 1770 diary (repr. 1979) as having 'a rather weak and uneven voice, not constantly steady as to intonation – but has a good person, a good shake, and much taste and expression', gave him a daily lesson in *solfeggio* for the first four months of his apprenticeship. Kelly received his instruction and living expenses free of charge and Aprile even paid his passage to Florence when he considered Kelly to be capable of making a living from performing. A generation or two later, Charles Santley, an English baritone who studied with Gaetano Nava in the 1850s, describes the importance of *solfeggio* thus:

The painter's perspective, colour, grouping; the surgeon's anatomy; the sailor's ropes and sails; the soldier's gun, sword, and bayonet exercises, and so on throughout the range of human occupation, are none other than scales and *solfeggi* in another form – the foundation, which must be formed of solid materials firmly and carefully welded . . . (Santley, 1893, p. 72)

The *solfeggi* were eventually replaced by *vocalizzi*, exercises on the vowel-sound 'ah'. These were often miniature concert pieces in their own right, developing not just fluent virtuosity but wider musical parameters such as smooth singing and dynamic range. Some found their way into drawing rooms as 'songs without words'. In a later passage Santley describes a typical lesson:

I commenced my lesson always with preliminary vocal excercises, taken in progressive order as I mastered them; the whole course, from the simplest combination of notes to the study of the shake, with which I concluded, occupying twelve months. I then sang one or two *solfeggi*, which after a few weeks, as I was already a good reader, were replaced by *vocalizzi*, though I still worked at *solfeggi* for the purposes of pronunciation at home; and I finished with the study of detached pieces from operas, in which the facility of vocalization I had acquired was most available. (p. 80)

Santley's dismissal of the *solfeggio* so soon after his strong endorsement of it is a symptom of one of the changes in teaching technique that occurred in the nineteenth century. A further difference between him and Kelly is that the latter was trained as a boy soprano from an early age, a practice that was no longer so rigorous in Santley's day. The serious training of an unbroken voice requires, like the *solfeggio* exercise, a 'natural' technique: *solfeggi* involve exploiting the agility of the throat, larynx and lips, giving a lightness to the voice. The *vocalizzi* were to develop long *legato* lines and the richness of tone associated with the *voix sombrée*, as Garcia termed the new singing appropriate for the music dramas of Verdi and Wagner (Garcia 1841/1872).

Since the early baroque period voices had undoubtedly been growing in size. The typical accompanying instrument of the late Renaissance was the lute, which underwent many design changes to increase its size and compass. The instruments of the lute family all have a wide dynamic range from a barely audible *pianissimo* to what in modern terms might be considered a robust *mezzoforte* (depending on the size of the instrument and on the maker). In the English lute song and French *air de cour* linear contrapuntal writing achieved its most expressive realisation. The scores contain nothing that a modern singer would recognise as dynamic markings (indeed, the first modern editors of lute songs felt obliged to add expression marks). Yet to assume that the music was sung without expression is to miss the point entirely. All singers of the period would have been familiar with rhetorical convention and all the information necessary to create an expressive performance was contained within the text itself. The balance of creative input between composer and performer was very different from the twentieth-century convention by which the composer specifies as many parameters as possible, leaving the performer reduced to the role of interpreter. The lute was the perfect accompanying instrument for such performances.

The declamatory style of the early seventeenth century was vertical and chordal with a minimum of counterpoint so that the text would always be clear. The words were, as Giulio Cesare Monteverdi put it, 'the mistress of the harmony and not its servant' (Strunk, 1981, p. 46). The scores of operatic recitatives are very minimal to look at, but they conceal the fact that many instruments played from the same bass line. All accompanying instruments increased in size during the seventeenth century to make the playing of recitative more efficient, larger harpsichords or lutes producing greater resonance which sustained longer. There was also an increase in numbers to take account of the larger buildings in which the music was performed. Inevitably, singers had to sing louder.

During the eighteenth century the lute family was eclipsed by the harpsichord. As an accompanying instrument the harpsichord is completely different from even the largest lute. Because the strings are plucked by quills which are affixed to jacks activated by a keyboard, the player has almost no control over the loudness of his or her playing, and none at all once the note has been struck (unlike the lutenist who can modify the sound with the finger-board hand after plucking). The instrument does resonate well: it produces many high frequencies which continue to decay in the instrument for longer than similar frequencies would last in a theorbo, and this proved well suited to combining with the cello as a small accompanying ensemble. The instrument increased in size during the eighteenth century, gaining an additional manual, with the possibility of tuning strings in octaves as well as in unison. The acoustic texture which results from a large harpsichord is such that the singer is precluded from the variety of expression that would be possible were the same piece to be accompanied by a member of the lute family. The implications are that singers were having to make more noise and perhaps to sing with less subtlety than their predecessors.

The performance circumstances of secular music, performed in the Middle Ages to a small number of *cognoscenti* often as a background to other sociable activities, changed considerably with the production of dramatic works. We know that the first performance in 1607 of Monteverdi's *Orfeo* took place at the palace of Margherita Gonzaga-Este in a room probably no more than 10m by 30m (Fenlon, 1984). Subsequent performances took place in larger rooms in order to accommodate the stage machinery required. The growth of public opera in the 1640s meant a move to theatres, which offered larger spaces for machinery, performers and audience. The Venetian theatre of SS Giovanni e Paolo, for example, was more than twice the size of the Gonzaga rooms (Worsthorne, 1968). The flexible scoring of continuo-based works meant that the most efficient use could be made of the acoustic space available. The castrati would probably have had no problems in projecting their voices over the larger instrumental forces increasingly employed, and this may have been another factor in their dominance of the music theatre at the time. As the size of orchestras, concert halls and theatres grew, there must have been considerable demands on the stamina of unmutilated singers. During the nineteenth century the addition of new and larger instruments and instrumental doubling, plus the introduction of sizeable dedicated concert halls, made more efficient vocal production inevitable. By 1832 Berlioz could devote several pages of his *A travers chants* to the problem of outsized halls in which only a few singers could project sufficiently.[1]

Although there was a general increase in the size of voices to keep pace with the demands of drama and technology there appears to have been no fundamental change in technique until the first quarter of the nineteenth century. In chapter 3 above I argued that the beginning of the seventeenth century saw a stylistic change in which both the 'decadent' florid singing of the sixteenth-century division school and the Renaissance school of text-setting based on word-painting as idea gave way to the 'realistic' speech-song of the early baroque. In purely vocal terms virtuosity lost its original function of highlighting the text and became an indulgence in display for its own sake. This cycle (or perhaps spiral) of development followed by a stylistic plateau appears to continue or begin again later in the seventeenth century. In the later operas composed from around the middle of the century onwards virtuosity again begins to predominate. There is a progression of increasing elaboration through Handel's extremely difficult castrati roles, to the coloratura soprano roles of Mozart and, finally, Rossini, in which the ever-increasing deftness of the singers in their improvised passages was incorporated into composers' scores, which would then be further extended by additional spontaneous cadential *roulades*.[2]

During this long period there is no evidence of a change in technique, despite the great changes in musical style. The singing was the basic light variety that had characterised secular music for centuries. The early-nineteenth-century technique expected by Rossini was probably not very different from that employed by the virtuosi of the sixteenth-century division school. Berlioz, conscious of living in a period of revolutionary change (and extremely ill-disposed towards Rossini), gives a vivid picture of singing in Italy during the 1830s:

What are undoubtedly more common in Italy than anywhere else are good voices, voices that are not only full and incisive but nimble and quick as well. But the prevalence of voices lending themselves naturally to vocalization and the public's instinctive love of glitter and display react on each other. Hence the mania for *fiorituri* which debases the finest melodies; hence those convenient vocal formulas which make all Italian phrases sound alike; hence that eternal device of the final cadence, which leaves the singer free to embroider at will but maddens many listeners by its perfunctoriness and dreadful inevitability; hence the constant tendency to break into *buffo* style which lurks even in the tenderest scenes of pathos; hence, in short, all those abuses which have made of melody, harmony, tempo, rhythm, orchestration, expression, plot, staging, poetry, the poet, and the composer the abject slaves and playthings of the singer . . . (Cairns, 1969, p. 212)

The similarity to the position in which Caccini found himself some two hundred years earlier is unmistakeable:

Moreover I see ill-used those single and double vocal *roulades* – rather, those redoubled and intertwined with each other . . . and I see vocal crescendos-and-decrescendos, *esclamazioni*, tremolos and trills, and other such embellishments of good singing style used indiscriminately. (Hitchcock, 1970, p. 43).

In all the manifestations of pre-nineteenth-century vocal styles there is no evidence of what would be recognised as a modern technique (as opposed to style). The age of the scientific investigation of the voice had not yet begun, though the basic workings of the voice were understood in some quarters. Today the physiology of the voice has been thoroughly researched (though a lot of work is still in progress) and by applying what is known today to the evidence of the past it is possible to be reasonably sure of some aspects of earlier 'techniques'. As an instrument, the voice consists of three elements: a power supply (the lungs), an oscillator (the cords, or vocal folds as they are sometimes called) and a resonator (the vocal tract, consisting of the mouth and throat cavities).[3] The airstream from the lungs passes through the folds, which vibrate, producing the raw material for speaking or singing. This raw sound is a complex one consisting of a fundamental frequency determined by the cordal vibration, and a large number of overtones or partials. As in any acoustic space there is a frequency at which the tract itself resonates. There are, in fact, four or five such resonances, known as formants, which have their own vibrating frequency (which, of course, changes with the shape of the tract). The closer the partials correspond to this frequency, the louder will be the resulting sound leaving the lips.

This relationship also determines the colour of vowels, a hugely complex process of continually shifting frequencies involving also the lips, jaw and tongue. This much is common to both speaking and singing. When a modern classical singer sings, a number of enhancements of this process takes place, the principal one being the lowering of the larynx (the small tube at the bottom of which the cords sit), which significantly increases the length of the vocal tract. The effect of this is to shift downwards all the formant frequencies with a marked effect on the first formant, which is associated with the larynx and the initial production of vowel sounds. This phenomenon, known as the singers' formant, produces additional resonance at the cost of no extra physical effort, to the extent that a solo singer can easily project his or her voice over a large orchestra.

The singers' formant and the low larynx position are also responsible for the 'coloration', the dark richness, of the modern voice. This in itself colours the vowels and gives the tongue less freedom of manoeuvre to distinguish between them. The lower larynx position is facilitated by the lower jaw position characteristic of modern singers, or a wider mouth opening (also a familiar sight). Both of these movements further modify vowels relative to speech. There is an additional effect, as the process is accompanied by a stiffness of the muscles of the vocal folds. This enables the lungs to work at higher pressure, producing more sound but at the price of some agility: the cords become slower to respond, making fast passage work difficult. It is important to bear in mind that these are generalised characteristics: there have been many examples of singers, such as Jenny Lind or Maria Callas, who have an unconscious, natural facility, clearly superior to that of their rivals, which is not easily explained in general physiological terms.

We know from Garcia's treatise of 1841 that the lowered larynx position (the *voix sombrée*) was a novelty in the 1830s and was not known earlier, and this enables us to make certain assumptions about a pre-Garcian voice. It is reasonable to assume that earlier singers sang with the larynx closer to the higher position used in speaking. This enabled them to distinguish clearly between vowels and made their voices light and agile: exactly the kind of voice one would need for the intimate performance of chamber music or the more florid ornamentation of the late Renaissance, baroque and classical periods. We know from countless illustrations of early singers that the forward jaw position found favour with many singers and would have effectively made their vowels sound more speech-like.[4] In the context of this pre-Garcian technique it is not difficult to see why the castrati were so highly prized. Their power combined with agility must have given them extraordinary ability. Although the castrati parts in baroque opera are invariably the show pieces, there is evidence in the increasing virtuosity of other parts (especially soprano lines) that the castrato phenomenon stimulated the other voices to greater heights. This must have meant a more systematised approach to breathing, though even post-Garcia the workings of the diaphragm, that indispensable muscle of the modern singer, were not properly understood. The celebrated turn-of-the-century *diva* Tetrazzini recounts how a potential pupil of hers successfully moved a piano with the diaphragm. Both teacher and pupil were confusing the diaphragm with the stomach muscles, as do many singers today (Caruso and Tetrazzini, 1909/1975, p. 14). The lack of a modern breathing technique was the other major difference between what we may call early and modern techniques: it is significant that the *cappella* singing of the sixteenth century was louder than its *camera* equivalent: it generally needed more than one voice to a part so problems of breathing could be rationalised (Uberti, 1981). This opportunity was not available to *camera* singers, who were dependent on their natural breath capacity which would have meant frequent breaths. There is no significant evidence of diaphragmatic breathing until late in the eighteenth century (a fact which has interesting implications for the recreation of a vocal technique appropriate for the works of Bach and Mozart).

The change from 'natural' to modern techniques was facilitated by a new school of scientifically orientated singing teachers. The scientific (or pseudo-scientific) nature of singing teaching reinforced the ideological function of pedagogy: all could aspire to the highest standards of professionalism or art which only a few would actually achieve. This process began early in the nineteenth century and was encapsulated by Garcia in his treatise *L'Art du chant*. Although Garcia's treatise is still held in high regard by many modern singing teachers, it is, ironically, his link with the previous era that receives the most comment, whereas what I find interesting for this study is his forward thinking. He considers, for example, the possibility of singing on the inhaled breath, and the technique that we would now call 'chant' (see chapter 7 below). As we would expect, he rejects both of these as having no practical application, but he is aware of their potential. Both are now standard extended vocal techniques. In 1830 Garcia had spent some time attached to a military hospital where he had unique opportunities to study the human vocal apparatus. Eventually, in 1854, he perfected the laryngoscope, an arrangement of mirrors (still used by throat specialists today) which enables the observer to watch the cords in action. Not only is his treatise the first to be based on genuinely scientific principles, but his science is remarkably well informed. Compare, for example, his summary of the vocal process with that of Johan Sundberg, one of the foremost living specialists in the field:

Garcia (1841): The instrument in which the human voice is produced is formed in three parts . . . a bellows or air duct (lungs and trachea), a vibrator (larynx), a reflector or tone modifier (pharyngial, nasal and buccal activities).
Sundberg (1977): Functionally the organ has three units: a power supply (the lungs) an oscillator (the vocal folds) a resonator (the vocal tract).

Garcia's quoting of Helmholtz, the leading acoustic theorist of his day, and his recognition by the French Academy of Sciences, show him to be in the forefront of knowledge. He was among the first to become aware of the *voix sombrée*, which he claimed to have taught since first hearing it in Italy in 1832. He discusses the new technique at some length and contrasts it with the more traditional *voix blanche* (translated by Paschke as 'clear voice'). The latter is essentially the 'natural' voice referred to above (Garcia quotes Tosi and Agricola, among others, as his predecessors), while the new technique involves a lower larynx position and can be recognised as the basis of modern classical technique. Sundberg's (1977) researches imply that a modern opera singer is by definition one who sings with this technique, whether or not he or she is aware of it. A lower larynx undoubtedly became the norm during the later nineteenth and twentieth centuries, to the extent that in the twentieth century it is taken for granted. Garcia himself saw his teaching as being in the mainstream of the traditional Italian school rather than a new departure, and in the second volume of his treatise he deals with vocal *fiorituri* and the conventions of traditional singing but in a far more comprehensive and scientific way.

The literature of the period has been extensively surveyed in Brent Jeffrey Monahan's *The Art of Singing* (1978) which analyses a comprehensive collection of statements on the subject made during the period 1777–1927. Monahan concludes that the beginnings of the 'scientific' school date from Garcia's publications and that by 1861 the number of 'scientific' works roughly equalled the number of 'empirical' ones. By 1891 he finds that almost every major new work on singing contained references to anatomy, physiology, breathing, phonation and resonance, and that the most important treatises of the time were written by physicians or scientists. This is in marked contrast to the pre-1840 period when every manual was written either by a practising singer or a singing teacher.

A further development in technique that has become part of the standard repertoire of twentieth-century opera singers was the extension of the chest register beyond the high tenor G to C. In traditional singing the higher notes made use of the 'head' register or falsetto, as the following extract from a letter from the tenor Domenico Donzelli to Bellini explains:

Chest tones . . . up to the G; and it is in that range that I can declaim with equal strength and sustain all the force of the declamation. From the G to the high C I can avail myself of a falsetto which, used with artistry and strength, is a resource for ornamentation. (Kimbell, 1981, p. 51)

In the first performance of Rossini's *William Tell* in 1831 the French tenor Gilbert-Louis Duprez amazed the audience when during Arnold's aria in Act IV he sang the top C in his chest register. Rossini, who had been expecting a falsetto note, thought the sound like 'the squawk of a capon having its throat cut' (Cairns, 1969, p. 539). Duprez was particularly associated with the *voix sombrée* and its lower larynx position would have accounted for the surprise experienced by the audience. The extension of the chest register to the upper fifth of the tenor range was a new and radical departure and is now characteristic of the twentieth-century operatic tenor sound.

Also associated with the new singing was a distinctive use of vibrato. In the sixteenth- and seventeenth-century treatises vibrato is rarely discussed, but by the second half of the nineteenth century the term appears in musical dictionaries and is clearly an issue. As with all aspects of the voice in the pre-gramophone era the subject is problematic because of the difficulty of knowing just what the sources mean. Mozart, for example, refers to the singer Meissner in a letter to his father:

Meissner . . . has a bad habit in that he often intentionally vibrates his voice . . . and that I cannot tolerate in him. It is indeed truly destestable, it is singing entirely contrary to nature.

but goes on to say:

The human voice already vibrates of itself, but in such a degree that it is beautiful, that is the nature of the voice. (Rushmore, 1984, p. 190)

H. F. Chorley, music critic of the *Athenaeum* and prominent anti-Wagnerian was not impressed by 'the habit of trembling'. He says of the baritone, Signor Fornasari (who made his London debut in 1843), that

The tremulous quality of his voice (that vice of young Italy, bad schooling and false notions of effect) became more monotonous and tiresome than the coldest placidity could have been. (Chorley, 1862/1972, p. 146)

Madame Medori, a Belgian dramatic soprano, arrived in England in 1853 with the 'habit of vibration so terrible . . . that on a long note it seems sometimes first too sharp, and then too flat, or vice versa, ere it settles itself' (Chorley, p. 331). This is a clear indication that the 'habit' is a pitch vibrato familiar to twentieth-century ears, rather than a vibrato of intensity which some voices appear to have naturally.

Some singers could make a pleasing effect with vibrato even on those such as Chorley who normally found it offensive to the ear. Of two of the noted tenors of the mid-century, one managed to use his vibrato to good effect, the other clearly did not:

. . . Signor Tamberlik had contracted the habit of vibration, which always, more or less, gives an impression of fatigue and premature decay, though in reality it is merely an ill fashion – a relic of Paganini's treatment of his strings, a peculiarity wondrously turned to account by Rubini when his sustaining power began to desert him and absolutely, in many of his best performances, producing an effect of emotion not attainable by any other means. (Chorley, p. 284)

Tamberlik (1820–89) was famous for his fast vibrato, and Rubini (1794–1854), a star of a previous generation, had been known for his high falsetto (for which Bellini wrote the high Fs in *I puritani*).[5] George Bernard Shaw also complained that vibrato was 'sweeping through Europe like the influenza' (Rushmore, 1984, p. 190). It is possible that what began as a means to cover failing technique became dramatically useful and then a commonplace of singing technique. There appears to be little direct connection between vibrato and larynx position, but given that higher-larynx singers use a vocal quality which is more closely related to speech (in which vibrato does not normally occur), there may be a case for dating the more indiscriminate use of vibrato from the second half of the nineteenth century. Peter Stadlen has demonstrated in a BBC radio programme, by slowing down various performances of *Pierrot lunaire,* that vibrato is an important criterion in defining the difference between singing and speech. The earliest recordings of Italian singers certainly show a tendency towards tremulousness, and by the time of universal recording very few singers appear to sing with no vibrato at all.[6] Extensive work was done at the University of Iowa during the 1920s and 1930s into the nature of vibrato. The voices of many famous singers were analysed, often by slowing down recordings of their voices. It was established that vibrato occurs in 95% of all sung utterances by trained singers, even though it may not be perceived by the listener. In untrained voices only one in five adults was found to have a natural vibrato as against nine out of ten singing students. Research was also undertaken to establish whether or not vibrato occurred in speech. It was found that the continuous pitch glides of conversational speech generally prevent vibrato from occurring (a stable pitch lasting at least 0·14 of a second is necessary for a single oscillation). When emotionally roused, however, speakers would use a certain amount of vibrato. This was particularly prominent in the actors analysed by the Iowa research team (Seashore, 1936a and b). I have a recording of Sir John Gielgud reciting Shakespeare in A minor which illustrates these points vividly. It is quite possible that the earliest systematic use of vibrato accompanied the return to the speech-like declamation required by Verdi and his successors.

There is a clear musical divide between the new technique and the brilliant but old-fashioned virtuoso style of Rossini who, although he supported his fellow Italian composers such as Verdi, was not at home with either the dramatic declamation or the circumstances in which it was used:

. . . I would add that the word expressive by no means excludes declamation, still less what is known as dramatic music, indeed I would assert that at times it requires such music . . . But I cannot deny a certain decadence in vocal art, for its new adepts incline towards the feverish style rather than the sweet Italian song that speaks to the soul. May God forgive those who were the first cause of this . . . (Gal, 1965, p. 239)

Rossini's letter to the music critic Filippo Filippi could hardly contrast more sharply with Bellini's letter to the librettist Carlo Pepoli:

Carve in your head in letters of brass: an opera must draw tears, cause horror, bring death, by means of song . . . Poetry and music, to make their effect must be true to nature, and that is all . . . (Gal, 1965, p. 251)

Verdi's letters to Varesi, who was to create the role of Macbeth, vividly demonstrate the new relationship between text and music:

I shall never stop urging you to study carefully the context and the words: the music comes by itself. In short I would like you to serve the poet better than the composer.

Of the witches' scene he says:

At this news you remain astounded and terrified

and of the appearance of the dagger:

This is a very beautiful point, dramatically and poetically.

then:

Notice that it is night: everyone is asleep: the whole of this duet must be sung *sotto voce*, but with a dark voice that inspires terror.

and then he gives a list of poetic ideas that should be particularly brought out. These extracts are from the the first of three letters in similar vein, which end with the instructions for the death scene:

you will be able to create a great effect if your singing is combined with well-thought-out acting . . . Let it be pathetic; but more than pathetic, terrible. The whole scene *sotto voce* with the exception of the last two lines; and here you must match your singing with action, breaking out with full force on the words 'Vil corona' and 'sol per te'. (Kimbell, 1981, p. 182ff.)

The *raison d'être* of Verdi's opera is as a forum for the expression of dramatic ideas rather than a vehicle for the *dolce cantare* of Rossini. His words echo those used by the seventeenth-century theorists examined in chapter 3, suggesting a return to the consideration of the relationship of text to music in much the same way that Caccini railed against the virtuosity of the sixteenth-century division school.

Wagner also gave deep consideration to the purpose of singing and the relationship between singing and text. He was himself an enthusiastic singer and before he began work on his major operas he was very conscious of living in a time when singing as he had known it was in decline. In 1834, having finished *Die Feen*, his first attempt at a full-length opera, and having not yet formulated his theories about the relationship between music and drama, Wagner wrote that 'the public, accustomed to faulty execution, overlooks the defects of the singer, if only he is a skilled actor and knows the routine of the stage' (Newman, 1961, p. 112). In 1850, shortly after the first performance of *Lohengrin*, he wrote in a letter to Liszt:

I have been so intent upon weighing and indicating the verbal emphasis of speech, that the singers need only sing the notes, exactly according to their value in the given tempo, in order to get precisely by that means the declamatory expression. (Henderson, 1938, p. 169)

Ironically, Wagnerian orchestration, even from the pit at Bayreuth, prevents a speech-like declamation by all but the largest voices. The amount of sheer volume required of the singers by Wagner's later works has led to the development of specialist Wagnerian singers in the twentieth century whose singing is so stentorian as to sound almost like pitched shouting. Indeed it is quite possible that research into the vocal behaviour of football crowds might reveal that the difference between the shouted chant of the fan and the singing of certain Heldentenors is more a matter of such markers as vibrato rather than tone production.

The introduction of the new singing was a gradual process. Because the public attention was drawn towards novelty and star singers of great individual charisma, there are few references to a break in tradition. The evidence tends to come from conservative commentators who feel a creeping malaise afflicting the entire singing world. Lord Mount Edgcumbe and Henry Chorley, two important observers of the opera scene from the end of the eighteenth century to the middle of the nineteenth, both have the tendency of older people reminiscing to condemn present styles of singing and composition while remembering fondly the experiences of their youth. Mount Edgcumbe, who published his *Italian Opera* in 1824 having not visited the opera for twenty years, had a hearty dislike of Rossini, whereas for Chorley, looking back from 1860, Rossini represented the last bastion against the evils of Verdi. They both agree, however, that the 'new Italian singing' is to be deplored. Edgcumbe says in his introduction that 'the taste of Italian professors, as well as singers and composers, is so much altered (and in my opinion for the worse)' (pp. x–xi). He writes that the shake (a fast, brilliant cadential trill) is 'entirely lost in Italy' though is still current in England (p.14). This kind of trill lingered later in England but by the end of the century was no longer used. An important indication that singers were singing louder is given in one of Mount Edgcumbe's own footnotes:

Modern music spoils the singers for concerts, especially in private houses. The constantly singing concerted pieces, adapted only for the theatre, gives them the habit of so forcing their voices that they know not how to moderate them to the space of an ordinary room. (p. 169n)

Chorley wrote his *Recollections* in 1862. The book consists of an examination of each season from 1830 to 1860, based on notes that he made at the time (presumably in connection with his critical writings for *The Athenaeum*). He had an encyclopaedic knowledge of opera singers, acquired both in England and from extensive travels in Germany and Italy. He too had a profound dislike of the new Italian singing. He takes it for granted that the more difficult passage work in Rossini's operas was usually omitted because the singers simply could not sing with the agility required. Bélart, the French tenor, was unusual in being able to sing all Rossini's notes (p. 374). This is surely evidence of a change of technique. He also mentions the tendency for vowel sounds to be less clear, noting that Tamberlik's speech-like recitatives show his singing in a poor light (p. 284). Those who sing in the older way are commended by Chorley. Donzelli, the Italian tenor, is compared favourably with 'the violent persons who have succeeded him . . . worse-trained folk who have since adopted the career of forcible tenors, partly from a wish to split the ears of the groundlings . . . ' (pp. 4–5). He tends to refer to the new style (and Verdi's music especially) with metaphors of violence. Singers in the new style are called 'declamatory artists' rather than singers. Chorley's critics have pointed to his failure to appreciate the historical significance of the young Wagner. From a singing point of view Chorley was in no doubt that Wagner was even worse than Verdi, summarising the mid-century period as:

The years during which singers' music has been stamped into bits as so much trash by the Wagners of New Germany, and bawled into a premature destruction of its voice by the Verdis of infuriate Italy. . . (p. 398)

An indication of the expressive possibilities of the new singing can be gained from a comparison of the late-eighteenth-century harpsichord and the newly invented piano. Haydn wrote a number of songs in the 1780s which he describes as 'Lieder für das Clavier'

('Clavier' meaning keyboard, as opposed to the more specific 'Cembalo', which meant harpsichord). His later English Canzonets of the 1790s are quite clearly also written for piano. If accompanied on a large harpsichord a great number of register changes is needed to achieve the dynamic markings that the composer asks for. A crescendo, or anything other than a terraced change of loudness is impossible. Although experiments were made with an arrangement described as a Venetian Swell, which controlled louvres in the lid of the instrument, such modifications could not compensate for the fact that the piano was touch-sensitive and had a dynamic range more like that of a large lute than that of a harpsichord. My own experiments with modern singers have produced startlingly different renderings of Haydn. Accompanied by an original fortepiano from around 1800, the singers were able to use a wide variety of dramatic expression which was completely lost when the song was repeated with a harpsichord. The early piano was also considerably quieter than the late harpsichord, and did not develop its characteristically full sound until the mid nineteenth century, by which time it, too, had undergone considerable technical improvements to enable it to compete with larger orchestral instruments in bigger halls.

The 'natural' empirical methods did not die out with the advent of the new singing though the decline of the castrati, and the spur this must have given to the development of more scientific methods, brought empiricism into something of a decline during the late nineteenth century. The dominance of the new technique resulted in huge voices (particularly in Wagnerian opera) but still left an unfulfilled need, not least among those teachers who could not cope with the new science. As Barthes (1984) has pointed out, bourgeois society is able to appropriate history and empty it of reality, substituting its own reality in the form of myth. One way of reinforcing the legitimacy of a pedagogy is to appeal to a golden age in which its principles reigned supreme, with the implication that given the appropriate application and discipline such an age may be regained.[7] This is more than the sentimental gloss which Mount Edgcumbe meant when he talked of a 'golden age' of Italian singing in his youth (p. xii). Though reality may become myth the process is not reversible, and seekers after the golden age are doomed to an endless search. In accepting the legitimacy of the search, however, they become beholden to the creators of the myth. Such is the case with bel canto. It is first used with a particularised connotation in

Italy in the 1860s to refer to the Italian style of singing, and, especially from the 1870s, to the beauties of that style compared with the crudities of Wagnerian dramatic declamation. The term became in effect a weapon in the propaganda war between the new Verdian style taken up by Wagner and the old virtuosic 'early' style, a war in which Wagner swept all before him, bel canto becoming an ideal (or lost reality) to which the losers could subscribe. The phrase did not enter dictionaries or text books until the twentieth century, by which time it had come to be associated with a style of singing developed during the seventeenth and eighteenth centuries, never precisely located and never surpassed. In appealing to this myth those who could not accept the more scientific theories of modern singing teaching would always have an important (and legitimising) criterion. The list of authorities claiming to possess the secret of bel canto grows yearly. Among the notable attempts earlier in the twentieth century is Klein (1923), a sometime pupil of Garcia, who associated it with Mozart. Lucie Manen (1987), the noted teacher of Peter Pears and Thomas Hemsley among others, entered the fray with a vehemently anti-Garcia polemic based on her own eccentric observations of vocal mechanisms. Perhaps the most balanced account is Celetti's *History of Bel Canto* (1991).

By the end of the nineteenth century classical singing had achieved a state of legitimacy implied in Bourdieu's definition of competence as

right to speak . . . right to the legitimate language, the authorized language, the language of authority. Competence implies the power to impose reception. (J. Thompson, 1984, p. 47)

It is only in the nineteenth century that the artistic use of the voice acquired the technique which would finally separate it completely from every other way of singing. The increasingly powerful middle class, which ensured a change in patronage from aristocratic to commercially dedicated concert halls, created the atmosphere in which a new concept of singer could flourish: the singer not just as artist, but singing as an exclusive art form, which required not just art but artifice. The new nationalism which inspired the revolutions of 1848 must also have furthered the circumstances in which a meta-language of singing could develop. The complex articulations of the class system ensured similar possibilities for exclusivity where it was needed: a music that was for the elite of society required a technique that was for its exclusive use. The modification of aristocratic conventions by the new bourgeoisie ensured that the concept of 'classical singing' and the circumstances in which it was consumed maintained a tradition of separateness from other musics.

Mount Edgcumbe disdainfully noted the change in lay-out at the Italian opera in London, the introduction of 'single seats called stalls, which may be hired by the night' and that 'Most improper company is sometimes to be seen even in the principal tiers' (p. 184). Chorley is appalled by what he calls the introduction of 'slang' by Mademoiselle Piccolomini, 'essentially a Vaudeville singer', and can hardly contain himself when Jullien, arch-populariser of the classics, is invited to compose an opera for Covent Garden. The musician in Chorley can see that Jullien was an able conductor, considerate and generous to his players, and he grudgingly credited him with 'a sort of pompous, comical, perverted enthusiasm'. He even refers to his 'lovely and inspired behaviour' but the fact that someone associated with mass music-making could be elevated to the Italian opera caused him 'utter disgust' (p. 320).

In England and other English-speaking countries this dominance was assured also by the relationship of the sung accents to their spoken equivalents. The early part of the nineteenth century seems to have seen the beginnings of what is now called Received Pronunciation (RP). The labyrinthine history of pronunciation in England, from the French-dominated medieval court through to the emergence of Southern English as a high-status form further complicated by monarchs of foreign origin, had meant that pronunciation had always had a wider social connotation than geography alone would produce. Phillipps, in *Language and Class in Victorian England* points to the increasing status of a non-regional way of speaking, and quotes Smart on the need to acquire:

. . . the standard dialect – that in which all marks of a particular place of birth or residence are lost, and nothing appears to indicate any other habits of intercourse than with the well-bred and well-informed, wherever they may be found. (Phillipps, 1985, pp. 135–6)

The 'standard dialect' requires an accent which 'demands a plumminess achieved by lowering the larynx and widening the oro-pharynx' (J. Wells, 1982, p. 283). In other words it operates in a similar way to the new singing technique. No research appears to have been done on the relationship between RP and singing and it is not yet possible to establish a specific link between them, but the ideological force of associating singing with high-status pronunciation in England can only have made classical singing more elitist. With the arrival of radio and recordings this tendency was compounded to the extent that almost all mainstream recordings of vocal music in English use RP whatever the linguistic origin of the performers. This has the curious effect of causing even native American music to sound quasi-English in performance, as for example in Copland's *In the Beginning* or Barber's *Reincarnations*. There is a considerable debate in the field of early music, where the revival of Renaissance vocal music has raised the possibility of reviving appropriate period pronunciation.

The term 'classical music' first appears in print in the second half of the nineteenth century. J. B. Macdonnell uses the term in the 1860 edition of *MacMillan's Magazine*. The *OED* gives 1885 as the earliest use and describes classical music as that characterised by an eighteenth-century sense of form and having 'permanent interest and value'. There is no word in the dictionary that expresses a concept of music that does not correspond to this definition, the inference being that other forms are impermanent and of no value (although 'popular' is used in connection with concerts from 1859 onwards). The word was almost certainly current for some time before the date of the dictionary entry, which is dependent on literary references. It is more difficult to establish a date for the currency of 'classical' singing, but it is logical to assume that during the nineteenth century this word was used to describe the elite form. The term is full of ideological echoes which embrace Aristotle, Plato and the Renaissance, and is a semantic and semiotic confirmation of a process that reaches a plateau towards the end of the century. Concepts need vocabulary in order to be adequately formulated and 'classical' at once separates the elite form of singing from other varieties and endows it with a moral legitimacy that is more than merely musical.

There are parallels between music and the sciences, and with literature. The new 'science' of singing is also an articulation of new ideas about the nature of human enquiry, which during the nineteenth century acquired a substantial new literature: science as a concept was changing. Similarly, the idea of a literary canon emerged during the same period, articulating the Romantic view of the artist as genius and his product as art. In sociological terms these phenomena are bound up with the rise of a dynamic bourgeois

ideological persuasion of the writer. In purely vocal terms I propose for the moment to apply the term popular to any variety of singing not described as classical. This will make it easier to analyse a range of singing varieties from community and domestic music-making to commercialised marketing and bourgeois entertainment.[1]

The 'relative' aspect of the terminology owes as much to the development of popular singing as to that of the elite form. The eighteenth and nineteenth centuries form the chronological terrain on which a struggle for the nature of the popular took place. The almost moral authority of classical music is due at least in part to a perceived lack of morality in various sorts of public entertainment. This apparent threat has been the subject of many reductionist analyses which see the constraints put upon popular music and institutions in terms of social control. There is plenty of evidence which would support this thesis: the repression of the church bands, the elevation of cathedral music, the creation of institutionalised music-making at a national level, and the attempts to regulate or suppress the pleasure gardens and music halls. Other scholars have developed a hegemonic model based on Gramsci (to which I shall return later) which accounts for the willing agreement of people to agendas with a sub-text that seeks to shape and control them. Dave Russell (1987) cautions against the use of even a Gramscian analysis, arguing that the element of control by the dominant class was in effect irrelevant, such was the degree of control and sheer enjoyment that the lower classes actually experienced in their music-making, which offered quantifiably pleasurable experiences as a relief from the tedium of work. A similar point is made by Susan Pennybacker (1987) in connection with the music halls: that the lower classes either used the attempted control to their own advantage or ignored it. It is certainly hard to tell who were the victors and who the losers in some areas of cultural negotiation, if only because it is impossible to measure morality and thought. There were also struggles which were won or lost as well as those whose outcome is still debated. The complex articulation of the popular, defined as 'struggle' in the sense that Richard Middleton (1990, p. 9) uses it, calls for a sophisticated extrapolation from Gramscian theory in which neither a reductionist view nor a post-modern 'poverty of theory' analysis applies (Middleton makes the point that articulatory theory accepts the relative autonomy of cultural and ideological elements within a cultural field). The maintenance of hegemony in nineteenth-century England at a time when the emerging bourgeoisie was seeking to define itself relative to both the old aristocracy and the lower classes is very much dependent on what Robert Gray (1979) called the 'hegemonic fraction', those elements of society who actually make it work in practice (as opposed to the ruling fraction who govern in the sense of making policy). As far as singing and music are concerned the hegemonic fraction can be found, for example, in the promoters of music hall as opposed to the licensing bodies, in the tastes of the professions who formed concert audiences or choirs.

William Weber, in his pioneering books *Music and the Middle Class* (1975) and *The Rise of Musical Classics in Eighteenth Century England* (1992) identified taste as the engine of musical division and the concert as the terrain on which such division can be most easily seen. Concerts, like music halls, had their origins in the tavern. Documentation on the earliest taverns-with-music is rare but there are references to music houses from the mid seventeenth century onwards, the most famous being those of Bannister and the legendary coal merchant Britton. During the Commonwealth the church, until then the main patron of choral establishments, was in effect suspended as a musical force. The court, the other principal patron of the arts, ceased to exist, a fact which gave new importance to the public concert series. After the Restoration, with its renewed emphasis on the arts, concerts began to take place in rooms assigned for the purpose (the earliest being that in York Buildings near Charing Cross, which was used for concert-giving from 1678, and the Music Room in Holywell, Oxford, which was actually built for concerts). The first public concerts were subscription concerts, which inevitably meant that considerable wealth was required by consumers since an entire season's tickets had to be bought at once. Throughout the eighteenth century the status of concerts increased, becoming almost entirely aristocratic with rigidly exclusive subscription lists (tickets could not be transferred outside the subscriber's immediate family by order of the king). As Weber (1992, p. 143) has pointed out in his more recent work, the aristocratic nature of the Concerts of Ancient Music was defined not so much by the peers who patronised them, as by the gentry and upper middle classses who 'looked to noblemen as patrons and aspired to participate in some manner in their social world'. The idea of a canon of important works that transcended the uncertain present and looked to a mythical past, was very much a feature of these events and established the conservative ideology of taste that has been associated with classical music ever since.

Taste, as Bourdieu (1986, p. 478) reminds us, is an investment in meanings which define our whole social being, what he calls the 'tacit contract' which defines 'us' as opposed to 'them'. In focusing on taste Weber, in his socio-musical analysis of London, Paris and Vienna, identifies an essential and often overlooked contributing factor to class difference. Weber categorised taste into two broad bands, the classical and the popular, the former divided into a high-status public and a low-status public. He drew attention to the importance of the family in instilling the middle-class values of discipline and respect for authority through the socialisation of children, something for which musical instruction is an ideal medium. Derek Scott (1989) makes the same point in his analysis of English bourgeois society. Middle-class families dominated concert life in England by the 1830s. Successful business owners, they tended to be anti-intellectual, enjoying virtuosity and display and value for money. They were efficient concert managers and promoters; they preferred the lighter 'classics' and virtuoso pianists to the German seriousness of Beethoven. The German school was favoured by a different kind of audience from the liberal professions and the proliferating bureaucracy. The importance of the non-economic professions in the construction of bourgeois taste cannot be over-emphasised. Money and display were not the prime consideration so the liberal professions were free to concentrate on art for art's sake.

Both of these taste publics were different from the aristocracy who had previously dominated concert life. The aristocracy had power and status but the Concerts of Ancient Music with their exclusively titled membership and quaint processions of nobility finally collapsed through inefficiency and indifference. The alliance of the nascent German 'classical' public with both the 'high-status popular taste' of the business families and the remnants of the nobility in the concerts of the Musical Union from 1845 onwards produced the chemistry of taste which ensured the elevation of the idea of classical music as the elite above all others. Musical Union events had high status because they were favoured by the aristocracy but they were also supported by successful businessmen who ensured that they ran on commercial lines, and they recognised that the definition of elite had to include talent and artistic sensibility, an element that would elevate certain sorts of music beyond the purely commercial (Weber,

1975). This sensibility encompassed the Romantic idea of the artist as genius, a key concept in the separation of taste publics.

Popular music in its wider sense was enjoyed by a lower-status public. Before the nineteenth century there was little organisation of working-class music-making. A wide variety of forms had existed from the earliest times. Athenaeus, for example, mentions the songs of labourers, shepherds, winnowers, bath attendants and even lawyers (Barker, 1987). Medieval iconography is full of illustrations of musical activity for which no music survives and which strongly suggests an oral tradition. Castiglione observes in his patronisingly pastoral way worksongs which have probably existed for thousands of years:

rude labourers in the fields under the burning sun will often beguile their heavy time with crude and rustic song. With it the simple peasant lass, rising before dawn to spin or weave, wards off sleep and makes pleasant her toil. This is the happy pastime of poor sailors . . . the consolation of tired pilgrims . . . and miserable prisoners in their chains and fetters. (Singleton, 1959, p. 76)

In Elizabethan and Jacobean England popular tunes were freely plundered for source-material by composers. Ravenscroft's *Pammelia* (1609), *Deuteromelia* (1609), and *Melismata* (1611) were the first song books to include a substantial amount of popular material, making him possibly the first folk-song collector (Bidgood, 1980). Street cries were used in surviving compositions by Gibbons (twice), Cobbold, Weelkes, Ravenscroft and Dering; the latter also produced a set of 'Country Cries' which parodied rural life while preserving a number of popular tunes. In much the same way as the music of the Italian improvisers has been preserved, so too have folk songs been legitimised by printing, removed from their oral origins and incorporated into literate and increasingly, urban, culture. The earliest Broadside Ballads were printed at the beginning of the sixteenth century and achieved sufficiently widespread popularity among all classes to be recognised by Shakespeare's audiences. A further stage in the upward mobility of folk song is the series of publications by John Playford in the latter part of the seventeenth century. These were produced for the domestic consumption of amateurs and professionals alike. The rising middle class had opportunities to sing both at home and in tavern and coffee house, for which the catches and 'free men's songs' of the seventeenth and eighteenth centuries were written. For all classes there were the pleasure gardens, which began to offer concerts towards the end of the seventeenth century and where proto-'classical' music could be heard in a more generally palatable form.

At about the same time as the first concerts were promoted, pleasure gardens began to provide a less rigorously musical form of entertainment. The gardens began as an outdoor (and therefore visual and seasonal) diversion, and could be anything from a tea-room to a park of several acres. They all developed their own idiosyncratic offerings of which music became an increasingly important part. Wroth (1896/1979) documented some sixty-five pleasure gardens spread over six main areas of London. Mulberry Gardens (on the site of Buckingham Palace) and Spring Gardens (near Charing Cross) were established before the Restoration but the heyday of the gardens was in the late eighteenth and early nine-teenth centuries. Marylebone, like many of the gardens, had a Great Room for concerts in which concert performances of operas were given. Ranelagh and Vauxhall both had Rotundas, impressive structures that housed an orchestra and an organ. All of the most successful singers in London performed at one or both (the tenor John Beard was particularly associated with Ranelagh, Thomas Lowe with Vauxhall). Music was always only one of a huge variety of experiences offered by the gardens. Patrons of Sadlers Wells could expect ballad-singers, rope-dancing, clowns and pony races as well as Charles Dibdin, masquerades and the 4,000 nights of Shakespeare that were promoted between 1844 and 1862. The musical events reflected a broad taste: Mozart appeared at Ranelagh, as did the castrato Tenducci; Vauxhall had a statue of Handel as Orpheus. Patrons could stroll in the extraordinary gardens (which covered twelve acres and were lit at one stage with 20,000 lanterns) or indulge in conspicuous dining. Socially the gardens attracted the entire gamut: Walpole and the Prince of Wales patronised Vauxhall, many others were closed by the magistrates when they fell into disrepute. The range of social and cultural phenomena which the gardens encompassed seems baffling to modern commentators, which perhaps explains why an adequate history of them to replace that of Wroth has yet to be written.

Changing tastes and class relationships were ultimately respon-sible for the decline of the pleasure gardens and their eventual replacement by music halls, which offered a similarly wide variety of entertainment. The fashion for gardens was centred on London and seems to have had no real equivalent in the provinces. The gardens reflected a classical and pastoral ideology that perhaps helped psychologically to keep the encroaching and enlarging urban developments at bay. The music hall was uncompromisingly urban, needed no vast acreage and could, in its earlier manifestations, be enlarged if demand was sufficient. Despite the credit given to Charles Morton and the Canterbury Arms in Lambeth, the first proto-music halls originated in the provinces and, like the first concerts in the seventeenth century, were an extension of convivial tavern activities which could be turned to profit in any part of the country. The very use of the name 'music hall' is indicative of the combination of improvement and profit. Until about 1860 the terms 'concert room', 'concert hall', and 'music hall' were only the most popular among many possibilities. These were, however, the same names as those given to the earliest concerts, which gave promoters the added bonus of a veneer of respectabiltiy. This case of the entertainment industry stealing its enemies' clothing was later repaid by the moralists and reformers who bought their own halls to get their message across (Russell, 1987; Davis, 1991). At their height the music halls were perhaps the largest form of mass music-making/ appreciation and were regarded by the establishment both as a possible threat to society and as a potential means of controlling it; the products of this struggle had the further effect of constructing or confirming beliefs in what constituted the popular, and by extension, what could be considered 'art'.

Music hall has a substantial literature ranging from the sentimental recollections of the early twentieth century to the academic research and debate of the present day. There is considerable argument as to who was controlling whom and who was the victor in the struggle for cultural control that music halls represent.[2] Like the gardens the halls appealed to a wide variety of tastes. Potential audiences could discriminate against each other according to which hall they attended, or how much they paid for admission. The development of music halls was extremely rapid, though exactly how many people attended and how frequently is unclear. Breaking down music-hall attendance figures by social group or even estimating rough attendance totals is notoriously difficult. Middleton (1991) is taken to task by Russell (1987, p. 73) for possibly over-estimating lower-class attendance figures. Ehrlich (1988) places music halls fourth in popularity mid-century behind drinking, fornication and sport (though it is difficult to know how he arrived at this conclusion). Pennybacker (1987) quotes a figure of 14 million annual visits in the early 1880s, based on the Select Committee Report of 1892.

By the late 1860s most major conurbations supported at least one music hall. After 1852 licensing was required for music and dancing, a legislative act which saw the end of the pleasure garden but a proliferation of music halls. Both sides of the industry were quick to organise themselves: in 1858 Ambrose Maynard's agency was founded (the beginning of the 'star' system), in 1860 the owners formed themselves into a Protection Society and in 1865 the performers attempted to protect themselves with a Provident Society. After the limited liability legislation of 1862, large companies and syndicates began to dominate the industry in a highly competitive market. The smaller halls and saloons were further hit by legislation in 1878 which insisted on more comprehensive safety measures and banned alcohol from the body of the hall. The larger halls were able to profit by the new legislation, adapting their premises and separating off a bar or promenade area at the back of the hall to keep apart the 'wet trade' and those patrons whose tastes were extra-musical. The improvements that resulted, combined with the regular attacks on certain halls by the Lord Chamberlain, helped to make the halls respectable. This in turn led to their metamorphosis into Variety Theatres, which could offer entertainment for all the family.

The repertoire of the music hall ranged from the semi-pornographic 'tableaux' of scantily clad women such as were on view at the Palace Theatre in the 1890s, or the 'nudge, nudge, wink, wink' skirt-raising of Cissie Fitzgerald, through 'serious' repertoire (Gounod's *Faust* was first performed at the Canterbury in 1859) to social comment and vast out-pourings of imperialistic and nationalistic songs. Strong, competing managements and agents were initially responsible for the rise of the celebrity singers who from the 1860s onwards traded in what we can now identify as 'music hall songs'. These highly charismatic performers (of which the 'lions comiques' were only the most well known) were in such demand that they could take in up to four halls per day, earning huge fees. The 'New Imperialism' of the later nineteenth century is reflected in a substantial number of songs that have been variously described as patriotic, nationalistic, imperialistic or jingoistic, though the ideological associations of these could change according to context.

Penelope Summerfield (1981, p. 210) has claimed that the various legislative attacks on the halls turned them into 'the residue remaining after the gradual reduction of those public forms of working-class self-expression which had come to be defined as less acceptable'. Susan Pennybacker (1987, pp. 135–7) supports the thesis that the legislative bodies deliberately moulded music halls into 'respectable' institutions but she points to the element of independence that remained to the working class, who happily accepted increased control if it meant increased comfort but refused to be constrained by moral strictures. Stylistically, the music enjoyed by patrons used a harmonic and structural language derived from classical music (and sometimes actually was classical music). This remained constant throughout all attempts to control the halls, presumably because the bourgeois legislatory bodies were happy with the degree of control that this implied. What is undoubtedly true is that the music hall phenomenon touched people of all classes, and those who attended the halls came to appreciate a commercially based music product.

The same range of musical repertoire also found its way into the home. The availability of cheap music and, in the latter half of the nineteenth century, cheap pianos, had a marked effect on the market for domestic music. Derek Scott (1989, p. 17) has drawn attention to the influence of English ballad opera on domestic drawing-room song. The incomprehensible style and language of the Italian opera beloved of the upper classes won little affection from the bourgeois audience. Scott points out that Mozart's operas depend on ensembles, whereas those of Balfe and his contemporaries tended to consist of a series of individual songs, the success of which could be measured in subsequent sheet-music sales. For this potential market vocal fireworks were a positive disincentive to those who wished to emulate the event at home. The ballad concert fulfilled a similar function: groups of four or five different voices would give recitals of solo songs, rarely all singing as an ensemble. Often the singers were paid to sing new songs or received a royalty from the sale of the sheet music. It is the commercial drive for quantity rather than quality (likened by Stephen Banfield (1985, p. 5) to the promotion of twentieth-century pop music) which accounts for the huge numbers of songs produced for domestic consumption in the late nineteenth-century. The vast majority of these are written off aesthetically by twentieth-century commentators; it is only with the end of the

royalty system when promoters actually made a feature of the fact
that their artists did not receive payment from publishers that it
became possible for composers to take the song seriously as an
aesthetic rather than a commercial medium. The need for an
operatic aria to be detachable and convertible into a drawing-room
song put severe constraints on operatic plots. The drawing room
required reassurance and *Gemütlichkeit* regardless of dramatic considerations. Scott (1989, p. 19) quotes Balfe's *The Dream* as being the
perfect detachable song, requiring no knowledge of the operatic
context to make sense. The 'refined folk air' (Russell, 1987, pp.
22–32), or pseudo-folk song, also went down well in the drawing
room. Partly reflecting a desire to attach the new urban culture to a
spurious past, partly refining the essence of a lower-class music so
that it could be incorporated into the bourgeois scheme of things,
and (as far as Celtic airs were concerned) partly reflecting nostalgia
for pre-Union days, the cultivation of folk song or the writing of
pseudo folk song was also a manifestation of the Romantic movement. British songs had a wide currency throughout Europe. Percy's
Reliques of Ancient English Poetry of 1765 was translated and imitated in
Germany, France and Italy by the leading writers of the day. Walter
Scott's *Minstrelsy* achieved a similar following (Pestelli, 1987, p. 181).

Similarly reassuring were the religious or sacred songs that
formed a significant part of the drawing-room repertoire. It is surely
the case that the sensibilities of such songs as *O Rest in the Lord* from
Mendelssohn's *Elijah* fostered the sense of rightness and morality
which the middle classes saw as their inheritance. The growth of the
Christmas carol owes much to the comforting ideology of the family.
Stainer and Bramley's anthology of *Christmas Carols New and Old* of
1871 was published at a time when this tendency was very visible.
The editors say in their preface that

The time-honoured and delightful custom of thus [i.e. by carol singing]
celebrating the Birthday of the Holy Child seems, with some change of
form, to be steadily and rapidly gaining ground. Instead of the itinerant
ballad singer or the little bands of wandering children, the practice of
singing Carols in Divine Service, or by a full choir at some fixed meeting, is
becoming prevalent.

Readers are further exhorted to celebrate the season 'with mirth
which shall not overstep the bounds of reverence'.[3] The carol books
were aimed by enterprising publishers at both the domestic market

and choirs, the latter having for a long time been a fruitful area for maximising the profit from spiritual and moral improvement. The tradition of church attendance meant that congregations shared and participated in a common body of music that had its own traditions and developments. As Temperley (1983) points out, the few descriptions of psalm singing in the seventeenth century are by professional musicians and extremely disparaging of the enthusiastic untrained congregations, which suggests a popular enjoyment of singing in a way not appreciated by professionals. This 'old way of singing', often extremely slow, was the subject of various attempts to reform and sanitize it, a fate mercifully escaped by the Pilgrim Fathers whose old way still survives in parts of the USA as an element of the Sacred Harp tradition.[4]

The Reformation in England had seen the end of the monastic schools in which basic notation and sight reading had been taught. This was in contrast to the effects of Protestantism on the mainland of Europe where liturgical reform was accompanied by a strengthening of the role of music in religious life. The influence of Luther and Calvin in the German-speaking countries ensured a simple and direct use of congregational hymn and psalm tunes. Perhaps as an acknowledgement both of the success of the continental primers and of the failure of traditional English music teaching John Day produced his *Whole Book of Psalms* in 1562. This was the first in a series of publications that were generally metrical psalters but also included religious tracts and musical treatises, the latter being a prime source of musical knowledge for the lower literate classes until the more formalised music lessons from the diploma-wielding nineteenth-century 'masters' made them unnecessary. Psalters were, as Bernard Rainbow (1982, p. 3) put it, an 'attempt to correct the continuing musical ignorance of the common folk'. The Prefaces invariably exhort the reader to more than musical ideals, either directly or by scriptural references. Day's title-page claims the authority of the Queen and has a quotation from James V of Scotland, as well as one from *Colossians*. He describes his publication as:

Very mete to be used of all sortes of people privately for their solace and comfort: laying apart all ungodly Songes and Ballades, which tende only to the norishing of vyce, and corrupting of youth. (Rainbow, 1982, p. 27)

Day had been granted a printing monopoly in 1559 and used it to produce copies of *The Whole Book of Psalms* almost exclusively. Known as the Sternhold and Hopkins psalter (after its translator/compiler), it was virtually the only version of the psalms used in the early seventeenth-century parish churches and became one of the most successful publications ever produced, running to several hundred editions over a period of three hundred years. Day was an early example of the entrepreneur who could fuse morality, music and sound business sense into one successful enterprise.[5] The writers of such psalters were invariably also the publishers and could make a more than adequate living by selling their volumes at classes that they themselves ran for aspiring teachers and pupils. One John French in his treatise of 1759 urges the tutors who will use it that

> as they often use the Words and Name of the omnipotent God, they will be the Example to their Scholars, not only in the Science of Music, but in their Lives and Actions; for the Behaviour of a Master has a great Influence over his Pupils; so yours ought to be particularly sober, modest, and discreet. (Rainbow, 1982, p. 97)

The manuals had an additional effect: as well as contributing to the financial well-being and moral satisfaction of their propagators they encouraged the development of popular psalm singing by congregations and the formation of choirs to lead them. The psalms were at first sung unaccompanied (possibly with improvised harmony) but by the late eighteenth century the choir had become a parish institution, part choir, part band and part social club. The membership in rural areas could comprise a wide variety of occupations from agricultural labourers to school teachers with the driving force coming from local tradesmen in the towns.[6] From the Reformation until the late eighteenth century, parish churches had enjoyed a remarkable degree of freedom compared with the more autocratic cathedral foundations. This extended to an enormous number of variations in the liturgy and a disregard for rubrics which was either tolerated or ignored by the church hierarchy, which was in any case loosely organised and riddled with absenteeism. Temperley (1983) cites the case of certain hymns which still have not been authorised by Parliament for use in churches. Against the background of such a loose ideological grip the choirs began to develop a certain autonomy of operation and style which became an important articulator of musical activity. Performances were often loud, idiosyncratic and verging on the secular by the late eighteenth century. New galleries were built in the west end of churches to accommodate the musicians, with the idea of giving a new prominence to psalm singing. In practice it gave even more prominence to the performers, who developed new repertoires of anthems and fuguing tunes and acquired a status and autonomy which the church authorities began to see as a threat.

In 1790 Bishop Porteus read a *Charge* to the London diocese urging the reform of country psalmody and the proper musical education of children. This was the opening salvo in a battle that was to see the end of the church bands and the demise of the itinerant psalm teachers who both taught and exploited them. By the 1860s the reform was complete (apart from pockets of resistance in the West Country), with the church bands ousted in favour of organs (or, if necessary, barrel organs) which could lead disciplined and controlled singing. The struggle was a bitter one, exquisitely fictionalised in Thomas Hardy's *Under the Greenwood Tree*, in which elite values triumphed over those of the ordinary people.

As the process of revolutionising church music continued efforts were being made to develop class singing as part of a national curriculum. This produced a different sort of treatise: the class-singing manual. Among the most successful of these was John Turner's *Manual of Instruction in Vocal Music* published in 1833 and aimed at both Sunday schools and the new National Schools (it was published under the auspices of the Society for Promoting Christian Knowledge). The body of his work is extremely practical but his early chapters on musical history and the need for a reform of psalm singing are quite plainly attempts to forge singing and godliness into one moral force. He quotes many authorities in his support, including the Rev. William Jones of Nayland who is said to have remarked:

Look out of Christendom into the kingdoms of China, Tartary, Turkey and the regions of the southern world, and you will discover no music but what is beggarly and barbarous, fit only to amuse the ears of children or savages. (Turner, 1833/1983, p. 19)

The question of music and morality in the nineteenth century has been dealt with at length by Russell (1987), Gatens (1986) and others who point to the extent that moral considerations formed the ideological back-drop to considerations of musical style and event. The connection between classical music and morality is most obvious in cathedral music, which was seen as a contribution to the act of worship. As Gatens points out, many Victorian sermons concerned themselves with the duty and privilege given to those responsible for choral worship. He goes on to quote W. H. Gladstone on the subject of the church composer, whose position 'has some analogy to that of the preacher' (Gatens, 1986, p. 46). The Rev. H. R. Haweis, whose *Music and Morals* first appeared in 1871 and was still being reprinted in the 1930s, says of earlier church composers:

> . . . whilst it must not be supposed that the fact of composing for the church makes a man holy, we cannot deny to these men as a class a great deal of exalted and often mystical religious fervour. Unhappily, this quality does not seem to be inconsistent with an occasional laxity of morals which cannot be too much deplored . . . (Haweis, 1871, p. 85)

Haweis also quotes the evangelical preacher Ward Beecher on the subject of singing hymns in church:

> There is a pleading element, there is a sense of humiliation of heart, there is a poignant realisation of sin and its guiltiness . . . and in singing you come into sympathy with the truth as you perhaps never do under the preaching of a discourse. There is a provision made in singing for the development of almost every phase of Christian experience. (Haweis, 1871, p. 115)

The second half of the nineteenth century saw an extraordinary revival in cathedral music. The foundations endowed in the sixteenth century or earlier had long been plundered by the clergy for other purposes and it was not until the Reform Bill of 1832 and the Dean and Chapter Act of 1840 that serious musical establishments could be contemplated. Musical excellence as an aid to worship (or, perhaps more accurately, as an end in itself) was an appropriate expression of the moral climate. As far as singing in the choir was concerned the religious expectations of the clergy and moralists were translated into codes of conduct in which music was inseparable from discipline as a day-to-day experience. Filson Young, writing in 1911 of his experiences as a choirboy at Manchester Cathedral has left a description of life in the choir:

> The discipline of the organ-loft was very severe, though it was entirely unwritten and unstated. There were no rules, but anyone who had the freedom of that place conformed to an etiquette as rigid as that of a German court. There were certain chairs upon which certain pupils might sit . . . there were certain places on which a hat or coat might be laid . . . There was a place where the music . . . books . . . were laid in their order, and from which they were handed up to the music desk at exactly the right

moment. There was a way in which the chant book was folded down inside the psalter at the end of the psalms, departure from which, one felt, would have threatened the existence of the foundation. (Young, 1911, p. 268)

Similar unspoken disciplinary codes are to be found in English cathedral choir vestries to this day.

Music as morality and singing as discipline were at the very root of Victorian church music and, by extension at the heart of the nascent national education system. Perhaps its prime exponent, who influenced generations of children and adults, was John Hullah, who together with James Kay introduced the 'fixed' solfa system of sight singing in 1842. Hullah was a failed opera composer turned educationalist (Dickens wrote the libretto to his *The Village Coquettes*, produced unsuccessfully at the St James' Theatre in 1836). Kay, as secretary to the Committee of Council on Education, had been impressed by Guillaume Wilhelm's successful teaching of large numbers of French adults and advised his Committee that such a method should be introduced into English schools. Hullah, a charismatic and successful teacher, was charged with the task of adapting Wilhelm's *Manuel musical* for the purpose. Hullah's method, with its fixed tonic which could only be transposed by destroying the sound-association idea on which the system was based, was in the end superseded by Curwen's 'tonic' solfa method with a moveable 'doh', but Hullah's teaching of the initial stages at his Singing School in London and through his book was enormously successful. Hullah is often wrongly credited with the invention of solfa, such was the impression made by his formidable approach.[7] Kay's 'Prefatory Minute of the Committee of Council on Education' which introduced Hullah's *Wilhelm's Method of teaching Singing adapted to English Use* is peppered with references to 'the lower orders' and 'the lower portion of the middle classes' (the potential pupils) and 'their Lordships' (his committee; Kay himself was a doctor). He notes that in infant schools 'singing forms one of the chief features of the instruction and discipline' and goes on to elaborate the civilising influences of vocal music, especially among the 'class of apprentices, foremen, and attendants in shops' who were formerly 'privileged outlaws in society' (Hullah, 1842/1983, pp. iii–ix). There is a description of Hullah's classes at Exeter Hall in Battersea which talks of matters of national taste, including the fact that 'the degrading habits of intoxication' which previously afflicted the Germans have all but disappeared since they started singing properly (pp. x–xiv).

Hullah, despite his successful rise through the system to become Chief Inspector of Schools in 1872, did not see his method applied as universally as he had hoped. John Curwen's system was far more flexible and enabled students to progress further. Curwen was a Congregational minister who had taught himself music with the aid of Sarah Glover's *Scheme to Render Psalmody Congregational*, published in Norwich in 1835. In Glover's Preface to her 1850 edition she implies that Curwen had been less than frank in acknowledging his debt to her work. The daughter of a Norwich rector, Glover grew up close to the dissenting and radical environment that also produced economist Harriet Martineau and prison reformers Elisabeth Fry and Amelia Opie (Hyde, 1991). Curwen immediately realised the potential of such a system, not only for Sunday Schools, but also for bringing the virtues of Christian music and temperance to the poorer classes in general. The combination of dissent and family business flourished with the Curwen dynasty as it did with Lloyds, Barclays and Cadbury, among others. The publishing firm that John Curwen founded to promote his religious and cultural agenda continued until the late twentieth century. Solfa brought cheap music within the financial and musical means of large numbers of people, fuelling the massed choir movement and the burgeoning teaching profession. One solfa edition of *Messiah* alone sold 39,000 copies (Pearsall, 1973). The benefits to ordinary working- and lower-middle class people in terms of sociable music-making are obvious. The success of the hidden agenda is impossible to measure: no one has devised a way of measuring the number of souls saved from the devil by solfa. The system persisted well into the twentieth century (many European countries, notably France, still use a version of solfa for training young children). The conceptual weakness of the scheme was its supposed completeness. In the end even Curwen's system could not account for the notational complexities that were the consequence of the complete emancipation of tonality in late-nine-teenth-century art music. Those who had learned, however studiously and comprehensively, from solfa, were barred from serious participation in the higher levels of the music profession. Hullah and Curwen (and Day before them) are examples of the hegemonic fraction at work, enabling all classes to have access to sufficient of the system to keep them happy while denying them any real power.

Solfa certainly produced an additional audience for choral music as well as choir-fodder, and this must have compounded the tendency inherent in the system to create a gap between professional singers and amateurs.

Discipline and music also combined in the institutionalisaton of the profession and its pedagogy, which ensured that singing could be defined and measured by certain 'standards'. It became very clear what was 'singing' and what was not, and an entire profession grew up to maintain this definition. Foucault (1977) has written at length on the ideology of discipline which was an essential pre-requisite of bourgeois society. Bourdieu and Passeron (1990, p. 200) describe the educational system as an institution for the exercise of 'symbolic violence'. In other words the legitimacy of education is such that those involved in it have no need to relate what is taught to universal principles since it is accepted as autonomous and self-perpetuating. In this way cultural hierarchies are produced and relations of cultural dominance maintained, as is the case with 'classical' singing, especially in its relationship to the teaching profession. In England the Royal Academy of Music was founded in 1823, and limped along as an under-funded institution run by gentlemen amateurs. In the second half of the nineteenth century 'conservatoires' as diverse as the Royal College of Music and the Royal Normal College and Academy of Music for the Blind opened their doors to aspiring musicians. The majority of applicants were pianists and singers, other instrumentalists being a very small proportion of the whole. There is no evidence that these institutions ever saw themselves as training musicians as performers (Ehrlich, 1988), performance in nineteenth-century England, as in ancient Greece, being seen as rather degenerate compared with music as pedagogy. The statistics for the 1883 RCM Scholarship competition are especially revealing. Of 335 female finalists 185 were pianists, 124 singers, with a total of 18 other instrumentalists (Ehrlich, p. 110). The products of the academies merely added to the private teaching profession which expanded at a spectacular rate over the same period. The emphasis on pedagogy as an end in itself contributed in a number of ways to the ideology of elitism that is one of the defining characteristics of classical music. Popular music only existed in performance; classical music could have an existence in written form and as a pedagogy completely independently of its performance. Access to these aspects of music was only possible to those with the appropriate knowledge, which those who had liked to keep to themselves. Academic knowledge (or, in the case of many nineteenth-century teachers, spurious academic knowledge) conferred a moral authority and status on those who acquired it. The study of singing, instruments, or musical notation are all functions that lend themselves to disciplined instruction, with a consequent effect that music itself becomes a matter of discipline rather than creative work.

The idea of discipline is still very much a part of learning how to sing in a choir, whether it be a choral society or a choir school, and singers are still subjected to discipline for its own sake. The following introduction is from *The Church Anthem Book* edited by Henry Ley and Walford Davies. Although it dates from the 1930s, it refers to a tradition that was long-established and the 1966 impression was still in use in some churches in the 1980s:

It cannot be too strongly urged that discipline is of primary importance in choir work. Regular attendance at practice is, of course, essential, and members of a choir must be prepared to sacrifice as much of their spare time as they can. The Competitive Music Movement, which is so widespread today, has done much to produce the highest possible standard. It is hoped that this standard may be generally applied to the ordinary routine work of a choir, and that the prevailing custom of one full practice a week may be regarded as insufficient to meet the musical demands of today. (Preface to the 15th impression, 1966)

English cathedral and college choristers of the recent past will recognise the ideological framework implied here. Many successful English professional singers will still involuntarily raise a hand if they make a mistake in a rehearsal (and I have even witnessed this in performance from certain singers). This is a legacy of the ritual humiliation whereby choristers are obliged to 'own up' to mistakes on the grounds that for maximum efficiency the choirmaster needs to know that the chorister knows he is guilty. Ley and Walford Davies, were products of the English public school system (both attended the Chapel Royal at St George's, Windsor). One of the functions of English public schools was to produce administrators and officers for the British Empire. Choir schools were often off-shoots of such institutions, and a musical discipline which had military overtones would not have seemed out of place.

Cathedral choirs meant, of course, high-status choral singing open to very few. The choral experience of most of the population was in locally organised choirs, some of which were very large. Although the social composition of choirs was quite varied, the leadership of such institutions was generally from the lower middle class. This is another example of the hegemonic fraction at work: the choirs were able to appreciate the importance of choral music while remaining themselves apart from the creative genius of composer and professional soloists. Weber (1975) quotes an article on singing in the *Westminster Review* of 1842: 'Since penal measures and moral exhortations fail to reach the hearts of the people – why not try to act upon them through the medium of their entertainment?' Large-scale choirs began to appear in the 1830s and were widespread by 1848. The choirs had a strong Dissenting membership and embodied a number of bourgeois ideals. Learning music and singing together meant self-discipline through musical training. Until the 1890s when amateur opera (especially Gilbert and Sullivan) became popular, religious music was the norm, contributing to the ideology of moral uprightness. The concerts also had a satisfying philanthropic element when they were given in aid of charity.

During the 1890s the competitive choral music movement began to find its feet. This, like its equivalent in the world of bands, was denigrated by those above such lower-middle-class activities. Competition led to an expansion of the movement, wider repertoire and higher standards of performance, and in building rapport with its ever-increasing audiences it increased that proportion of the population with a respect for classical music. Choral singing probably raised its status towards the end of the century. Certainly the works of Stanford, Elgar and others are now regarded as important in the classical canon.

Dave Russell (1987, pp. 250–1), in his social history of popular music, warns against the use of crude models of social control in which the working class 'dance like well-schooled puppets', pointing out that the musical activities which took place outside the cultural elite were not only relatively freely entered into but produced music of 'real worth'. He is also wary of what he calls neo-Gramscian approaches which are concerned with the 'downward flow of ideas' and patronising assumptions that the working classes never fulfilled their historic destiny. There is no simple answer, but the evidence does suggest a general rationalising of social and economic relationships and institutions in which the traditional and localised customs of much working-class music-making gave way to organisational norms. As Weber (1975) tellingly put it, 'Society now codifies what it formerly just did.' There was an attempt by the new bourgeoisie to impose middle-class values on the lower classes. This was a considerable cultural realignment: the old nobility had generally felt secure enough to leave the lower classes to their own devices. The effect was to instil bourgeois values as absolute norms, with the result that classical music, and the unique variety of singing which characterised it, became ideologically fixed as the elite form.

The period has been eloquently summarised by Vic Gammon (1981, p. 83) in his article on the church bands:

> In order to elevate the culture of the elite it was important that the culture of the poor be devalued . . . paternal tolerance gave way to middle-class condemnation. Once the poor accepted this devaluation of their culture (if only partially) a new kind of hegemony was negotiated, an acceptance (if only partial) of the value system of the ruling elite as superior, and a perception of the world refracted through elite eyes. Thus all art should be judged by elite standards; that which fails to reach them is bad art, that which cannot be judged by them is not art at all.

Bourdieu (1986, p. 19) is undoubtedly oversimplifying when he says that nothing more clearly affirms one's class than tastes in music. Yet the sheer variety of musical activities throws up taste markers which offer key insights to sociologists. Bourdieu points to the sanctity of concerts, the perceived spirituality of musicianship. The bourgeois world sees its relationship to the rest of society 'in terms of the relationship of the soul to the body in which insensitivity to the purity of music becomes an 'unavowable form of material coarseness'. Singing became during the nineteenth century one of the major ways in which this intimate relationship between class and music was articulated.

CHAPTER 6

Armstrong to Sinatra: swing and sub-text

Until the development of recording at the end of the nineteenth century all analysis of singing styles and techniques is inevitably limited to what can be gathered from written sources. Recording allows direct access to the primary source, albeit one that has been manipulated by both technology and commerce. It also enables the singing of popular music to be analysed on similar terms to classical singing. Working directly with the primary source material means that it is possible to show clearly the progression of singing style in all its phases within varieties, as well as to analyse the relationship between the classical and the popular. In American popular singing, jazz established, and then lost, its dominant status over other popular varieties as it went through the three-stage process of development, decadence and renewal. This chapter explains how the process operated in the popular music field during the first half of the twentieth century, with particular emphasis on the roles of Louis Armstrong, Bing Crosby and Frank Sinatra.

Even the earliest recordings were intended to be 'performances' despite the novelty of projecting them by remote control into listeners' living rooms and the circumstances (without a 'live' audience) of capturing performances using the new technology. Recording, as opposed to public performance, is a private medium in which a one-to-one relationship is established between singer and listener who are probably unknown to each other and who will probably never see one another. This immediately changes the socio-musical significance of singing and gives a new prominence to the question of meaning in singing. Before the availability of performances of songs on record, the semantic analysis of a song in given historical contexts is limited to deducing the composer's intentions from his written score (he is usually male), reports of his own thoughts and/or those of the performers, or on written descriptions of its perception by listeners. Listening to a recording the listener has direct access to the meanings laid down by the singer, which may or may not coincide with those of the composer. To this mix, the listener will bring his or her own meanings, modified perhaps by the circumstances in which the song is heard. It is immediately obvious when listening to a song (as opposed to reading one) that the concept of truth takes on different meanings in the context of any sort of performance: a song is *about* something, it is not the thing itself. To sing is to dissemble, to invest the performance with a reconstructed reality which allows the performer to offer the listener many layers of potential meaning.

At the same time as the music halls and variety theatres were flourishing in Europe a wide range of musical entertainment, loosely known as vaudeville, was performing a similar function in the USA, but in very different circumstances. At the end of the nineteenth century the relatively recently United States, purged of most of its native population, covered an area many times that of Europe, but with a much smaller and more disparate population of émigré Europeans and Africans, the latter descendants of recently emancipated slaves. Slavery was almost as old as colonisation itself and many black people had an American lineage as long as that of many whites. Trading in slaves had been banned throughout the British Empire in 1807/8 and institutional slavery abolished in 1833. Most other countries imposed a slavery ban over the next fifty years.[1]

The Americanisation of the country's African population was a gradual process. Baraka (1963) forcefully suggested that the only aspects of African culture which survived were those with no artefacts as end-products: religion being the most significant. As conquered people the newly enslaved Africans had a certain respect for the victors' gods, which made the translation to Christianity almost inevitable. Some aspects of old religion found syncretic equivalents in the new (in much the same way that Roman Christianity took over parts of its diverse predecessors). The total immersion of Baptist rites recalled ancient river gods, and the ring shout, with its shuffling movements, was a compromise between the African love of dancing and the Church's abhorrence. African languages merged into English, vocabulary first, adapting African grammars to produce the characteristic black patois, and white hymns to produce the negro spiritual.

The Post-Emancipation period saw the ex-slaves having to come to terms with a social and political economy that saw them as a sub-class of cheap labour to be kept as separate as possible from the mainstream of white society. The church's monopoly on the social life of black people ended and the dispersion of ex-slaves from the old plantations filled the (segregated) towns. In New Orleans, where successful creole communities had flourished before the segregation laws were passed, the Napoleonic marching bands were an inspiration to black musicians to form ensembles of their own. At the same time the multifarious forms of entertainment available to black people, the medicine shows, minstrel troupes and salons and saloons of every kind, ensured a precarious living for certain sections of the community.

White people knew little of black culture in the earlier part of the nineteenth century, but constructed their own images of racial stereotypes to reinforce notions of racial superiority. As early as 1768 in England Charles Dibdin had developed his black character Mungo, which he went on to use in his one-man shows until his death in 1814. Storace, too, wrote 'primitive' songs for negro characters in his operas. These and other composers of the period assumed that, as second-class human beings, the African-Americans' native music would approximate to second-rate drawing-room music of the period. There was an endless fascination with Afro-American dialect and the perceived simplicity of negro life. During the first quarter of the century black characters played by white entertainers appeared increasingly in theatres and songs in the USA in entertainments that were similar in character to those found in the English pleasure gardens. Sometime in the twenties the first black-faced whites appeared, taking the ridicule of black Americans one stage further. By the forties 'blackface' had become so successful that entire evenings were given over to minstrel shows in which white singers and actors in black make-up performed a range of European music but in which the main attraction was the 'negro' song. 'Plantation songs' appeared during the forties and fifties, making a connection between the sentimentality of the European drawing-room ballad and similar sentiments assumed to be felt by the 'negro' about his life on the plantation. While these were often comic songs at the negro's expense, these minstrel offerings saw black people as human, with human emotions (unlike the minstrel songs of the previous generation) and they undoubtedly helped the abolitionist cause in the years before the civil war. After the war black entertainers themselves began to appear in minstrel troupes and from the eighties onwards the minstrel show began to be replaced by vaudeville, an offshoot of the European music hall. Many black performers found they could earn a living in vaudeville. This reinforced the duality of black musical experience: economic and social success was possible in the white market but it was the myth of Africa that provided the possibility of cultural depth. The first blues singers and the gospel singing of the black churches provided a different sort of experience, fusing European musical structures with a rhythmic vitality that was absent from white performing tradition.

Although there were black musicians who could read music and had had some musical training, many took up their instruments for inspirational rather than vocational reasons and acquired a technique by listening to other players and, if they were fortunate, sitting in with bands. How jazz came to develop its improvisational character is by no means certain. The blues, which shared a background with many aspects of jazz and gave its form as one building block for jazz forms, probably began as an improvised music. The solo field holler is one possible blues prototype, with the A-A-B form a consequence of the singer repeating his first line while thinking up the next one. The ring-shout formula of movement in a line combined with call and response singing surfaces in many areas of American music from funeral processions to Stephen Foster's 'Camptown Races' (Floyd, 1991). Baraka (1963) proposed the ring shout as the origin of the twelve bar blues structure. Many slave songs had texts which included nonsense, a kind of precursor of scat, and were possibly improvised. This enabled the black man to shield his real meanings from his white masters. The chanted sermon with its improvised interjections, itself derived from African praise singing, may also have encouraged a tendency towards spontaneity. Few working-class black people had access to the kind of pedagogy that would have moved them into the European tradition of reading from scores, so learning had in any case to be primarily by ear. Learning from records also increased the improvisational tendency. Even if they could buy the sheet music, potential performers were more likely to learn by ear from the record (just as new young rock bands do today). Even those who could read, such as Lil Hardin, Armstrong's pianist and second wife, preferred not to when playing dance music. Dispensing with the music was also linked with the pragmatics of performance: jazz at funerals happened on the move and competitive performances from the backs of trucks were also common.

The issue of race has tended to blur the terrain on which jazz discourse has engaged with questions of culture, race and class. It is undeniable that jazz was an expression of working-class (or non-working) black people. It is also true that some of the earliest successful jazz musicians (such as the Original Dixieland Jazz Band) were from the white working class. Conversely there was also a small but significant number of middle-class black musicians (W. C. Handy, Will Marion Cook, Scott Joplin, for example). The term 'black' has subsequently acquired significant cultural meanings, and for many commentators, especially black musicologists, what may have been a class issue has become a cultural one. Ultimately, social relations must become the site for cultural analysis, but the issue is almost impossible to approach objectively in the current climate where 'white' historical guilt intersects with the 'black' cultural agenda (Tagg, 1989).

As it emerged from the other varieties of dance music of which it was a part, jazz took on its most revolutionary musical aspect. At some point during the first two decades of the century some bands began to apply a new concept of tempo to the already syncopated binary rhythms of ragtime.[2] Syncopation had been a feature of European music for many centuries; the novelty of ragtime was its insistence which was almost structural. The subtleties of tempo on many early jazz records cannot be written down adequately with a conventional notation system. The music was often not actually written at all in the first instance and inverted the European model of notation first followed by performance. Jazz could only be written down after the event, and in a notation system that cannot support rhythmic complexity without becoming unreadable. In classical music notation has traditionally been a barrier to rhythmic development. Debate about rhythmic modes was central to the development of the earliest polyphony, but the arguments were symbolic and intellectual and not of the body. Similarly the multiple time signatures of the fourteenth-century *Ars Subtilior* and the rise and fall of *isorhythm* were intellectual and mathematical conceits which were reasonably well catered for by the evolving notation system. Later tempo 'revolutions', the baroque concepts of *notes inégales* and *sprezzatura* which were concerned with a rhythmic and expressive freedom not unrelated to swing, were, like jazz inflections, unable to be notated.

This phenomenon of tempo is referred to by various names ('hot' is characteristic of the early twenties) but roughly equates with the modern term 'swing'. Gunther Schuller (1989, pp. 223–5, 855–9), who has made a more comprehensive attempt than most to define the phenomenon, makes a distinction between a general 'foot-tapping' meaning of the term and a more specific one. The former meaning applies to any music sufficiently rhythmic for the listener to want to participate, the latter is something infinitely more subtle. Schuller goes on to elaborate four additional criteria: there must be a regular pulse, the pulse and the position of the notes between it must be felt rather than counted, there must be a 'perfect equilibrium between horizontal and vertical relationships of musical sounds', and there must be peculiarities of attack and release that contribute the feeling of swing. He gives spectrographic illustrations of the latter. Schuller's criteria can be amplified yet further. One of the essential differences between jazz and other dance music of the twenties and earlier is that non-jazz almost invariably uses binary rhythms (Joplin playing his own rags is a case in point). Even today 'jazzification' of a piece of music will almost certainly mean giving a ternary feel to what would otherwise be a binary piece.

An early defining characteristic of jazz was said to be the 4/4 swing tempo, and this is presumably what Schuller means by a 'regular steady pulse'. Attempting the fruitless task of transcribing one of Louis Armstrong's early solos would only work if the quavers (or eighth notes) were considered 'inégal' (in the manner of French baroque music, for example). A more practical solution might be to use a compound triple time signature such as 12/8, but this would not account for all the rhythmic elasticity. Early jazz and blues performers did not always use drums or percussion (the drum 'kit' evolved when the cymbals and bass drum of the marching band were able to be played by the same person, the latter being played with the foot rather than hand[3]). The key to the tempo then resides in the rhythm instruments, perhaps a banjo, wash-board or piano, whose players feel the tempo as a consistent reference point but with beats two and four (in a notional 4/4 time) almost imperceptibly ahead of or behind a strictly accurate tempo, depending on the essential character of the piece. Similar characteristics can be heard in early blues singing. Blind Lemon Jefferson, for example (the first rural blues singer to be recorded) created his tempo by emphasising the main beats, leaving space both for voice and guitar improvisation. There is evidence to suggest that this notion of the tempo being both 'there' and 'somewhere else' goes back to the slave songs of the nineteenth century and earlier. Schuller himself, in an earlier (1968) publication, quotes the editor of an 1867 book on slave songs:

One noticeable thing about their boat songs was that they seemed often to be sung just a trifle behind the times [i.e. behind the rhythm implied by the oar strokes and the rattling of the rowlocks]. (Allen *et al.*, 1867/1965)

The basic perception of the tempo is 'swung' not only by what happens in the space occupied by beats two and four, but also by what happens between all the beats from the moment the main tempo beats have been felt by the performer. The result may have a ternary feel to it (the brain perhaps assigning a ternary value to anything repetitive and not obviously binary) but close analysis may reveal something more like a proportion of five to two or three to two, or even, conceivably, a golden section between the main beat and what is 'swung'. Even this may be approximate and will vary depending on the speed and the overall shape of the phrase of which it is a part. Exactly why ternary rhythms should be so satisfying has not been researched. Binary rhythms subdivide the beat in equal proportions, and are therefore ultimately predictable. It may be that ternary, or rather non-binary rhythms, offer an open-endedness on a micro level that may not have a completely predictable outcome. A binary rhythm that is not strictly binary is unsatisfactory and is not a binary rhythm; a notional ternary rhythm, though heard as such, may be far from a strictly accurate proportion. This irregularity is a feature of speech, and is at a very deep level unsettling and exciting, with the smaller part of the proportion arriving at an unspecified time. Metaphorically, and actually, the immediate future cannot be predicted. Schuller's spectrograms would produce in their raw state a print-out sixteen feet long for each second of music, which makes very close analysis impractical. Nor is it generally desirable, since these tiny variations are very much part of each performer's identity and account for the individual magic which makes swing so intangible and difficult to describe.

The development of recording, and the early dominance of it by white musicians, make it difficult to document proto-jazz in any detail. It is certainly the case that some bands recorded certain pieces with a binary feel and others which sound more ternary. The Original Dixieland Jazz Band's 1918 recording of 'Clarinet Marmalade' is in a fast, stomping ternary throughout with an insistent '4/4' beat. It gives the impression of being a fully developed style that the band had presumably used for some time. Unfortunately, there are not enough surviving recorded sides to be able to tell how far this was typical of all their playing, however. King Oliver's Creole Band of 1923, which included the young Louis Armstrong, recorded three titles in October of that year. The first, 'Chime Blues', is a curious mixture of binary and ternary textures. The first two rounds of the tune (a modified blues sequence) feel only just ternary and the ensemble reverts to binary proper for the third and fourth statements. The fifth and sixth rounds consist of Lil Hardin's binary piano solo (the 'chimes' of the title), which are followed by a lazy binary/just ternary seventh statement, reverting to binary for the eighth and final statement. Armstrong's own 'Weather Bird Rag' on the other hand is swung in a ternary tempo throughout (as opposed to the rigidly binary of Joplin's rag recordings of twenty-five years previously). The third side, 'Froggie Moore', is a subtle amalgam of binary and ternary, notable for Honore Dutrey's deliberately unswung binary solo which cuts through the fast ternary of Oliver, Armstrong and Johnny Dodds' clarinet. All of these songs have a rhythm section consisting of Hardin on piano, Bill Johnson on banjo and Baby Dodds on drums. Dodds is very insistent with his solid 4/4, often seeming to use the bass drum on every beat. The emphasis on beats two and four is absent from these recordings, in contrast to the recording of 'Dr Jazz' by Jelly Roll Morton's Red Hot Peppers of 1926. Here Andrew Hilaire's drumming is much less insistent, and under Morton's recitative-like vocals the tempo is felt but not foregrounded. Armstrong dispensed with a drummer for his Hot Five sides recorded between 1925 and 1927, adding Lonnie Johnson on guitar to the rhythm section for the later recordings. His most famous song of the period, 'Heebie Jeebies', is almost cool, Louis playing at the lower end of his register for much of the piece, and delivering his first scat solo over the binary banjo of Johnny St Cyr. The scat seems rather clumsy compared with what Louis and Crosby were to achieve later, but its effect on Armstrong's fellow musicians was phenomenal. Jazz musicians in Chicago would greet each other with phrases from his scat solo (Leonard, 1964, p. 64). Armstrong claimed that he had spontaneously invented scat when his music for 'Heebie Jeebies' fell off the music stand (Friedwald, 1991, pp. 23–5). This is quite probably the first occasion on which

Louis had scatted but the technique had been used before by Cliff Edwards and, possibly, Jelly Roll Morton. Although it was one of the most celebrated records of its day it is difficult today to understand the excitement generated by 'Heebie Jeebies'. Mezz Mezzrow (Mezzrow and Wolfe, 1946) recounts how he and several other musicians were so taken by their first hearing of it that they drove in the middle of the night to wake up Bix Beiderbecke, who, having heard it himself, set off round Hudson Lake to play it to anyone who would listen.

By the time of 'I'm not Rough' in 1927 two of the main ingredients for the future development of jazz are in place: Armstrong's deeply felt vocal, and a sense that anything is possible with tempo manipulation. The piece has both binary and ternary elements as well as an extraordinary double-time passage towards the end. The doubling of tempi for the final statement of a slow piece (perhaps harking back to the return from the cemetery after New Orleans funerals) became a jazz cliché. Here it only takes a bar or two before reverting to the original speed.

Jazz history is written in terms of instrumentalists and most authorities assume an instrumental origin for jazz. Unfortunately the earliest performances of what might have been jazz pre-date the development of recording and the earliest recordings are instrumental. It is also assumed when comparing vocal and instrumental styles that jazz singing was heavily influenced by jazz playing. In fact the relationship between singing and playing must have been very close and there is no particular reason to assume that the influence was all one way. Ogren (1992, p. 13) quotes Kid Ory and Bill Matthews on Buddy Bolden as well as Willie 'the Lion' Smith and Danny Barker in support of a church (and therefore primarily vocal) origin of jazz. Church services certainly would have produced the combination of accentuated rhythm, audience participation and emotional depth that separates some jazz from other dance music. There are many examples of performers drawing parallels between playing and singing. Barker, for example, says of the trumpet player Chris Kelly that 'his masterpiece was "Careless Love", preached slow and softly with a plunger', and that ' . . . he also played church music, especially "Swing Low Sweet Chariot". He really moved the people. He should have been a preacher. But he preached so melodiously with his horn that it was like somebody singing a song.' (Shapiro and Hentoff, 1992, pp. 51–2). The strong link between singing and trumpet playing is reinforced by technical considerations. Both need powerful lungs (although the microphone was available in the mid-twenties it was still customary to perform acoustically even in the early thirties). The vibrato which is so much a hallmark of Louis Armstrong's playing, especially as applied to the end of a long note, is exactly what classical singers do to make their breath go further. Louis does it with his singing too (and was performing in public as a singer while he still lived at the Coloured Waifs' Home and before he took up the trumpet). Billie Holiday and others share the same technical trait.

The question of what happens between the beats, between the attack and release of a note, is specially pertinent to singers. Gunther Schuller (1989, pp. 855–9) gives computer analyses of four performance extracts, each played by two players. One is a recording of the original artist who swings the music, the other is a version played by another musician who plays the music 'straight', or unswung. These visual representations of swing, especially the swung attacks in Schuller's diagrams, show a much closer alignment with speech patterns than the cleaner, more 'accurate' renderings of the non-swung versions. I do not know of a similar analysis being applied to jazz singing, but David Howard's (1992, pp. 51–2) study of singing styles shows a similar difference between spoken and sung phrases.

Figure 1 shows the phrase 'more fools than wise' spoken by me for approximately one and a half seconds. The darker area at the bottom of the graph represents the fundamental pitch, with the higher frequencies giving the colour of the text. Figure 2 shows the same phrase sung in a classical way. The contours even out into a more regular and predictable pattern, as they do in Schuller's representation of unswung playing. Comparison with Schuller's diagrams confirms that swung playing shares some of the characteristics of speech, but is markedly different from unswung playing and unswung singing. Swing, in other words, is a factor in enabling singing to carry a text more effectively in a way which was not available to singers before the beginnings of jazz.

The difference between jazz singing and more conventional dance-band singing can be heard in the 1947 version of Hoagy Carmichael's 'Rockin' Chair' sung by Armstrong and the trombonist Jack Teagarden. The piece begins with the band supporting Armstrong who plays the tune as an introduction (curiously, somewhat sharp, in contrast to the just intonation of his singing). Even

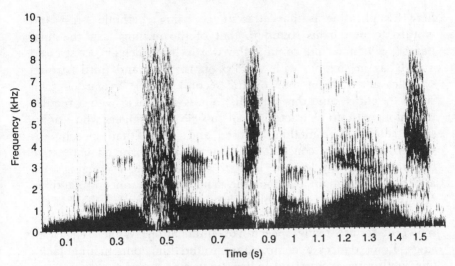

Figure 1 'more fools than wise' (spoken)

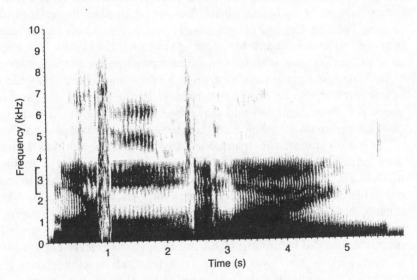

Figure 2 'more fools than wise' (sung)

here his phrasing is that of a singer, using rhythmic stress and
vibrato to match his sound to that of the unsung text: the final
phrase, which would contain the words 'rockin'chair', is stressed
exactly as in singing, with vibrato on the first and third (strong)
syllables and straight tone on the second (weak). Teagarden then
sings the entire tune through. His tone is sustained, with a regular
tremulous vibrato characteristic of sub-classical singers who understand singing as something stylised and 'other' than speech. His
vibrato is virtually constant and does not perform an expressive
function, it merely lets the listener know that he is 'singing'. He
anticipates the main beats in the syncopated manner of ragtime.
His pronunciation is careful, with a rolled *r* in 'Harriet'. Many
singers of the period (Ethel Waters is a good example) were
reluctant to use really speech-like enunciation. While Teagarden
sings, Louis dances a commentary round him, punctuating Jack's
lines with interjections and hollers (including a perhaps ironic 'sing
it father', followed by 'dig this' as Louis prepares to take over the
tune). In fact Louis avoids the tune, preferring to stick to one note
for as long as he can (a favourite Armstrong device: his versions of
'Sunny Side of the Street' get progressively less tuneful). He also
manages to avoid singing for most of the time, declaiming the text
in a speech-like way, with no vibrato except where he phrases a long
note. When he changes pitch he often glides – something else which
is a feature of speech rather than music. In the playout Teagarden
plays the tune Louis should have been singing with Armstrong
playing a descant, ending in a long glissando, again perhaps an
ironic comment on the trombone playing. Almost nothing Louis
does until the last two lines of his sung verse coincides with the
main beats. He is never far away from it but it is often very hard to
tell where exactly his attacks start, and his decays (again, like
speech) peter off into nothing in contrast to the sustained 'singing'
of Jack Teagarden. Throughout, Louis' singing is based on speech
shapes. From the beginning of his attack until its release each word
is energised at the level of the syllable, each syllable given its
appropriate weight, and the whole related to the tempo. The sum of
all these factors means that Louis swings and on this occasion
Teagarden, who went on to become one of the most respected of
jazz blues singers, does not. The performance is full of irony. The
text was originally written by Hoagy Carmichael. Here is the
version sung by Armstrong and Teagarden:

Jack Teagarden	**Louis Armstrong**
Old rockin' chair got me	Old rockin' chair got you father
Cane by my side	Your cane by your side?
Fetch me a drink of water there son	No ain't no water you want father
Or I'll tan your hide	Gonna tan my hide
Can't get from this cabin	What cabin, chokin' father?
Ain't goin' nowhere	You ain't goin' nowhere no
Just sittin' here grabbin'	Grabbin'
At the flies round this rockin' chair	Rockin' chair oh lord
You remember old aunt Harriet	Aunt Harriet mm
Along in heaven she be	Heaven she be . . . (*scat*)
Send me a sweet chariot	Oh chariot oh
For the end of the trouble I see	My sweet cheri
Old rockin' chair get it	Old rockin' chair giddit father
Judgement day's almost here	Judgement days yeah
Chained to my old rockin' chair	Sing it father, look at that father
	Dig this

Armstrong	**Teagarden**
Ole rockin' chair got you father	I sure is beat
Your cane by your side	Can't even pick that up no more
I ain't got no water father	Well you'd better start runnin'
mm you gonna tan my hide	You said it you said it
You can't git from this cabin	(*unintelligible*)
No father but you ain't goin' nowhere	oh ah mm mmm
You sittin' here grabbin'	yeah
Grabbin'	yeah
You grabbin' the flies round his ole rockin' chair	It sure is bothersome isn't it?
Rockin' chair	
Remember old aunt Harriet	Yeah along in heaven she be . . . (*unintelligible*)
Way up in heaven she be	I hope (*scat*)
O fetch me a chariot a chariot	I've got you a ride
End of the time of trouble I see	Yes sir
Old rockin' chair giddit	yeah
Old rockin' chair giddit	yeah
An' judgement day oh judgement day	
yeah judgement day	mm
You sittin' yeah chained	
your rockin' chair	yes . . . (*unintelligible*)

Hoagy Carmichael's text paints a picture familiar to millions of Americans: the old head of the family on his verandah addressing a servant. Carmichael had in mind an old black woman of his acquaintance who liked to relax within easy reach of her gin bottle, and the song was originally popularised by Mildred Bailey. Roger Hewitt (1983) has pointed to the racial stereotyping that this scene seems to suggest, and criticised Armstrong's role in propagating such ideology. Hewitt's analysis appears to be based on the published text, which is considerably different from the one embroidered by Armstrong and Teagarden, and a close reading of the actual performance reveals a far more complex sub-text than Hewitt allows. Teagarden initiates the text; it is he who has the 'chair' and who asks his 'servant' to fetch him a drink of water (not gin, as in the published version, though alcohol is obviously the intended meaning, and ironic in view of the fact that many of the listeners would have been aware that Teagarden himself had an alcohol problem). The main irony of Teagarden's introduction would also be there for those who knew the sub-text to discover: Teagarden is a white male (of German, not Indian extraction, as has been claimed); the stereotype requires a black female (the song had been a nationwide hit for Mildred Bailey in 1931). Both the expected roles and the genders are reversed. The idea of gender reversal is latent in the text itself: Beecher Stowe's character Harry was one of the successful escapees to reach Canada in *Uncle Tom's Cabin* and he did so by becoming a girl called Harriet (also Beecher Stowe's own first name). In the song Harriet is described as being 'way up in heaven'. Heaven, far from meaning the clichéd spiritual heaven that Hewitt assumes, was one of the code names given to Canada, the last stop on the Underground Railroad that helped slaves to freedom (Southern, 1983). The scene of the Carmichael song is a 'cabin', just such a one as Stowe asks her readers to remember as a permanent memorial to the martyrs of slavery. From the opening of the song it is clear to those who know, that this is much more than an apparent example of 'Uncle Tomming'. Louis panders to Jack during the first verse and when he takes over the tune he does not adopt the first person but adapts the text as a commentary which appears to maintain a subservient attitude to the white 'boss'. Teagarden uses conventional American English, Armstrong uses black dialect with its interjections and attentuations. He calls Teagarden father (as he called Bing Crosby father). One can imagine the eye-rolling that may have accompanied his apparent subservience. The dissembling is extremely sophisticated, with one set of meanings offered to those whites who wish to see such meanings, and another for those who can read the code.

Carmichael was Jewish and a friend to many black musicians. Armstrong was the most celebrated jazz musician of his time and his collaboration with Teagarden was an important milestone in desegregating studio recordings (Smith and Guttridge, 1960). It is possible that there is latent racism in Carmichael's work, as Hewett suggests, but it is equally likely that his sense of irony was sufficiently developed to be aware of the dissembling possibilities that his music gave to black performers. The first verse appears to recall minstrel songs and to be patronising to negroes. In the second verse, however, the listener realises that 'in one sense the colored minstrel was poking fun at himself, and in another and probably more profound sense he was poking fun at the white man' (Baraka, 1963, p. 85).[4] Although Louis appears to continue in a subservient role, he actually sings his part with far more confidence and increasing irony, and his speech-related technique eventually overcomes Teagarden altogether as he rejoices in the fact that Teagarden is stuck in his chair and he, Louis, will survive him. The relationship is briefly reversed when Armstrong has the 'chariot' line, which Teagarden then arranges for him. He never does get the water. Furthermore the apparent capitulation of Teagarden at the end is by consent, by which time the layers of meaning have become so complicated and absurd that laughter is the only possibility. The two protagonists have been playing a metaphorical game of 'dozens', the negro game of exchanging insults which eventually become so absurd that the 'victor' has his opponent incapable of further play because he cannot speak for laughing. Louis' behaviour is exactly what both white and black sections of society would expect, providing simple entertainment for white listeners and a sub-text for black people which works in a protective way in order to explain the past, alleviating the sting of a particular black–white historical relationship.

The practice of reversing meanings dates back to slavery when black slaves would often appear to be singing cheerful songs by inventing antiphonal structures to hide their true meaning from white listeners. Frederick Douglass, whose classic slave narrative provides a mid-nineteenth-century witness to relations between blacks and whites, was often surprised to encounter white people who assumed that the singing of slaves was an expresssion of their contentment. White dominance required blacks to appear happy in order to justify the system. This process began on the slave ships, where the slaves were regularly 'danced' for exercise and were whipped for non-compliance. Reality for the slaves was that you did what was required of you in order to survive. As Richard Wright (1937/1989, p. 280) put it, speaking of his adolescence in the South:

I did not want to lie, yet I had to lie to conceal what I felt. A white censor was standing over me and, like dreams forming a curtain before sleep, so did my lies form a screen of safety for my living moments.

Dissembling was, in any case, an essential part of African culture: praise singing and its opposite, blame singing, were concerned with social and commercial realities rather than objective truth, so there was a pre-existing tradition of not meaning what you sing. It was therefore easy for black slaves to sing 'I love to shuck corn' and 'we'll make the money boys', knowing that neither was true. Songs would also acquire coded meanings: 'I don't expect to stay much longer here' meant to the white boss that the singer looked forward to a better life in the next world, but to the slave that he was looking forward to escape. The Underground Railroad often used specific songs for this purpose: Harriet Tubman, an ex-slave who returned to the South many times to rescue slaves, had special 'alerting' songs, such as 'Steal away' or 'Swing low Sweet Chariot' that would announce her presence to potential escapees (Southern, 1983, pp. 143–4).

The protective dissembling so essential to slave and post-slave culture has been codified by Henry Louis Gates (1988) as a specific 'fundamentally black' rhetorical practice. Gates underpins his theory with the image of Esu, a mythical African trickster figure who stands 'at the crossroads of destiny', where two (or more) possible modes of discourse meet. The term 'signifying' had been used by black Americans in a general sense to describe their vernacular word-play, but Gates extrapolates from this a semantic system that is a metaphor for textual revision. Text is here meant in an oral sense (and Gates spells his version of the word with a bracketed final *g* to symbolise the 'black difference' suggested by its omission in black vernacular speech). Gates does not mention singing but David Brackett (1992), in an extrapolation on Gates' idea, applies the theory to the work of James Brown. Brackett's analysis of Brown's work in terms of the Bahktinian 'double-voiced utterance' in which he points to Brown's songs as a celebration of black 'difference' could in principle be applied to Armstrong. In the recent (1980s/90s) cultural climate, Brown appears to be 'politically correct': it is quite clear that his sub-text implies a refusal to submit his 'blackness' to white dominance.

Cultural and political attitudes change over time and the tortuous path of black studies attempting to come to terms with the appalling slavery and post-slavery past may lead to a re-evaluation of so-called Uncle Tomming. Harriet Beecher Stowe, the author of *Uncle Tom's Cabin*, is now seen by some scholars as a proto-feminist. Tom's martyrdom is seen as a triumph and not an act of submission, and the book as whole taken as a proto-feminist attack on capitalism, with slavery 'the ultimate expression of a culture dedicated to buying, selling and accumulation' (Baym, 1988). The book began as a serial in an abolitionist journal and was republished in book form in 1852. It was highly partisan politically, exposing slavery as morally and intellectually indefensible. Whatever the interpretation put on the book by subsequent commentators, its effect was undoubtedly perceived at the time as a powerful argument in favour of the dignity of black people. Armstrong's position does appear to have been at least open to misinterpretation at various points in his life. His eye rolling seems particularly to have offended some of his fellow musicians (Dizzie Gillespie and Miles Davis to name but two; Miles Davis' autobiography is particularly scathing about Armstrong), but his sense of humour also led him to poke fun at all sorts of things including his own physiognomy and his trumpet playing. His occasional forays into what was seen as Uncle Tomming were surely of a Bakhtinian nature, where 'the word in language is half someone else's. It becomes "one's own" only when the speaker populates it with his own intention, his own accent, when he appropriates the word, adapting it to his own semantic and expressive intention.'[5]

Armstrong's duetting with Teagarden and other white singers, especially Bing Crosby, did a great deal to legitimise the new music among blacks and whites alike. His application of jazz singing to the songs of Tin Pan Alley was a further step in changing popular singing style for good. After the success of the Hot Fives and Hot Sevens in the mid-twenties he concentrated increasingly from 1929 onwards on larger dance bands and on popular songs rather than original compositions, giving equal prominence to playing and singing. Not long before this Bing Crosby had begun his career with the Paul Whiteman orchestra, a popularising band that took jazz-influenced music to concert halls (where it sat, sometimes uneasily, beside 'classics' such as the 1812 Overture). A natural with a microphone (not all singers are), Crosby also managed to incorporate jazz phrasing and style into the commercial music of Tin Pan Alley. He was also from a poor background (though poor white in the Crosby household was very different from poor black in that of Armstrong). He had become interested in jazz and dance music at an early age and was heavily influenced by Louis Armstrong whom he first heard in Chicago in the mid-twenties. Crosby had been something of an actor in his childhood, winning medals for public speaking and elocution, ironically taking elocution lessons at the same time as many black people were doing the same thing. The linguistic division between black and white communities, and between certain white accents which were perceived as either desirable or undesirable, were important factors in opening up a universal speech-related singing. It is not known whether Armstrong had elocution lessons (probably not, given his tendency to satirise his own speech) and his 'natural' way of singing is part of the swing revolution. Crosby was also considered a 'natural' singer, his speech lessons presumably having left him with a clarity of diction and an accent which sounded 'natural' in a country where there was no real concept of a high-status accent, but a wide variety of geographical ones.

Crosby's first public performance as a singer was at the age of twelve. He also played the drums. His early consciousness of both rhythm and text enabled him to make the best possible use of his natural gifts as a singer (C. Thompson, 1975). He made his first record in 1926. It was followed by a series of sides with the Whiteman band, of dance music heavily influenced by jazz. His 'Mary (what are you waiting for?)' of 1927 is typical of the period, superficial, with Crosby using a lot of vibrato and the Whiteman band unable to decide whether it is playing at a salon or a saloon. By the time of his first big hit with 'I Surrender Dear' in 1931 Crosby has toughened his sound (the opening chorus seems curiously prophetic of Elvis Presley's ballad sound). The following year he recorded 'St Louis Blues' with the Ellington band. This is the mature Crosby showing that he can sing the blues like a black man without blacking up. The song opens with anguished wailing from trumpet and trombone and Crosby enters almost speaking the text. He only uses vibrato sparingly and at the end of long notes, a distillation of Armstrong's style. His voice is that of Armstrong on the wordless 'West End Blues' of 1928, light, straight but with a strength and swing derived directly from the blues. In not pretending to be black he took black musical concepts to the mass white audience, erasing the memory of minstrelsy. His use of the microphone enabled him to put all his energies into text/tempo creation, unencumbered by the need to project which had given him so much trouble when singing live in larger halls.

In commercial terms the expansion of jazz-influenced music was effected by Jack Kapp, the co-founder of Decca Records. Kapp, a man of ruthless business sense and uncommonly wide musical taste, had been managing Crosby since 1931 and from 1935 onwards also had Armstrong under contract. He ensured that they used their talents in the broadest possible way, seeking the maximum market for all his artists (who included Billie Holiday, Basie, and the three great women singers Mildred Bailey, Connee Boswell and Lee Wiley). The resulting commercialisation ensured that jazz could no longer be perceived exclusively as appealing to a black audience. Towards the end of the twenties there is a noticeable change in the character of the music and lyrics of jazz. It is possible that black musicians wanted to re-value their music in the light of a perceived need to make it more acceptable to a white market (Hansen, 1960). More likely is that the hegemonic nature of white popular culture began to appropriate its meanings for itself, foregrounding social, as opposed to cultural relations. The lyrics of Armstrong's music towards the end of the decade tend to posit a more general agenda: the signifying sub-text is increasingly absent from his performances. As Leonard (1964) has pointed out, such songs as 'When you're smiling' and 'When you Lover has gone' have nothing especially 'black' about them and could equally well be sung by white singers.

The success of Crosby and Armstrong in appealing to a wider audience propelled popular attention towards singers rather than players. This is a crucial turning point at which jazz style evolves into the swing movement. 'Traditional' jazz, as it came to be called, continued as one of an increasing plurality of jazz styles, but it became decadent, in the sense that it no longer carried the message it once did (and was in fact freed to carry quite different semantic codes, especially when 'revived' by European musicians during the fifties). Jazz-influenced singing, on the other hand, was increasingly taken up by the mainstream. By the beginning of the thirties jazz singers were losing many elements that had initially marked them off from other, non-jazz, singers. The layers of meaning became diffused, meaning less but to more people. At the same time essential elements of jazz style were appropriated by dance music which did not claim to be jazz in the rough, raw sense that it had been in the early twenties. The technical aspects of jazz singing style, swung, speech-related rhythms, were ideal for the dance bands that proliferated towards the end of the decade. Jazz singing achieved a breakthrough: it became a viable way of singing in the mainstream. As instrumental jazz reached a stylistic plateau, public attention tended to focus on the singers. The make-up of bands began to change, with the somewhat larger dance bands incorporating a formulaic version of jazz forms. Jazz composers, such as Ellington (building on the ideas of Jelly Roll Morton before him) disciplined performances into more architectural structures. 'Jazz' began to redefine itself as something exciting and essential to white middle-class youth. By the beginning of the thirties jazz had much of the discipline of classical music, as befitted its new status. There was less improvisation and written arrangements became the norm. Benny Goodman, for example, rehearsed at great length, played from written arrangements and applied the criteria of classical music to his performances: they had to be in tune and together in the same sense as classical pieces (Goodman and Kolodin 1939, pp. 241–2).

A further ingredient to be found once a new dominant style is established is an authenticising myth. In the seventeenth century this took the form of a 'return' to Classical Greek musical thought; for jazz it was contained in the heritage of Africa and the rise of black consciousness. The real legacy of the African past is slowly being unearthed: in the twenties it was the jungle themes to be found in urban nightclubs that gave a spurious legitimacy to the new music. Ellington is a case in point: he achieved national fame with his broadcasts from the Cotton Club, a Harlem night club catering exclusively for white people, in which the floor shows consisted of 'jungle' exploits involving clichéd ideas of the negro's African past, while the black musicians played a suggestive accompaniment. Ellington and his men were no doubt signifyin' to their own satisfaction and were handsomely compensated for doing so.[6]

The lack of women singers in twenties jazz bands is striking. The position of women in Afro-American society, the economic dependence of black women on either their husbands or white employers, left them with very few opportunities for self-advancement. For many, a career in vaudeville offered one way of escape. The relationship between singer and audience in American vaudeville was no different from that of the English music hall: the singer was there to entertain and her performance referred to what were considered to be topics of mutual interest. Adelaide Hall's 'The Blues I love to sing' is a good example: it is not a blues, but features Hall making trumpet noises and generally enjoying the playing of Ellington's men. The great Bessie Smith herself was not above pure silliness if she thought it would entertain her audience ('Cake walkin' Babies from Home', for example). The blues gave the singers an opportunity to create a different relationship with their listeners. The so-called Classic Blues singers, Ma Rainey, Bessie Smith and their contemporaries, learned their singing in minstrel shows and vaudeville, often developing powerful voices as they learned to cope with the dead acoustic environment of the tent shows. Such passionate and powerful delivery was used for more than merely entertaining the audience. Blues tends to be directly expressive of a limited, but powerful, set of emotions, externalising publicly what is normally expressed in private. It was this commitment that influenced succeeding generations of singers.

Ma Rainey, whose career immediately before she successfully fronted her own band was as one half of a vaudeville duo, sang in a strong but often stilted manner. The five takes recorded in 1924 (with a band that included Armstrong) reveal a classical-like sustained vibrato and a use of her chest register that takes her well away from the speech-related techniques that are essential to swing. The songs are in binary tempi and the band gives the feeling that it would burst into something far more swinging if Ma were not there. Many of the women were obviously influenced by European role-models (which they would have encountered in vaudeville). Ida Cox and Ada Brown use, if anything, more vibrato than one would expect to find in a classical singer of this period. Bessie Smith's more shouting style sounds more worldly, at once harsher and more sophisticated. Her minimal version of Handy's 'St Louis Blues' gets right to the heart of the song. Her songs often signified on drink and sex ('Me and my Gin', 'Take it right back'). She was one of the few women blues singers who worked successfully with the microphone: in her 1929 sides where she is accompanied only by a piano her delivery is toned down quite considerably.

Susan McClary (1991) and others have drawn attention to the fact that gender roles are socially constructed in music. The question of empowerment is at the heart of all socially constructed reality and this aspect of gender relations in the early part of the century undoubtedly conditioned the roles that women singers could play. Both the classic blues singers and the so-called 'torch' singers projected narrowly specific agendas to a clearly identified audience. The blues ladies articulated powerful complaints about poverty, infidelity, drink, sex and love in the notional context of black working-class women. The torch singers (white, and working in white clubs to white audiences), confined their texts to the theme of unrequited love implicit in their name. The repertoire of male singers from the period is much more general, and it is possible that the roles in which women singers could project themselves were too narrow to achieve the widespread success of the men. There were exceptions to this, however, and some women singers probably exploited their sexuality from a position of power in much the same way as McClary has recently claimed for Madonna.[7] Many singers sang songs that were also recorded by men (Bessie Smith's version of 'St Louis Blues') or dealt with issues of sexuality in a hyper-male way (the 'gutbucket' songs that middle-class whites found so offensive). After jazz-influenced singing became the mainstream it was possible for Billie Holiday and her successors to draw on the experiences of the classic blues, torch singers, and the Armstrong–Crosby legacy. The working conditions and opportunities for women in a profession that was socially and economically dominated by men also meant that only the strongest and most persistent women singers were likely to succeed. Even when more opportunities for 'canaries' arose in the thirties, life on the road was often extremely hazardous for women musicians. There were very few female band members, and singers had no union representation. Singers fronting bands were expected to maintain and pay for a substantial wardrobe, whereas the mostly male band members were provided with a uniform (Dahl, 1989).

The dominance of the medium by Armstrong, Crosby and their male imitators certainly made it difficult for women to find a place in jazz. Black women were in any case confined to race labels, which restricted their potential market still further. The move towards bigger bands at the end of the decade created marketing opportunities for entrepreneurs such as Jack Kapp, who was anxious to combine the commercial appeals of glamorous women singers and successful bands. His first success in this direction was with Mildred Bailey and a group of Paul Whiteman sidemen. In 1931 (the year of Bailey's first hit) Duke Ellington hired Ivie Anderson, who would remain with the band until 1942. Anderson is clearly influenced by Crosby but there is little of the passion of Armstrong in her delivery. Ellington was unsure of the best way to use a singer at first but by the mid-thirties Ivie had adapted herself to the needs of the band. Her version of 'Oh Babe, maybe Someday' could be Crosby: entertaining and fast enough to dance to, with plenty of breaks for solos (both improvised and arranged).

Also under Kapp's control were the Boswell Sisters. Largely inspired by Connee Boswell (who had a career of her own after her sisters married in the mid-thirties), the Boswells brought a new strength and breadth to popular singing. Their arrangements were complicated, almost amounting to recompositions. Although Kapp vetoed their more avant-garde efforts, the sides that were released often take jazz-influenced pop into new territory. Friedwald (1991, pp. 155–6) rightly gives some two pages to an analysis of 'Shout, Sister, shout!' of 1931, with its many time changes and blues-inflected scatting. These are the hallmarks of the Boswells' work (a total of some seventy sides produced before the group effectively disbanded in 1935). Friedwald also quotes a letter from a radio listener who wants to know whether the sisters are black or white, an indication that the influence of Armstrong and the Classic Blues singers also characterised their singing. The influence of Armstrong, together with that of Bessie Smith, is also to be found in the singing of Billie Holiday. In 'You can't loose a Broken Heart' and 'My Sweet Hunk o'Trash', the two duets recorded towards the end of Holiday's Decca contract in the forties, the two singers use exactly the same speech-related phrasing, with its displaced accents, that Armstrong had perfected in the twenties. The chaotic and often tragic nature of Holiday's life found expression in her songs, which ranged from the melodramatic 'Strange Fruit' to the erotic 'All of me'. Her intensity of expression perhaps marks the high point of what Friedwald (1991, p. 311) calls 'adult pop'.

Crosby's style was imitated by literally hundreds of singers during the thirties and forties (Dick Haymes, Russ Columbo, Perry Como and Dean Martin to name but four extremely famous ones). Those who refined it still further were relatively rare. Three stand out as managing to keep the hegemonic status of jazz-inflected popular

singing viable: Billy Eckstine, Mel Tormé and Frank Sinatra. All
have elements of classical technique, especially a tendency towards
vibrato (in most Eckstine and in later Sinatra); all have impressive
breath control. Eckstine is important for two additional reasons: he
was the first black male singer to be wholly accepted by a white
public as a singer of love songs. His band was also instrumental in
bringing together Dizzie Gillespie, Charlie Parker, Miles Davis and
the creators of bop (he also 'discovered' Sarah Vaughan).[8] His tone
could range from a smooth, vibrato-free, speech-like quality (a sort
of ultra-refined Crosby), full of innuendo ('Blues the Mother of Sin')
to heavily vibratoed louder passages ('Jelly Jelly'). Tormé, a great
manipulator of the microphone (he really was a 'crooner'), is also a
great manipulator of a text. His 'Getting to be a Habit with me' is so
understated and intimate as to be almost embarrassing. His best
work was done with very small ensembles, usually a trio, which left
plenty of space for him to realise the text. He too, could sing high,
sustained notes with an even vibrato in the manner of a classical
tenor using his head voice, but he preferred to let the microphone
energise the text for him. This means that his words are always
absolutely clear. The double-time section of 'Oh you Beautiful Doll'
shows this to pefection: even when the music is very loud, Tormé
appears to be making very little effort.

Frank Sinatra stands astride the period from the late forties to the
present and encapsulates what was, for much of the earlier period,
the mainstream style. He has had many imitators (Vic Damone,
Buddy Greco, Sammy Davis) and at least one who would be his
successor (Harry Connick). As Friedwald (1991) points out, Sinatra
was the first to think of himself as an artist, and his 'art' contains the
passion of the Classic Blues singers, the phrasing of Armstrong and
the diction of Crosby or Tormé. 'Birth of the Blues', recorded in
1952, and previously recorded by Crosby, among others, shows the
singer at the peak of his powers:

> These are the blues,   1
> Nothing but blues.
> Oh they say some people long ago
> Were searching for a different tune,
> One that they could croon   5
> As only they can.
> They only had the rhythm so
> They started swaying to and fro;

They didn't know just what to use.
This is how the blues really began.   10
They heard the breeze in the trees
Singing with melodies,
And they made that
The start of the blues;
And from a jail   15
Came the wail of a down-hearted frail,
And they played that
As a part of the blues.
From a whippoorwill way up on a hill
They took a new note;   20
Pushed it through a horn until it was worn
Into a blue note.
And then they nursed it,
They rehearsed it,
And then sent out that news   25
That the south lands
Gave birth to the blues.
They nursed it,
Then they rehearsed it,
And they sent out that news   30
That the south lands
Then gave birth to the blues.

The song begins with almost no introduction. Sinatra emphasises
'blues' (line 1) and holds it with a downward glissando on the final
consonant when the word is repeated (2). This is picked up by an
answering scream from the band (three trumpets, three trombones
and four saxes, but sounding like twice that). Sinatra then pauses on
the 'Oh', making the line quite a long one to do in one breath. He is
really singing here, and in no sense crooning. In line seven he makes
a rallentando at 'They only had the rhythm': a reminder that this is
concert music, not for dancing. Each subsequent line is taken in one
breath, with every consonant clearly audible: as Sinatra himself said,
'You got to get up and sing but still have enough down there to make
your phrases much more understandable and elongated so that the
entire thought of the song is there' (Friedwald, 1991, p. 314). These
are the thoughts of a man who thinks, from a technical point of view,
like a classical singer (indeed Sinatra himself once described his
singing as bel canto). Sinatra makes another rallentando into 'They
heard the breeze' (11). His diction is immaculate during this verse:
the *t* of 'that', both times, is perfectly judged. It is surely more

refined than in his normal speech (another classical trait). The bridge section (19) is invested with yet more energy, which becomes more concentrated as he moves through the verse, punctuated by the muted horn section, and with a spectacularly long line at 'Pushed it through'(21). There is another rallentando into the chorus section (23), with a small croak on 'they', his only concession to human frailty during the entire song. With a final repeat of the chorus Sinatra and the band build up to a tremendous climax, with soaring high notes and more feats of breath control. This is Frank Sinatra at his most eloquent: faultless technique executed with total commitment. The band is superb, the whole production exuding American confidence and Sinatra's personality. What you hear is what you get: no sub-text is signified here, unless it is to claim the blues for crooners (despite the reference to the South). It is the song of a man at the peak of his powers celebrating his own success. It is about excellence, the production of musical commodity of the highest quality, and Sinatra went on to produce hundreds like it (and is still, at the time of writing, attempting to do so).

There is now nothing else that Sinatra can do except to try to fulfil the expectations of his market. Artistically, he is complete. The music appeals to those sections of society for whom such criteria are important. It does not have the appeal to the young that it had in the forties. It is no longer radical and full of latent potential. The style begun by Armstrong and Crosby has become a tradition (here with its own mythology in the curious mix of references to 'blues' and 'crooners'). It can (and does) continue to appeal to listeners who are themselves older, more successful, or interested in performance techniques, but it can no longer appeal to those listeners who first enabled the style to function, and who were increasingly (in 1952) turning to the raw excitement offered by rock'n'roll.

CHAPTER 7

Early music and the avant-garde: twentieth-century fragmentation

There is a common-sense view of music history which says that until Mendelssohn 'rediscovered' Bach all music was contemporary music, which was then discarded in favour of more contemporary music. In fact, the idea of performing music from previous generations is as old as music history itself. The chant repertoires codified by Gregory into the corpus that (rightly or wrongly) bears his name are an early example; the Prague manuscript known as the *Codex Speciálník*, which dates from around 1500 and contains French *Ars Nova* pieces as well as Franco-Flemish polyphony, is inscribed with a presentation date of 1611; Monteverdi is known to have ordered copies of Josquin's masses for his singers; Hawkins and Burney, compilers of eighteenth-century musical histories, had an academic interest in earlier music; Bach performed Palestrina at Leipzig and the Academy of Ancient Music in nineteenth-century London promoted concerts of Handel and Purcell, among others. In the early twentieth century, Landowska and Dolmetsch were responsible for re-kindling interest in historical instruments, and Nadia Boulanger performed Monteverdi's madrigals. Since the beginning of the century scholars have made performing editions of medieval and Renaissance music. Until recently, however, the singing style adopted for the performance of pre-Romantic music was invariably that of current post-Romantic practice, with no concession to the idea that the music may have sounded completely different when it was first performed.

In English cathedrals and at the universities of Oxford and Cambridge the works of Byrd, Tallis and other Renaissance composers have remained in repertoire from their composition until the present day. Eighteenth-century English composers such as William Croft and Maurice Greene also continue to be performed alongside works by their Victorian and Edwardian successors Wesley, Stainer,

Dyson, Sumsion and others. New commissions (such as the annual new carol from King's College, Cambridge) may take their place within a core repertoire that goes back a very long way. Perhaps because of this there is an instinctively retrospective taste among those boys and adults who sing in such choirs. Despite the revival of English cathedral music towards the end of the nineteenth century, most English cathedral singing was not noted for its musicianship, style or beauty of sound until Boris Ord, building on the foundations laid by A. H. Mann, applied rigorous standards of intonation and style during his tenure as organist at King's College, Cambridge between 1929 and 1957.[1] The Christmas broadcasts and many records made by the choir under Ord and his successor David Willcocks not only made the choir a household name but also inspired other cathedral and college choirs to adopt a more efficient and professional approach. Choral scholars from Cambridge (and, to a lesser extent, Oxford) began to sing professionally during the sixties (the Baccholian Singers) and seventies (the King's Singers and the Scholars). Individual soloists who had been choral scholars became internationally known (Robert Tear, a rare success in opera, and Nigel Rogers, as a baroque specialist).

The first singer of note to give serious attention to old singing styles was Alfred Deller, who joined the choir of Canterbury Cathedral as an alto lay-clerk in 1940 at the age of twenty-eight. The male alto, an adult using a falsetto voice, is particularly associated with the English cathedral tradition. Deller's voice was very different from the bland and unreliable alto of his contemporaries and he preferred to call himself a countertenor (the two terms are currently used interchangeably, although there is a school of thought which argues that an alto is a falsettist, whereas a countertenor is a tenor with an extended upper register).[2] The extraordinary and idiosyncratic quality of his singing was noticed by Michael Tippett in 1943 and Deller was invited to take part in concerts at Morley College, subsequently singing in the inaugural concert of the BBC's Third Progamme. From 1947 onwards he was able to make solo singing a full-time career, the first time any falsettist had been able to do this. Claims that the countertenor is a revival of a historical solo voice are difficult to justify. The vocal lines marked 'countertenor' towards the end of the seventeenth century (when the term is first used as the name of a voice as opposed to a musical line) are clearly high tenor parts. E. H. Fellowes' pioneering editions of Elizabethan church music, begun in 1913, transposed the music where necessary to bring it within the range of male altos, thus unwittingly furthering the myth. It was perhaps the attempts of nineteenth-century altos to cope with earlier music composed for high tenors that gave the English cathedral alto its slightly comic reputation. There have been periods on the European mainland when countertenors have flourished, notably in sixteenth-century Spain and in the Rorantist chapel in seventeenth-century Cracow, but there are very few known examples of prominent countertenor soloists. Deller's work, though problematic historically (his voice had probably not existed in the sense that he thought he was reviving it) did open people's minds to the idea of a fresh aproach to historical music. It was for Deller that Britten wrote the part of Oberon in *A Midsummer Night's Dream*, the first of many significant countertenor roles composed by him and other composers which were later to include Maxwell Davies, Ligeti and Reich. Just as important, however, was Deller's decision to perform Dowland lute songs accompanied by a lute (rather than a piano). Deller's success enabled other countertenors to become full-time professionals. Although there is an American tradition (Russell Oberlin, John Angelo Messana and, more recently, Derek Lee Ragin), and a European one (René Jacobs, Jochen Kowalski), England has been the most prolific producer of post-Deller countertenors. All of these have had experience in cathedral or college choirs (John Whitworth, King's College, Cambridge; James Bowman, New College, Oxford; Paul Esswood, Westminster Abbey; David James, Magdalen College, Oxford; Michael Chance and David Cordier, King's College, Cambridge, to name only a few from a very long list).

The English choirs also produced tenors and basses with the light voices required by the new early music aesthetic. Attempts to reconstruct Renaissance and medieval vocal sounds had been made by Michael Morrow using the voice of soprano Jantina Noorman with his group Musica Reservata at the end of the fifties. The 'Reservata holler', as Howard Mayer Brown (1978, p. 166) called it, failed to sustain its initial impact. Noorman's folk-influenced and often strident singing was too much of a departure from the comforting warmth of the choral scholar sound.[3] It was not until David Munrow formed his Early Music Consort of London in 1967 that early music singing was perceived by the public as attractive to listen to. His singers were the countertenor James Bowman, the tenors Martyn Hill and Paul Elliott (ex-King's College, Cambridge and Magdalen College, Oxford, respectively) and the bass Geoffrey Shaw (St Paul's Cathedral), and he could reinforce this line-up with a larger group, all of whom had sung in Oxford or Cambridge choirs. In the BBC Promenade Concert nine months before his death only one of the singers (the bass, Terry Edwards) was not from this background.

During the seventies former Oxford and Cambridge choral scholars (or ex-choirboys) formed the nucleus of the post-Munrow groups such as Pro Cantione Antiqua, the New London Consort and the Medieval Ensemble of London, the same singers often appearing with different ensembles. These groups explored the Renaissance and medieval repertoires sometimes as adjuncts to reconstructed bands and sometimes as *a cappella* vocal groups which began to reclaim for solo voices what had in the the more recent past been considered to be choral music. There were larger groups, such as the Monteverdi and Schütz Choirs, and the Clerkes of Oxenford, who also employed women singers, most of whom were also graduates of the two universities (Oxford produced Emma Kirkby, perhaps the most successful early music soprano). In the eighties the same elite was to be found in the Hilliard Ensemble, the Taverner Choir, the Tallis Scholars, the Gabrieli Consort, the Sixteen and Gothic Voices. Groups with singers who did not make the accepted Oxbridge sound (such as the Dufay Collective and Synfonie) were consistently marginalised. The nineties saw a new generation of successful ensembles with a strong ex-Oxbridge membership, although a slightly less sweet sound can be detected in groups such as the Cardinall's Musicke. Singers with larger voices tended to gravitate towards baroque music, which even today tends to use 'unreconstructed' singers although conductors will often go to great lengths to secure 'authentic' players.[4]

In effect, singers from the two universities have been able to establish a dominant style of their own in parallel with the main classical style. British early music has its own career paths and educational programmes and has become a major exporter. Many of the ensembles mentioned above do as much work abroad as in Britain and the English style of singing early music is imitated all over the northern hemisphere. This position of authority has been achieved with the minimum change to the techniques that the singers learned to gain their choral scholarships, and with almost no concession to the little academic work that has been done on historical singing. There have, however, been changes in attitude to the enunciation of texts. The Ord/Willcocks style of text presentation at King's involved exaggerating consonants and vowels far beyond the demands of clarity. Latin was pronounced in a broadly Italianate way but with certain idiosyncrasies, such as softening the Italian *c* to something like *sh*, which was considered to be simply 'better' than the Italian paradigm (I suspect that similar notions are behind the recent recording of Haydn's *Insanae et vanae curae* by Norwich cathedral choir, which uses a soft pronunciation for the second *g* in 'negligas'. There are no precedents for this in any spoken Romance language, *g* being always hard before *a*). Where two phrases were to be sung in the same breath (succeeding lines of a hymn tune, for example) a crescendo would be made out of one phrase and into the next. This does not add to the listener's understanding of the text (and may even make nonsense of it) but it does demonstrate disciplined breath control. Such was the eminence of the choir that these quirks of style and pronunciation became the norm for parish church choirs thoughout the land (and generally remain so). The stylised pronunciation was a by-product of the music-as-discipline approach and a striving for an abstract notion of excellence. The pronunciation established criteria by which excellence could be measured, and the singing was judged in part by the excellence of its pronunciation rather than by the success or otherwise of strategies to put across the meaning.

The Munrow approach to text declamation was very different. He was not himself a singer, but a bassoonist turned virtuoso player of exotic wind instruments. He worried less about the sound of the text as words and more about its articulation as music. He expected his singers to reduce their vibrato and sing in a more instrumental way. In practice this meant breaking up legato melismatic passages as though they were tongued woodwind phrases. This can be clearly heard in the BBC recording of one of his last concerts, the Promenade Concert of 1975. In the performance of Isaac's *Agnus Dei*, each quaver is separated from the adjoining one. The effect is to prevent the comprehension of the text as a complete entity. Like the King's College singing, it is not an efficacious way of singing a text, which meant that if early music singing was to develop further, more experiments with articulation would have to be made. Some sign of this was seen in the late seventies and early eighties, especially by the

New London Consort which attempted to reconcile a historically informed approach with a speech-like declamation in a form that was acceptable to audiences. Significantly, Catherine Bott, the singer featured in almost all the group's recordings and performances, did not have an Oxbridge background and had been a member of Swingle II, the successor to the Swingle Singers (who sang in a very speech-orientated way using microphones). Bott's performances, informed by historical sources and pop music, showed that it was possible to move beyond the choral-scholar influenced sound of the seventies towards a declamation that was genuinely speech-related. More recently, as the group has become more successful, her style has shown signs of becoming more singerly, and other soloists employed by the group tend to come from the mainstream Oxbridge background.

The Oxbridge singers tend to share a similar kind of spoken accent which is also reflected in the way they sing. This sits awkwardly with potential attempts to devise a way of singing which would be appropriate to earlier periods. England has been a plurality of linguistic communities since pre-historic times. The Norman invasion in the eleventh century resulted in what linguists call *diglossia*, with French joining Latin as the official and artistic language for several hundred years. English presumably continued to be the language of folk music, and the increasing national consciousness of the English court eventually saw the return of English as a high-status language. It was a language of many varieties, that of the South in general and the court in particular having the highest status. By the Elizabethan period (the earliest for which there is a substantial body of evidence) English had made inroads into religious music, previously only set to Latin texts, and in the English madrigal (adapted and developed from Italian models) there existed a vernacular secular music form which was widespread among the upper and emerging middle classes.

Madrigals are a substantial part of the core early music repertoire in the late twentieth century. At the time of their composition (in England roughly between the last quarter of the sixteenth century and the first quarter of the seventeenth) they were sung by both professional and amateur musicians and there is no evidence to suggest that the pronunciation used was anything other than that appropriate to the locality. Fellowes (1948/1972) shows the major madrigal composers as having professional positions in houses, schools and cathedrals throughout the country. Alan Durant (1984, p. 164) has pointed out that this variety in accent is not reflected in current recordings and performances of madrigals, which use Received Pronunciation (RP) as a kind of cultural absolute, implying a narrow definition of culture rather than 'a continuing process of renegotiation and reform within which present musical practices are an important defining activity'. There is, however, a phonological reason underlying this ideological condition. If Elizabethan singers sang with a relatively high larynx position, it would have been fairly easy for them to enunciate the texts and still retain an accent similar to that used in their speech. Domestic music-making would not in any case require projecting the sound much above speech level. Classical singers of today use the lower larynx position with its consequent rounding and darkening of the sound, and ability to be heard in larger acoustic spaces. RP also involves the lowering of the larynx, which gives it its distinctive colour. Modern performers have no option but to sing in RP if they wish to maintain a technique appropriate for modern concert halls and acceptable to modern audiences. This ideological problem has compromised all attempts to re-create the pronunciation of earlier periods.

One reason that it has taken so long for language to be problematised by singers is that pronunciation is indeed assumed to be a cultural absolute, and inevitably so, bearing in mind the educational background of the vast majority of English early music singers. The problem first surfaced when more rigorous editing in the sixties had to deal with the fact that in the sixteenth century the ending *tion* (as in 'generation') was pronounced as a disyllable and would have to be pronounced as such by modern performers if the musical text was to remain intact. This attempt at 'authenticity' was the first move away from strict RP but in practice sounded like an exaggeration of it: it was possible for the innocent listener to believe that such singers might use such pronunciation even in their speech. During the eighties, researchers (notably Harold Copeman and Alison Wray[5]) began to give serious attention to the problems of performance based on historically informed pronunciation. When they were composed, Elizabethan songs were sung as extensions of speech, a combination of regional accent and applied rhetoric. In the sixteenth century the class connotations were different from those of today: the language of the court influenced its speakers and those who aspired to courtly position, but there was little institutionalised class

coding according to geography, except insofar as the court was in
the south of the country. Today's classical music, as a high-status
activity, customarily uses the high form of the language in which to
express itself, which means that early music is generally sung in RP,
an accent that does have class implications. If modern RP-speaking
singers use their natural accent they perpetuate class coding in a way
that has nothing to do with the song as it was originally conceived.
If, on the other hand, they try to reproduce an 'Elizabethan'
pronunciation they risk compromising their own integrity by singing
in a language that they are, in effect, inventing, and they also risk
incomprehension on the part of the listener. Unlike singing in a
foreign language, a reconstructed pronunciation of one's own language can appear to the RP-speaking listener as quaint, comical, or
even perversely obstructive.

Different singers have asked themselves (or failed to ask themselves) different questions, using as much reconstructed language as
their modern techniques will allow. By keeping relatively modern
'singerly' traits such as vibrato they appear reluctant to go too far
towards a speech-related technique. The Hilliard Ensemble experimented with Elizabethan pronunciation for records of Dowland and
Byrd and also with Latin pronunciation appropriate to Tallis. These
efforts were also compromised by a reluctance to depart too far from
the recognised sound of the ensemble. The group has since abandoned its attempts to use old pronunciation except where the text
cannot be satisfactorily modernised, in which case a reconstruction
may be attempted and a translation provided for listeners if necessary. The minefield of infinite possible varieties of medieval and
Renaissance Latin is avoided by using what the group calls 'Hilliard
Latin', a pronunciation based on early English consonants with
fairly bright RP vowels. Red Byrd, a group started towards the end
of the eighties with the aim of addressing questions of class as part of
its agenda, has grappled with the problem by singing Renaissance
music in modern regional accents, each singer using a local accent
with which he or she is familiar. The intention behind this is to relate
something of the linguistic circumstances of the original to a speech-
related singing technique, thus attempting to satisfy vocal, musical,
linguistic and class criteria. The message that the listener is intended
to receive is that this is not class-based music-making. Audience
response has ranged from excitement that the music can be sung in
this way (especially in Germany, which has a diglossic language with

considerably fewer class implications than English) to horror that the singers use, as one reviewer put it, 'vowels that choir trainers spend years trying to eradicate'. Some listeners view the project with distaste on the grounds that the singers sound 'common' or 'rough' and it is possible that listeners with genuine regional accents hearing records of what would normally be an RP activity might feel patronised by them. Ironically, despite the group's insistence to the contrary, many critics have assumed they were being offered Elizabethan English and judged it accordingly.

Adopting a high larynx position would enable reconstructions of Tudor singing to be attempted and would mean that singers could reclaim from the past a rhetorical style of delivery based on textual criteria and direct emotional expression. It would have none of the social and musical constraints that are currently a feature of early music singing. However, the existence of early music as a high-status alternative to mainstream music is dependent on early music being perceived as 'excellent' and restrained. By using RP, singers of early music identify sufficiently with current classical singing not to be a threat to it. The kind of singing that would emerge from a systematic attempt to reconstruct Renaissance or baroque technique would use regional accents and would have the 'natural' sound of an untrained voice, probably not dissimilar to that of a folk or rock singer. Strip away the rock rhetoric of Sting, Phil Collins or Freddie Mercury, and you are left with a basic sound that may be much more appropriate for early music than that made by most of today's specialists. Many rock singers use an upper register which is a non-falsetto head voice corresponding to (and in many cases exceeding) the male alto range, which would conveniently solve the problem of Purcell alto/tenor lines.[6] This would, of course, put most professional early music singers out of a job and could have very serious implications for the social basis of western art music, which currently depends on a small number of people having access to elite skills. Enlarging the pool of potential performers would be seen to 'devalue' the art, especially if performance criteria were to be redefined in terms that by-passed conventional concepts of excellence. The likelihood is that early music singing will continue in its professional niche. Although it does not satisfy criteria for historical truth, it is very much a part of the contemporary aesthetic. It is comfortingly small-scale, concerned with the maintenance of certain standards and legitimised by a musicological profession that takes itself very seriously indeed.

Early music is only one of the many varieties of singing which have evolved alongside what we think of as classical singing (which perhaps reached a plateau towards the end of the nineteenth century). The dramatic declamation of Verdi very quickly gave way to the very large voices required by Wagner, Mahler and Schoenberg. Schoenberg was himself aware of the problem of voice size: he had introduced a speaking part in *Gurrelieder* (1900–11) but the huge orchestral forces required often overwhelm both the speaker and the solo singers, causing both distortion of the speech into something like song and distortion of the singing to the point where the text is incomprehensible. He experimented again with a mixture of speaking and singing in *Die glückliche Hand* (begun in 1908, though not completed until 1913). He described the work as a drama with music and it is written for two mimes, baritone, a chorus of six men and six women, and orchestra. As with Verdi's operatic declamation and that required for the 'New Music' of Caccini and Monteverdi, the experiment in new declamatory techniques begins at that point where drama, text and music interact. The two main characters do not speak at all, and the chorus sing and speak in a manner that recalls ideas of the classical Greek chorus, the composer notating the 'spoken' passages in traditional notation with crosses through the stems. Changes in singing techniques have inevitably involved new tone colours, but the basic function of the voice until Schoenberg was to carry a text or a melodic line. Schoenberg's chorus in *Die glückliche Hand* significantly develops the idea of voice-as-texture by using sung and spoken pitches simultaneously, this time over the rather smaller ensemble that he used for *Erwartung* rather than the gargantuan forces of *Gurrelieder*.

All these ideas were refined in his *Pierrot lunaire* of 1912. His theatre works up to this point (and also the programmatic *Verklärte Nacht*) had been characterised by a tortured sense of melodrama often with disturbing psychopathological overtones. In 1911 Schoenberg had given a series of lectures in Berlin, where he met the actress Albertine Zehme, who suggested he set the Giraud poems for her. Schoenberg actually described *Pierrot lunaire* as a melodrama and in it he made his major experiment with 'Sprechgesang', in the context of Giraud's brooding expressionistic poems. The melodrama had its beginnings in the late eighteenth century in the experiments of Rousseau. Its history is linked to the German *Singspiel* and to the ballad opera, which explored the expressive possibilities of heightened speech. As a socio-musical field it never achieved the status of opera, but many leading composers were attracted to it (Benda, Pfitzner and Richard Strauss, among others). The technique of melodramatic declamation involved a vocal repertoire that ranged from speech to something approaching classical singing and was the province of the reciter (*recitant, diseur/diseuse*) whose normal milieu was the cabaret or theatre rather than the concert hall. What Schoenberg envisaged was a pitched speech which would not be used episodically as was usually the case with the traditional melodrama but integrated into the form of the work as a kind of arioso. In his preface Schoenberg says that the notes are not meant to be sung but should be transformed into 'Sprechmelodie'. He gives two instructions for creating the vocal sound he requires:

1. The rhythm must be kept absolutely strict, as if the reciter were singing; that is to say, with no more freedom than he would allow himself if he were just singing the melody.
2. To emphasise fully the contrast between the sung note and the spoken note, whereas the sung note preserves the pitch, the spoken note gives it at first but then abandons it either by rising or by falling immediately after. The reciter must take the greatest care not to fall into a sing-song form of speaking voice; such is absolutely not intended. On the contrary, the difference between ordinary speech and a manner of speech that may be embodied in musical form, is to be clearly maintained, But, again, it must not be reminiscent of song. (Wellesz, 1971, p. 139).

Although the Berlin performance, preceded by its forty rehearsals, was a success, Schoenberg was rarely happy with the result of his instructions not to 'sing' a pitched text (and his own recording of the piece in 1942 favours speech very much at the expense of the pitches). He abandoned five-line notation in favour of a single line stave for the *Ode to Napoleon*, *A Survivor from Warsaw* and *Jacob's Ladder* and made many contradictory statements on the subject during his lifetime. His unhappiness was largely due to his lack of understanding of the way voices produce text. At the time he wrote the piece it is inconceivable that a classically trained singer would sing without vibrato. Vibrato is not a component of speech, as can be demonstrated by slowing down a recording of a sung phrase and comparing it with a slowed down spoken one. It is not physically possible to speak Schoenberg's pitches unless the reciter uses no vibrato. If vibrato is used, the result is singing rather than speech. It would be possible for a rock singer of today (Sinead O'Connor, for example) to sing the piece in the way that Schoenberg envisaged. The only way that would have worked during the composer's lifetime would have been to abandon fixed pitches altogether, which would have undermined his sense of the function of the composer.

Schoenberg was not alone in his attempts to experiment with musical text declamation. His ideas, born out of the composing tradition of the German Romantics, were less radical than those espoused by the poets and artists of Futurism and Dada. Both movements, which are closely related to each other, have been claimed by the fields of art, literature and music. Common to both was an emphasis on performance which blurred the boundaries between previously separate artistic disciplines. Both were strongly against art in the forms it had come to take in bourgeois society. The first Futurist events in 1910 were a devastating shock to those expecting performances in the accepted genteel manner. Marinetti's evenings of 'dynamic and synoptic declamation' featured 'parole in libertà' (literally, 'words in freedom'), a particularly anarchic way of performing texts which themselves may be purely graphic and with no conventional typography at all. The beginnings of Dada in 1916 at the Cabaret Voltaire saw similar performances of texts such as Huelsenbeck's 'See how Flat the World is', 'sung' to the accompaniment of a large tom-tom; or Ball's 'gadji beri bimba . . .', for which Ball, dressed as an obelisk, was carried onto the stage to sing his poem. The text consists entirely of nonsense syllables intended to represent an imaginary African language (Richter, 1978).

Dada and Futurism did represent a liberation of the word from the confines of a formal technique-based delivery. Marinetti's sound poems were an advance on Schoenberg's thinking about voice and texture, but totally outside the German tradition of European classical music: a piece can be what the performer wants it to be. More importantly, the ideas of Futurism and Dada tilted the balance between composer and performer back towards the latter. They made it possible for singers to invest their performances with an infinite variety of meanings provided they chose a medium that was outside the dominant style. At the same time as black Americans were realising the value of singing as a subversive activity within the medium of jazz, itself outside the mainstream of American dance music, similar principles were being applied in Europe on the fringes of the artistic field. Where speech-related singing became the agent of renewal in popular singing, the attempts of the Dadaists and Schoenberg took longer to have a wider impact.

The freeing of singing from classical technique did not immediately revolutionise singing. In Germany and the USSR there were experiments with speaking choirs, which pursued Schoenberg's ideas a little further, but Futurism as a movement ultimately became associated with Fascism, condemning itself to the musical sidelines.[7] Both Futurism and Dada had begun with the intention of subverting bourgeois art forms and especially the concept of performance, which was to be extended to include anything the performer could think of. Instead of causing the collapse of art, however, the most successful practitioners (especially of Dada) allowed themselves to become a part of the very ethos which they had so decried. Duchamp's urinal or Man Ray's lavatory seat undoubtedly changed the nature of art, but in doing so became a part of it and thereby acknowledged the existing hegemony.

In musical terms John Cage can be seen in a similar light. He was strongly influenced by Duchamp and Dada, and what linked him to the Europeans of the sixties was his interest in theatre. He wrote very little music theatre that was specifically vocal, but his *Aria*, for solo voice is a theatrical *tour de force* for the performer, who has to adopt a number of vocal personae to interpret the piece. The title suggests something distinctly classical, but the various styles in which the sections of the work are performed imply a complete emancipation of vocal style. Many composers of the sixties and seventies extended the principle of emancipation to the text–music relationship, seeing words as texture or tone colour, one musical resource among many. It is through Cage that the apparently anarchic vocal performances of Futurism and Dada become part of the mainstream classical repertoire. A work such as *4′33″*, for silent performer, could have revolutionised the field by allowing non-specialist performers (or even non-musicians) access to it. In practice *4′33″* is almost always performed by persons distinctly over-qualified. Cage's instructions to perform his pieces with any number of players/singers and any sound-producing materials (as in *Variations IV*, for example) should have democratised the medium but often ironically reduced the performance of such music to a small elite. Like the Futurists, Cage also saw a link between music and graphics. He had a large collection of scores, many of which found their way into his book, *Notations*.

Although Cage's ideas have been accepted into the mainstream his influence on musicians working outside the dominant style is also considerable. Graphic scores were very much a part of the 'scratch' movement of Cornelius Cardew. Cardew described scratch music as 'halfway between composing and improvising'. A sometime assistant to Stockhausen and collaborator with Cage, Cardew summed up his philosophy in his book, *Scratch Music* (1972), a manifesto that could equally well have been written by Cage or Marinetti, which includes texts and graphics to be realised by singers and/or players. There is an almost anarchical commitment to consider as a 'score' anything that the performers wish to perform. Cage's influence is still at work; in *Solo* by Sylvano Bussotti (who has a background in graphic design) it is perfectly possible to 'perform' the lighting diagram, which is graphically similar to the actual score.

Post-war composers were keen to exlore the voice as a sound source. This was a logical development from sound-poetry and parallelled the experiments in creating new sound sources by means of electronics. The use of tape, however, greatly reduced or even eliminated the singer as performer. Stockhausen's *Gesang der Jünglinge* (1955–6) was written directly to tape using a treble voice for its raw material. Many composers since the fifties have preferred to use the voice simply as source material. Trevor Wishart, for example, in his *Red Bird*, created in the University of York Electronic Music Studio (1973–7) gives credit to five people for 'voice source-material'. The work, in its disc form, is complete and does not require performance in the conventional sense. Other composers have used the voice as source but also added the living voice as a performance element, often interacting with their own voice on tape. Henri Pousseur's *Songs and Tales from the Bible of Hell*, composed for Electric Phoenix in 1978, uses the group singing a Dowland polyphonic song ('Flow my Tears') as its source material. Material derived from the song was sent by Pousseur to England with instructions for recording. The finished source-material was returned to the composer in Belgium and he then treated the material and produced a mastertape and score. This was performed using amplified voices with and without electronics operated by the singers. Noa Guy uses a similar technique in her *Who Knows the Secret?* The solo voice sings to the accompaniment of a tape made from raw material provided by his own voice which has been subjected to electronic treatment and multi-track elaboration. There are no live electronics but the singer is required to act out the texts, which are based on creation myths. Although the composer in effect shares responsibility for the piece by incorporating a substantial element of performance, the freedom of the performer is severely curtailed by the real-time clock that is the tape.

The idea of extending the range of meanings that could be derived from vocal performance also interested Stockhausen. His *Stimmung* of 1968 is a seminal work, which brought the singing of reinforced harmonics (or overtones) into the repertoire. The singers sustain for the seventy-five minutes of the piece twenty-one different vowels whose harmonic content is associated with the second, third, fourth, fifth, seventh and ninth partials of B flat. The technique was at first so difficult that only the Collegium Vocale of Cologne could attempt it successfully. After some persuasion Stockhausen eventually agreed to the British group Singcircle performing and recording the piece, and it is now in the repertoire of many student ensembles. Singing reinforced harmonics, or 'chant' as the technique is sometimes called (after its Tibetan antecedents) has been particularly developed in the USA. The Harmonic Choir, directed by David Hikes, has a substantial repertoire entirely of pieces which use reinforced harmonics. William Brooks' setting of *The Silver Swan*, one of his four *Madrigals* composed for the Extended Vocal Techniques Ensemble of San Diego, is constructed from a phonetic analysis of the vowels of the text. Having established the harmonic spectra for each vowel the piece then 'wrote itself' in four parts notated on eight staves, each singer singing the fundamental note and reinforcing the overtone that produces the required vowel (Brooks, 1982). In a sense having both vowels and harmonics is tautological: an American speaker could theoretically produce the effect with either information set. A second madrigal, *Osannga*, explores more fully the harmonic possibilities of four people 'singing' in eight parts.

Fundamental to extended vocal techniques is a concern for the breath. Breathing in singing is traditionally associated with discipline and support for tone colour which then produces text. In extended vocal techniques breathing is explored at a much more basic level, that of breath as sound production. Diaphragmatic breathing in its conventional sense is of limited use because it is designed to provide consistent support for exhaled breath over long phrases. Many of the new techniques are gestural, such as sighing or gasping, or use mouth air (various clicks and other percussive sounds) or inhaled breath. Singers have always envied the circular breathing of wind virtuosi such as Heinz Holliger and Vinko Globokar, and some singers and composers have experimented with trying to create a seamless sound alternating between inhaled and exhaled breath. Joan La Barbara's *Circular Song* was an early attempt at this (1975). James Fulkerson took the idea a stage further with his *Antiphonies and Streams II*, in which the solo singer, highly amplified, builds up polyphonic textures by manipulating the multiphonic sounds that occur as a result of the action of mucus on the cords in a more or less constricted windway. There are various other multiphonic possibilities that use the mouth as a sound source in addition to the vocal cords. The most obvious method is to combine breath sounds with those produced by the voice, whistling and singing at the same time, for example. The face or throat can also be used as a resonator though the act of hitting one's self may signify extra-musical meanings which inevitably limit the use of such a technique. More useful, but far more difficult, are multiphonic sounds produced by dividing the cords themselves. One of the most successful performers of multiphonics was Roy Hart, for whom Maxwell Davies wrote *Eight Songs for a Mad King* (1969). The chords in this work were finalised in rehearsal between the composer and singer and were based on Hart's repertoire of multiphonic sounds. In 1975, Hart, who also worked with Henze and Stockhausen, was killed in a car crash and successive performers of the *Eight Songs* have only managed an approximation of the original score. Hart's work was based on the ideas of Alfred Wolfsohn, who had formed a group of singers during the fifties for the purpose of extending the range and possibilities of the human voice, which Wolfsohn believed to be the most direct expression of the soul. His experiments were remarkable for their time, and he and his pupils gave concerts and demonstrations which included multiphonics sung by singers with ranges of up to seven octaves. Roy Hart took over the leadership of this group on Wolfsohn's death in 1962, establishing the Roy Hart Theatre as a kind of commune near Lille. The group studies and teaches singing in a very broad sense, aiming to draw out the potential voice of any individual. Many of its members have vocal ranges that considerably exceed the expectations of bel canto.[8] Swiss singer Tamia Favre has a similar multiphonic repertoire covering several octaves.

Luciano Berio has probably contributed more than any other

living composer to the study of vocal semantics and semiotics. He was fortunate in having as his collaborator his first wife, Cathy Berberian, a virtuoso soloist whose natural tendency, like Jane Manning after her, was to sing with a conventional modern technique, but whose imagination and broadmindedness knew no bounds. This basis of legitimate vocal strength enabled her to perform more unusual effects without fear of damage to her reputation. Berio referred to her as his second 'studio di fonologia', and a substantial number of her repertoire of sounds appears in his *Sequenza III*, which was composed so much with Berberian's talents in mind that he has considered arranging a three-part version to be certain of getting the effect he requires.[9] As it stands, it is a solo voice work to a text by Mark Kutter, and it is currently the only vocal work in a series of solo studies otherwise devoted to the exploration of individual instruments. The work is a catalogue of what have become known as extended vocal techniques (evt): there are signs for approximate pitch, breathy tone, whispered sounds, laughter, inhaled breath, mouth clicks, coughs, closed mouth, hand over mouth as well as a 'dental tremolo', an effect similar to shivering at which Berberian was particularly adept, and which the composer re-used in several subsequent pieces. Berio asks for some forty emotive states, in a piece which lasts only a few minutes. Together with *Pierrot lunaire*, this work is one of the milestones of twentieth-century 'classical' vocal writing. Berio and Berberian succeeded in defining extended vocal techniques and created new ways in which vocal semantics could operate. The text is never delivered in a conventional way, but broken up, distorted and recycled as though sung by someone unhinged. Like Pierrot, the subject is a woman, perhaps on the verge of madness, and looking for new ways of expressing her predicament. Berio uses the voice as a sound-generator, as a palette of colours, each one summoning up a mood, only to be dismissed by yet more vocal wizardry.

Berio's interest in language was given concrete form when he met Umberto Eco in the fifties. They soon discovered a mutual interest in onomatopoeia, which led them to collaborate on *Thema* (*Omaggio a Joyce*), an attempt to transform the onomatopoeia of the eleventh chapter of Joyce's *Ulysses* into musical ideas using a spoken voice as source material. In this and all his subsequent vocal works Berio has been preoccupied with syntactical and semantic transformation. In *Sequenza III* the text itself is fragmented and re-integrated, as is the performance, which continually transforms itself from speech into song and vice versa. Despite Berio's complicated instructions the work, though instantly recognisable, never sounds the same in any two performances, as each performer discovers new semantic possibilities within the composer's prescription.

Although Berio has continued to experiment with different aspects of singing (the ethnic styles used in *Coro*, for example) ideas begun in the vocal *Sequenza* seem to have reached their apogee in *A-Ronne*. This work began life in Belgium as a radio play for five actors. Berio describes *A-Ronne* as documentary on a poem of Sanguinetti, whose text consists of quotations from a list of writers ranging from the Bible to Barthes. The quotations are concerned with three themes: beginnings, middles and ends, and are in English, Greek, German, Latin, Italian and French. The text is repeated some twenty times during the piece, during which it undergoes a number of semantic or semiotic treatments, the same words given entirely different meanings according to the context in which they are uttered. Berio makes only occasional reference in the score to the particular situation that he had in mind for each transformation of the text. In its live version, written for the eight singers of Swingle II, the performance took place in complete darkness except for torch beams aimed from a darkened music desk at the singers' mouths. The audience's attention was thus concentrated on the relationship of the mouth to the ear, and semantic transformations of the text which happened between the two. Berio subsequently agreed to a more fully realised stage version, but staging the work did not add to the dramatic or semantic content of the piece and was semiotically tautological, the action merely duplicating what was being done with the voice. The piece begins with the performers greeting each other as at a party. This transforms into the speech of a dictator being harangued by his opponents (or supporters), who turn into a hospital ventilator used as the background to a speech-therapy session. This is followed by sections that appear to take the text to the confessional, the barracks, a tennis match in which the vowels and consonants are exchanged between two protagonists, a boxing match, a bedroom scene, gossiping, a radio/TV commercial, singing practice, folk song, scatting, a lyrical baroque-sounding section supporting a self-consciously boring 'actor', until the piece comes to an end with a gasped 'ette, conne, ronne' (the last three letters of an old Italian alphabet) after a lumbering musical section which recalls the sonorities of big band music. New meanings are continuously being generated, showing the limitless expressive potential of language, which composer, performers and listeners are continually rediscovering.

In *A-Ronne* Berio uses all the devices of extended vocal techniques which are efficacious in text realisation. He has not been able to add anything further on the subject, and I would suggest that the piece represents a moment at which a cycle of development in the field of extended vocal techniques is complete. The compositions of the eighties saw some new techniques enter the mainstream, but if anything the repertoire of sounds contracted, despite significant works from James Dillon, Georges Aperghis and others. Textual clarity has been more satisfactorily realised by singers working in early music, who have found themselves in demand for contemporary pieces. The light, relatively vibrato-free tone is ideal for the textual demands of the simpler 'post-modern' compositions of Reich, Pärt and others, which have developed alongside the fading avant-garde. More recently there have been attempts to marry extended vocal techniques with jazz. Jazz singers have had occasion to use techniques familiar to evt singers: Ella Fitzgerald could scat in octaves with herself, for example. Bobby McFerrin has inspired many people to explore the sound-producing capabilities of their own bodies and his commercial success, both on record and in television advertisements, has probably stimulated a wider interest in what is now a decadent style. Toby Twining's compositions and performances owe much to McFerrin (whose workshops he has attended), but he also incorporates extended vocal techniques and improvisation.

This sense of completeness is confirmed by the various attempts to codify the repertoire of possible sounds. The Extended Vocal Techniques Ensemble of San Diego was established in 1972 at the Center for Music Experiment operating in conjunction with the Linguistics Department at the University of Southern California. Its members, all virtuoso vocalists, produced a *Lexicon* of seventy-five sounds on tape, containing examples of seventy-five different sounds ranging from 'car crash' to 'slurp'. The sounds were the basic repertoire of the group and went on to fulfil a similar function for the British groups Electric Phoenix, Singcircle and the London Sinfonietta Voices. Trevor Wishart, in his *Book of Lost Voices* (1980) made a similar catalogue of possible sounds which he updated in

1985 in his book *On Sonic Art*: chapter 12, 'The Human Repertoire', is a comprehensive description and discussion of the sounds Wishart has been able to discover using his own voice (from 'quarter-WAMP' to 'lip-fart') . There is an accompanying tape of 170 examples which illustrate his text. Defining and codifying the repertoire creates a legitimacy for extended vocal techniques which can then be incorporated into the mainstream. They can be studied in a formal pedagogic context and tend to lose their subversive and exploratory connotations. In effect, a smaller hegemony is established in parallel with the main classical style, as it has been in early music. Like the commercially successful early music composers and performers, new music has its own niche in the fragmented market of the late twentieth century.

CHAPTER 8

Elvis Presley to rap: moments of change since the forties

A similar stylistic fragmentation to that which occurred in classical singing can also be found in pop singing in the second half of the century. In chapter 6 I proposed that jazz singing, the dominant popular style from the late twenties onwards, reached a stylistic plateau with the singing of Frank Sinatra. In fact, by the end of the forties popular singing style as represented by the successors of Armstrong and Crosby was showing the typical signs of decadence that precede a significant change in popular taste. Crosby himself was at the peak of his powers and had many imitators, whose often well-crafted Tin Pan Alley ballads monopolised the record industry's sales charts. The introduction of weekly published charts of best-selling singles began in the USA in 1940, and although the charts were not immune to interference they do provide a better guide to popular musical taste than any indicator previously available. Under segregation the separate markets for 'black' and 'white' audiences could be easily identified and targeted by the record industry. The first Billboard Best Selling Singles chart was, in effect, a measurement of sales to white buyers. Sales to the black audience were soon sufficiently large for the addition of a separate chart. In 1949 this became the Rhythm and Blues chart, and a Country and Western chart was added at the same time. The commercial success of these two minority fields was itself an indicator of the diversity of taste that mainstream music had become increasingly unable to represent. The three categories of chart represented broadly separate markets, each with its own performers, radio stations and shops. Within each category, however, there could be a wide variety of music: the 'white' list would contain the products of the major record companies: Tin Pan Alley ballads, novelty numbers reminiscent of variety, jazz bands and dance music of all sorts enjoyed by the fairly affluent middle class; R&B charts reflected whatever (working-class) black people were buying at those retail outlets which took part in the chart-creation process. R&B records were produced in relatively low volume by smaller, so-called independent labels, and ranged from the aggressive urban blues of musicians such as Howlin' Wolf to close harmony sung by black vocal groups (such as the Orioles' 'Crying in the Chapel' of 1953). Country music, or Country and Western (C&W), as it became, was stylistically a rural 'cowboy' music which combined a folk mythology with a sentimental simplicity appealing to the white working class.

The folk music of rural American whites has a history stretching back to the arrival of the earliest European migrants. In the south and west of the country, musical traditions evolved in isolation from the more heterogeneous stylistic developments that occurred in urban areas. It is not possible to document the unrecorded ancient history of country music with any certainty (though the stylistic history of tune families can be researched). It was a domestic and sociable music, preoccupied with similar themes to English folk music, and was characterised by a vocal sound that is frequently described as harsh, nasal and uncultivated. During the thirties and forties radio brought the music to a wider audience, who tended to associate the hillbilly nasal twang with things backward and primitive. The earliest commercial successes, groups such as the Carter Family and the Weavers, undoubtedly modified their tone to make it more acceptable to more people. The Carter Family's 'At the End of the Road', for example, has a southern-accented full-throated soprano carrying the tune, and the harmony chorus contains a real bass. It is an unsophisticated, religious song sung in a stylised way.

Country music reached its most efficacious expression in the singing of Hank Williams. Williams' style was still sufficiently nasal to link him with the roots of country music, but there is little sign of a southern accent. He uses his chest voice to produce a very straight, speech-sounding tone with occasional swoops into falsetto at the ends of phrases (reminiscent of Jimmie Rogers, and perhaps ultimately derived from cattle-calls). His songs articulate the economic and emotional lives of poor southerners and they have a seriousness, a desperation even, that is entirely absent from mainstream popular music at the time. Williams achieved this by using a much less stylised, more speech-like delivery, where the listener's attention is immediately drawn to what he is singing about, rather than the quality of his voice. C&W is primarily a white man's music, but

Williams 'underscored the connections between whites and blacks' in addressing problems of class that were common to all races (Leppert and Lipsitz, 1990, p. 271). Williams' success was only on the fringes of the mainstream during the forties, although he did have national hits before his death in 1953. The commercial development of a mass market for country music came about largely as the result of Chet Atkins' attempts to make the music more relevant to wealthier, urban record-buyers. The 'Nashville sound' associated with Atkins' RCA artists dropped the traditional fiddle and steel guitar (increasingly an anachronism for all but the oldest players) in favour of two acoustic guitars and background vocal harmonising. It was this sound which Elvis Presley appropriated when he signed for RCA and took on the Jordanaires (a resident Nashville studio group) as his backing musicians. Atkins' singers were much more polished than their predecessors. The charts in the mid-fifties frequently registered hits by C&W singers who owed more to the ballad tradition of Tin Pan Alley than to traditional music. Frankie Lane ('Cool Water'), Tennessee Ernie Ford ('Sixteen Tons'), and Jim Reeves, represent the acceptable, adult face of country music. Their tone is fuller, stronger and multi-registered. It is impossible to listen to Jim Reeves without being aware of the quality of his voice (a light baritone). None of the classical voice categories adequately describes Williams' voice, whose sound owed much more to the thin, high sound of Jimmie Rogers, and it is this sound (and attitude to text delivery) that influenced the younger generation of 'rockabilly' singers (those singing the faster, dance music that was to become rock'n'roll), while the more rounded, commercial sound of Nashville entered the decadent phase that still continues today.

Southern country singers could not avoid contact with black singers. The two cultural traditions, though segregated, shared the hopelessness of permanent poverty and alienation from white middle-class America. Williams himself acknowledged a debt to black singers, and many young white singers grew up listening to rhythm and blues on local radio stations. Blues and country music share a common terrain, foregrounding themes of alienation and loss, using a limited number of musical formulae realised through standardised performance practice. Their debt to European music predates the jazz era, and the more developed forms of post-jazz popular music had only a limited place in either music. The earliest blues musicians were itinerant singer-players who did not expect to make more than enough to keep themselves alive. Of all the many forms of music to be found in black culture in the early part of the century, the blues come closest to the simplicity of country music.

The term 'blues' covers a multitude of singing styles which have interacted with other varieties at many points since the twenties. The full-voiced style of Bessie Smith and the 'Classic' blues singers of the twenties, which exhibits a European classical influence can be heard in Jimmy Rushing's jazz blues of the thirties. Rushing, although described as a blues singer, was a specialist in fast, jazz blues, outward-looking dance music rather than the introspective country blues. T-Bone Walker and Joe Turner both sang with jazz bands and smaller ensembles. Their voices had the rich quality of Rushing's that probably appealed to a wider spectrum of middle-class listeners than the more specialist urban blues singers. Turner sang with Basie's band and with blues-orientated smaller combos. Walker had performed with Ida Cox and Ma Rainey early in his career, and grew up guiding the country blues singer Blind Lemon Jefferson, who was a family friend. The band leader Cab Calloway also kept alive a non-crooning vocal style, and much of his dance repertoire ('Duck Trot', for example) anticipates rock'n'roll.

Many of the smaller bands that followed the collapse of the Big Band movement in the forties were direct forerunners of rock'n'roll. Louis Jordan is the prime example. His 'Keep on knockin'', of 1939 was surely in Little Richard's mind when did his own version (known in the trade as a 'cover') in 1957. The song itself is even older, probably having an earlier incarnation than James Wiggins' 1920s version (C. White, 1984). Jordan's 'Ain't that just like a Woman' (1946) was later recorded by Chuck Berry and Fats Domino. Jordan's sung declamation is very close to speech, and quite unlike the developed technique of Sinatra and his contemporaries. This can be heard quite clearly in 'You run your Mouth', in which Jordan starts with a spoken introduction and then moves into singing with an ease that Schoenberg would surely have wished to hear in *Pierrot lunaire*, and which young rock'n'rollers found more appealing than main-stream models.

Singers such as Jordan, Calloway and Walker were successful in a wider market than just that area known to the charts as R&B. Within the latter field there was a thriving market of small labels, the most successful of which (during the early fifties) was the Chicago-based Chess. Chess supported many black singers who made a living on the R&B circuit, including Muddy Waters, John Lee Hooker and Howlin' Wolf, some of whom eventually had national hits as a result of their songs being taken up by white singers. It is important to point out (in view of the romantic blues myth that permeates so much of the writing on the subject) that the small independent labels were only small because of the size of their market. They operated on exactly the same commercial principles as the 'majors'. Willie Dixon, the Chess musical odd-job man, was a career bluesman, just like the other Chess performers. He joined the company in 1951 and first recorded Muddy Waters three years later. He played bass on all Chuck Berry's early hits and was a member of Berry's first road band. His compositions included 'Little Red Rooster', 'Hoochie Coochie Man', 'My Babe' (each recorded by more than fifty different bands) and some five hundred other blues numbers (Dixon, 1989). The Chess brothers were capitalist entrepreneurs who thought they could sell the blues. It was a world of hustle and ambition, and a far cry from the 'romantic' poverty of Blind Lemon Jefferson or Robert Johnson. It was the more aggressive, up-tempo numbers from urban blues singers which appealed to young white C&W singers, who were themselves always on the look-out for songs which would make them a decent living. Rhythm and blues singing had developed a range of expressive possibilities far in excess of anything used in most country music, and it was the possibilities inherent in the singing of R&B that appealed to young white country singers.

Much has been made of the influence of black singers on white rock'n'rollers, who are often said to have copied the style of black singers. The evidence for this is not conclusive: the point is that the emerging 'white' style of singing transcended country singing and appeared to ignore the pseudo-classical style of the Tin Pan Alley ballad. There is little evidence that Bill Haley, for example, thought he was singing with a 'black' voice. The sound he makes is conditioned by his background listening in 'black' music (and, more especially, in the straight sound of C&W). It is difficult to pin down specific aspects of his style which derive from black singers. His is the sound an untrained, 'natural' voice makes when delivering a text. The delivery uses a similar rhetorical style to that employed by some blues singers. The lack of either the more obviously nasal or mellow sounds of C&W, plus the direct rhetorical delivery by a white singer are the stylistic traits that enable an ex-country singer to become a rock'n'roller.

The form that this synthesis took was often a cover version of a recent R&B hit. Haley's first hits were either cover versions of R&B songs, or parodies of the style. 'Rock around the Clock' had been previously recorded by Sonny Dae, 'Shake, Rattle and Roll' had been a hit for Joe Turner. The Comets' repertoire included Willie Dixon's 'Seventh Son' and Tommy Tucker's 'Hi-heel Sneakers'. The band also had a repertoire of instrumental music, a fact often overlooked by commentators on the rock'n'roll phenomenon. Haley's band numbers used a cut-down big-band horn section which enabled them to play popular mainstream tunes in a frantic, up-tempo fashion, with none of the finesse of a conventional dance band but with plenty of rough excitement. 'Harlem Nocturne', 'Skokiaan' and Ellington's 'Caravan', are substantial pieces for a rock'n'roll dance band, and put alongside his country numbers ('How Many') and the occasional novelty ('Skinny Minnie') locate him at the site of convergence of several streams of competing styles. Dance was what had kept bands alive during the forties and Haley would have found a ready audience for his brighter versions of old dance tunes. There is also a suggestion of doubt, as though he himself is not entirely confident of the way forward and was glad to have the legitimation that existing repertoire conferred. It is possible that instrumentals are also symptomatic of a lack of confidence in singing generally. In the period before the Beatles had their Number 1 hit with 'Please Please Me', there were also many bands who were successful without singers. On 2 February 1963, the day 'Please Please Me' appeared in the British chart, the top three were instrumentals and there were four more in the Top Thirty (Rees *et al.*, 1992, p. 123).

In the mid-fifties records began to appear simultaneously in two or more charts. This simply meant that Bill Haley's 'Rock around the Clock', for example, was bought in sufficient numbers by black fans to appear in the R&B charts, or that Chuck Berry's 'Maybellene' was also bought in large numbers by white people. It did not mean that Berry was perceived as white or that Haley was considered an R&B artist. The first person to appear simultaneously in all three charts was Elvis Presley, whose first two hits of 1956, 'Heartbreak Hotel' and 'Hound Dog' both went to Number 1 in all three charts (with the exception of 'Heartbreak Hotel' which only made Number 5 in the R&B charts). Elvis' success in appealing to all three categories of record-buyer has led scholars to assume that his music represents a synthesis of three existing styles, and that this fact accounts for the dynamism and initially enormous success of rock'n'roll.

Elvis' early history certainly suggests links with working-class music in both black and white communities. He was born in East Tupelo, Mississippi, where he first experienced the (white) gospel singing of the Pentecostal church, and he undoubtedly heard 'white' country music, 'black' rural blues and popular songs on the radio. When he moved to Memphis at the age of thirteen he would have been able to experience the urban blues tradition at first hand. His first records were made in Memphis for Sun in 1954. The first two appeared in the local Memphis country charts and in 1955 he was voted 'Number 1 Up and Coming Country and Western Artist' by Billboard disc jockeys, having had two more hits nationally and toured on the C&W circuit.

Presley's very first Sun disc, Art Crudup's 'That's Alright', was an easy transference from R&B to C&W and was typical of the time: 'cover' versions were a significant feature of the charts in the USA, and, after 1952 when the first chart appeared, in Britain. The song was still a separate entity from its performance, could be orchestrated and 'interpreted' in a similar way to a European classical piece, and the bulk of the profit would be realised in the sale of sheet music. The 30 April 1955 British Top Twenty contains only thirteen songs, the remaining seven being alternative versions competing in the same market. These ranged from ballads such as 'A Stranger in Paradise' getting different treatment from Bing Crosby and Don Cornell, to the Crew-Cuts' 'Earth Angel', originally an R&B hit for the Penguins, here covered by a white group. In this very competitive environment, Elvis' background in C&W, white gospel and R&B was an exploitable resource, at a time when there was a great deal of fluidity between listening publics that had previously been considered separate. 'That's Alright' opens with Scotty Moore's arpeggiated country-style guitar chords and Elvis adding a few interjections on his own instrument. Although the song uses a three-chord blues structure it is firmly C&W in feel, as is the subject matter (telling his mother about his girlfriend problems). The guitar solo is a limited exploration of the fingerboard typical of cowboy songs of the period. What is unusual about it is the direct engagement that Elvis makes with the listener, a kind of creamy urgency that is unsettling to listen to.

Presley's second Sun single, 'Good Rockin' Tonight', is a step further into new territory. It is a dance song, reifying 'rock'n'roll', which was still a nascent concept, perhaps a state of mind rather than a set of musical parameters at this stage. The balance has shifted away from C&W (though the influence is still there) and towards R&B, especially in the more bluesy guitar solo and Elvis' more aggressive delivery, which must have reminded some of his listeners of the black R&B singers of Memphis. The use of the term rock'n'roll to describe the new music was common by the mid-fifties. American disc-jockey, Alan Freed, claimed provenance on the name, having used it in 1951. It was undoubtedly in use before that, probably in the black community and with sexual overtones. Ella Fitzgerald's 1937 'Rock it for me' has a text that sounds twenty years in advance of its time (and, ironically, includes a line about 'the nifties swinging down the fifties'). The song celebrates a new dance ('let's rock') and Ella commands 'satisfy my soul with the rock'n'roll'.

At the end of 1955 Presley's Sun contract was purchased by RCA and in February 1956 'Heartbreak Hotel' was released. In May it entered the British chart at Number 15, where it peaked at Number 2 in June (possibly because RCA also rushed out a Presley version of Carl Perkins' 'Blue Suede Shoes', which may have diluted the market). 'Heartbreak Hotel' has almost nothing to do with C&W. Musically the song has its roots firmly in urban blues and jazz blues. After a few rhetorical chords Elvis sets off accompanied only by a string bass. This, together with the stop-time declamation is a jazz technique from the twenties, as is the final two chord 'goodbye' ending on an unresolved seventh. The instrumental playing moves to the blues 'steps' (a guitar riff which moves step-wise from the fifth to seventh degree of the scale and back again while the supporting chord remains constant). Elvis' singing enters an entirely new rhetorical domain. He sings with a menacing, aggressive restraint, which at times has the vibrato and lyricism of Crosby and then suddenly switches into barely-audible muttering. The references to loneliness are sometimes actually spoken, or as close as the singer can get to pitched speaking. He forces the language to accommodate his thoughts: the tension between what he is thinking and what he is singing can almost be felt by the listener. The artificial reverberation (the only remnant of country music to survive in the song) often seems to blur the words, the sentiments of which seem to be so shocking that the singer can hardly get them out. His hyper-pronunciation of 'baby' (something Jonnie Ray had done before him and generations of white singers were to do subsequently) is full of implication, affect rather than effect. He emphasises beats that a country singer would have considered weak (what Richard Middleton (1972, p. 152; 1990, p. 18) calls 'boogification'): by accenting the text in unexpected places he forces the listener's attention towards the text in a way that links the words directly to rhythm and, by extension, to dance. This foregrounding of the guts of the text, which brings a surrogate physical presence to the words, does for the text declamation what swing did in the twenties: removes it from conventional rhetoric to a terrain where new realities can be constructed by the listener. The surface-level meanings of the text are modernist and open-ended, and channel listeners into particular sets of meanings but leave them free to construct their own outcomes. The text is a revelation, compared with the bland professional ballads that kept it company in the chart, the hotel in question being a place of loneliness and desperation such as teenagers might find in their minds but which Sinatra's 'swinging lovers' would probably go a long way to avoid. Elvis' rhetoric is visceral and erotic. The implied equation of sex and death has a long history in European art music, but such sentiments had not been expressed in popular music since the twenties. Presley challenges his listeners to enter his world, or to reject it, or to invent one of their own, and this is exactly what future generations of rock singers were to do, and exactly what the ballads of Sinatra did not do. The overall impression is one of roughness, as though Presley is making it all up as he goes along, articulating his most personal thoughts as they occur to him (it is only the repetition of the second strophe that reminds the listener that the drama is pre-planned). The immaculate wholeness (and wholesomeness) of the Sinatra school, and its feeling for craft and excellence, are entirely absent from Elvis' singing of 'Heartbreak Hotel'.

Elvis' releases following his initial success explored in individual detail some of the elements that are present in 'Heartbreak Hotel'. 'Hound Dog' is a raw rocker: no vibrato, subverted text ('cry-hing'), a blues guitar solo (and curious, close-harmony backing vocals), Bill Haley out of Johnny Ray. 'Love me tender' is a ballad, the theme from the singer's first film, which sees Elvis developing his lyricism with a Crosby-like fluency; this song, which joined three other Elvis sides in the British chart in December 1956 was perhaps something of a surprise to his youth following, but it probably broadened his appeal to their parents, as did his recording of Rogers and Hart's 'Blue Moon'. C&W had a long ballad tradition, and, more significantly, so did Tin Pan Alley. In capturing the middle of the road Elvis ensured that that very terrain would be open to future 'boogification'. His version of 'Blue Suede Shoes' was not his only cover version: 'Rip it up' followed versions by both Little Richard and Bill Hayley. Hayley uses a straight chest-voice delivery, uninflected with the coloration that gives the text the potential for additional meanings. Presley's rhetoric is far more sophisticated, even in this fairly simple dance tune. Haley urges the listener to dance, Presley uses a much wider range of expression to suggest many other possibilities. Haley's singing is very close to what the listener imagines his speaking voice to be like. Presley heightens his speech more radically. This does not make him into a classical singer, but it gives him the power, through the tension and release of phrases and even individual words, to make a very personal statement, and through this to allow the listeners to make their own.

Elvis encapsulated and transformed a number of pre-existing styles: he did not invent any of them. The charts of the early fifties were dominated by ballad singers and crooners. In Britain, the week after 'Heartbreak Hotel' reached Number 2 (June, 1956) Frank Sinatra's LP, *Songs for Swinging Lovers* reached Number 12 in the singles charts, the highest position ever attained by an album until the Beatles' *With the Beatles* reached Number 11 in December 1963. Sinatra's album represents the last and one of the most successful manifestations of the old style: a perfectly worked synthesis of all the developments within the mainstream since the twenties. It has many of the attributes of classical singing and is underpinned by a concept of excellence: this is Sinatra 'at his best'. Others without Sinatra's swing went even further towards classical singing, and classical tenors such as Mario Lanza and David Whitfield were capable of selling records in very large numbers. Whitfield's 1954 hit 'Cara mia' spent ten weeks at Number 1 in Britain and entered the US Top Ten, and he became the first British male vocalist to have a million-selling record in the USA. Whitfield was a classical tenor who happened to sing popular songs: the technique was classical, but the rhetoric was that of pop music. Popular stars who adopted a classical-like technique included Eddie Fisher and the more well-known Dean Martin and Perry Como. Women singers (of whom there were many) also used vibrato and breath control in a pseudo-classical way: Doris Day and Vera Lynn were sopranos in all but name and Rosemary Clooney would have made a passable mezzo.

Elvis' position relative to classical singing is ambiguous. His embodiment of elements from all the prevailing styles does not of itself account for his extraordinary success. The answer to that must lie in the nature of his voice, given that most people's exposure to visual material of him would have been relatively small (despite his appearance on the influential Ed Sullivan show). His voice at the time of the first hits does have a maturity which is noticeably different from that of other young rockers: it is fully formed. It is also very rich and colourful, and he comes close to a classical light baritone sound when he sings ballads. Crosby and Eckstine used a similar technique. The German Heldentenor, Peter Hofmann, who also has a parallel career as a rock singer, is an interesting mirror-image of the same phenomenon: his recent pastiche album of Presley songs does not involve him in a huge change of technique. By choosing mainly ballads and singing with a higher larynx position than he would normally use but keeping the possibility of using vibrato, he produces a sound that is uncannily like that of Presley. Listening to Hofmann, imagining him firming up on a note (by lowering his larynx and starting to project) it is easy to see what a short step it would be (in purely vocal terms) to move from 'Love me tender' to *Lohengrin* if the singer has the means and the inclination. It is unlikely that anybody perceived Elvis as being another Mario Lanza, but when Elvis sings a ballad there is undoubtedly a vocal link between him and the classical-style crooners as well as a rhetorical one.

In addition to ballads there were other songs around which were quite different, both from ballads and each other. The wide variety of alternatives is a symptom of the decadent state of the mainstream ballad. The idea of novelty for its own sake resulted in a pseudo-genre of its own which could produce anything from 'The Happy Whistler' to 'The Yingtong Song'. The novelty records are an important indicator of change, a case of the new waiting to be born, while the old dies (as Antonio Gramsci might have put it). Both listeners and performers were searching for new territory but were unsure which direction to follow. Louis Armstrong had something of a revival in the fifties. The music is that of the mainstream: post-big-band European-style orchestrations that made few demands on the listener, but the singing style is the same as it always had been:

speech orientated and direct, owing little to European classical technique. The few other black stars also offered an alternative, more speech-related singing style: Louis Jordan from R&B-influenced jazz, Harry Belafonte from calypso, and Nat King Cole in the more conservative tradition. Belafonte's 'Banana Boat Song', although marketed as an 'ethnic novelty' (Clooney's 'Mambo Italiano', the Andrews Sisters' 'Rum and Coca Cola' are other examples), is musically extraordinary: Belafonte was a 'product' of the industry and was a trained singer, but his delivery in this song is in a real Jamaican accent, complete with non-verbal vocalising that could be interpreted as signifyin', and the momentum of the song itself is carried along by the absence of a first beat in a striking anticipation of reggae. Like Presley, Belafonte used resources from a variety of musical possibilities. What might have been just another novelty song tapped into Jamaican roots, adding another ingredient to performers' and listeners' potential vocabulary.

Nearer to the black singers than to the pseudo-classical white balladeers was Johnny Ray (described by Will Friedwald (1991, p. 222) as 'the first Rock'n'roller'). Ray was an outspoken opponent of racism who performed in black clubs and claimed black singers as his mentors. He was marketed on CBS' 'race' subsidiary, Okeh, as one of the very few white singers aimed specifically at a black audience. His performances did not draw on black rhetoric (he could not have done that without losing his integrity as a white performer), but used the R&B singers' style of text subversion coupled with vibrato-free delivery. His 'Cry', which reached Number 1 in the USA in November 1951, draws on a number of different styles. The opening close-harmony oohs and ahs (by the Four Lads) suggest something much more bland than the opening lines of Ray's vocal, which positively assault the eardrums with their intensity. He is a master of what Friedwald (1989) calls 'the hyphenated style of singing'. In the first line

> If your sweetheart sends a letter of goodbye,

the *y* of 'your', the *s* of 'sweetheart' and the *l* of 'letter' are all, in effect, vocalised upbeats (something that Elvis Presley was to exploit to great effect five years later). The second syllable of 'goodbye' trails off in a downward glissando, vibrating as it disappears. This is an instrumental effect well known to Armstrong, who used it to imitate the voice: here it is a voice imitating an instrument imitating a voice.

The song unfolds over a steady strumming which places it firmly in period, but many singers were using the same techniques a decade later. Also significant is the fact that the tune was composed not by a Tin Pan Alley professional, but by a night watchman in a Pittsburgh dry-cleaning plant. Presley's physical presence often electrified those who witnessed his performances at first hand; Ray, many of whose songs were too slow to dance to, had had a similar effect several years earlier.

Even established singers in the conventional mould were capable of producing songs that related to the emerging new style. Rosemary Clooney, who vowed never to rock'n'roll, recorded 'Come on-a my House' in 1951. This stomping rocker is unlike anything else Clooney ever did. A jazz-band singer in the forties, Clooney was reluctant to embrace rock'n'roll but was certainly capable of doing so. 'Come on-a my House' owes something to the ethnic novelty style that Mitch Miller found so successful in his Columbia artists, but the lyrics are extremely suggestive and the song is driven by a jazz-orientated harpsichordist, supporting Clooney's vibrato-free insinuations. The music was ultimately not to her taste but that such a song could be recorded in 1951 is a clear indicator that rock'n'roll had quite recognisable beginnings a good deal earlier than the mid-fifties.

If we accept that record sales are an important indicator of public taste it is possible to draw a number of conclusions about the critical moment at which one style gives way to another. The singing of the main authoritative style, that required for the Tin Pan Alley ballad and its derivatives, had evolved from the jazz singing of the twenties and became dominant when elements of the singing style, largely though the mediation of Armstrong and Crosby, were adopted for mainstream dance-band singing. By the late forties this style had moved from its revolutionary origins and become a singing style that represented the norm. As such it began to take on a sophistication that was foreign to its original terrain. As the music ceased challenging its listeners, so did the singing, which increasingly adopted some of the characteristics of classical singing (vibrato, supported breathing). The meanings expressed in this medium became increasingly irrelevant to those who felt themselves outside the establishment that this style symbolised. By the beginning of the fifties this decadent variety found itself competing with other, emergent, styles, any of which could theoretically replace it. This phase in the evolution of style is characterised by an interest in novelty, an unquestioning newness for its own sake, indicative of a lost sense of direction. Some singers (such as Rosemary Clooney) went further than this and incorporated elements of what they considered to be a threatening new style into their own performances. It is also possible that the surge in sales of Sinatra's *Songs for Swinging Lovers* was in part a reaction by audiences who felt threatened by a possible new music.

The potential replacement styles are in evidence from the early fifties onwards. The most likely candidate was some form of country music, and Frankie Lane, Slim Whitman and others had successful singles in the national charts. The singing was unthreatening, a safe alternative to the mainstream style. R&B was a less likely possibility, given the segregated markets, but as jazz singing had originated in the black community it was theoretically possible that blues singing of some sort might become the next mainstream style. In practice country singing, in the form of the Nashville sound, was rapidly entering a decadent phase itself, with an insufficient range of emotional and rhetorical potential to attract the wider audience that would be necessary for it to become a dominant style (despite the commercial successes of Nashville). Country singing shared with certain varieties of blues singing a speech-like vocal delivery. It was largely this that enabled the hybrid style of rock'n'roll to emerge. The resulting music, appealing to relatively affluent teenagers, flourished briefly before it, too, became decadent. The blues form, which was the basis of most rock'n'roll, was simply not able to sustain the wider range of meanings that a new mainstream style must carry.

The new style was democratic and breached the stylistic hegemony of the decadent jazz-based style: anyone could do it, realising an individual vocal expression without needing what was conventionally thought of as a 'voice'. As with any singers, some were perceived as better at it than others, and this is the real significance of Elvis Presley. Elvis was not simply a synthesis of what had gone before. His singing cannot be described by the catch-all term 'crossover': he was only one of many singers who were influenced by country, blues, and mainstream 'adult' pop. Similarly, the music he represented was more than the sum of the various parts claimed for it. He surely succeeded because he was not black, not a blues singer, not a country purist, but a dynamic performer who could make something new from those ingredients that was at once uniquely his, and at the same time was able to articulate the commonality of desires shared by a substantial number of those who had previously been satisfied (or not) with something less. In purely vocal terms he was capable of transcending the limitations of his various influences, and his example enabled other young 'non-singers' to grasp the possibilities of singing a range of music in ways that they could make their own.

The challenge of rock'n'roll effectively broke up the existing monolithic taste market and facilitated the parallel existence of a plurality of markets. Thus in 1958, when Elvis Presley released 'Jailhouse Rock' and 'Don't', he had to compete with Perry Como's 'Magic Moments' and 'Catch a Falling Star' in the British charts. All four were extremely successful, but it is unlikely that either singer's fans bought each other's records. The C&W sound of Frankie Lane was still selling well, as were newer singers with a country pedigree (such as George Hamilton IV) and others with a rockabilly background (such as Buddy Holly). The success of white singers' cover versions of R&B songs had led white record-buyers to explore the black singers' originals, and Little Richard and Fats Domino could be found along side the increasingly old-fashioned dance music of Ted Heath and Eddie Calvert. The rock'n'rollers' sound and image was increasingly used in the performance of blander material, and this was important in establishing the new, 'natural', singing as the norm. Much of the ballad repertoire of singers such as Cliff Richard and Adam Faith (and Elvis Presley) could have been sung quite happily by Andy Williams or Tony Bennet, but the rhetoric would have been that of a previous generation. Older singers generally did not do this, presumably to avoid drawing attention to the generation gap, or simply because it would have been ideologically difficult for them to do so. This also helped to secure a musical middle ground for Paul McCartney's variety of ballad, making the new singing acceptable to a much wider age range and confirming the irrelevance of the older style.

By the beginning of 1963 the post rock'n'roll confusion is still evident in the British chart: there is a large number of purely instrumental pieces and it is the playing (especially of guitars) that seems to have all the life. The singing is of a universal blandness: Cliff Richard, Frank Ifield, Mark Wynter, Kenny Lynch, Susan Maughan, Bobby Vee and Mike Berry represent what was by now the mainstream of singing style; Mel Tormé, and Frank Sinatra and

Sammy Davis ('Me and my Shadow') maintain the old style, while Ray Charles has a cover version of Hank Williams' 'Your Cheating Heart'. Elvis Presley's 'Return to Sender' is vigorously declaimed, and Rolf Harris' 'Sun arise' and Chris Montez' 'Let's dance' stand out from the rest as using their voices in a non-standard way, but otherwise the singing is characterised by a distinctly unerotic inoffensiveness. There is none of the danger of the mid-fifties: the blues-influenced declamation has lost ground to a cleaned-up country sound of limited dynamic range (at its most typical in Cliff Richard's 'Bachelor Boy'). There is a feeling that the middle ground has been successfully claimed for the new singing style, but that the revolution has rather quickly lost touch with its roots.

In some European dance halls and clubs there were much more dynamic things happening. For some years the Liverpool and Hamburg club scenes in particular had been witnessing the evolution of a British music that looked back to R&B for its legitimisation, often re-working rock'n'roll tunes in the light of the post-Haley/Presley late fifties successes by black R&B singers. The Beatles' live recording of their final Star Club appearance in 1962 reveals a catholic choice of material, all of it performed with far more drive and verve than anything then currently in the charts. They include several Chuck Berry numbers as well as revived country-based standards such as Carl Perkins' 'Matchbox' and rock'n'roll standards such as Gene Vincent's 'Be bop a lula'. There are covers of current hits, such as Frank Ifield's 'I remember you' and songs from musicals ('A Taste of Honey', 'Till there was you'), as well as two of their own songs ('I saw her standing there' and 'Ask me why'). They had had a minor hit with 'Love me do' but their extraordinary rise to stardom was still in the future. The singing of McCartney and Lennon recalls Little Richard at his gutsiest (closer to shouting than Chuck Berry ever gets). Their prime aim was to make people get up and dance. There is none of the ponderous pseudo-naïve seriousness that afflicts chart music of the time. By the end of 1963 this re-invigorated style had translated itself into records and the Beatles sold almost as many records as the rest of the competition put together.

The Beatles were unique among the countless numbers of groups who emerged from Liverpool in the early sixties. Liverpool's position as a translatlantic port probably made it easier for influences from the USA to permeate the local music. John Lennon had been an Elvis Presley fan from an early age, and Ringo Starr was brought up on country music. Ringo had a country-style song on each of the Beatles albums and had a post-Beatle career as a country singer of sorts (Clayson, 1993). Other Liverpool groups had strong links to Country and Western: the Searchers were named after a cowboy film, and Gerry and the Pacemakers included a cover of Hank Williams' 'Jambalaya' on their first LP. Unlike many of the other groups, the Beatles quickly outgrew the musical material that first brought them together and began to write their own songs. The importance of this in relation to the actual singing cannot be over-emphasised. From the Beatles onwards the singer had the opportunity to become the song in a way that had only been available in the past to blues singers. Even when blues singers were not singing their own songs they brought a personal 'blues' quality to the music which enabled them to make the song their own, rather than an interpretation of someone else's feelings. The Beatles, apart from their flirtation with Chuck Berry's R&B rockers, did not make significant use of the blues, but their complete control of their own material personalised their songs in a similar way to blues singers. It also meant that they had to sing in their own vernacular accents: the pseudo-American used by most British singers would have compromised their unspoken claim to *be* their songs. For the first time in a significantly popular music the singers were creators and not just interpreters.

It was this ingredient which enabled the emergent rock'n'roll-based singing style to come close to completing a cycle of development and become the main legitimate variety. As early as the second album the Beatles rejected the wholesale use of pseudo-American pronunciation, even in the six non-original cover versions. The language has the liveliness and phrasing of speech. Country influences are still there (notably in Ringo's solos) but the important influences are relatively obscure (to British audiences) black singers such as Smokey Robinson ('You really got a hold on me') and Barret Strong ('Money'). The inclusion of 'Till there was you' (from the musical *The Music Man*) on the second album was a crucial decision for the future of the style. Until this performance the only non-jazz-based ballad singing was either American or in some way country influenced. McCartney's singing of a conventional ballad, accompanied only by guitar, in a completely unsentimental way, sanctioned the performance by hard-line rockers of even middle-of-the-road ballads as something legitimate and normal (the Stones' 'Lady Jane' was still in the future at this point and had a similar effect). By the time of *Rubber Soul* even the R&B songs had gone, and the group recorded its own songs exclusively, songs which could not be easily taken apart and analysed in terms of their influences.

The possibility that the new style might simply be a new way of singing middle-of-the-road material was averted by the Rolling Stones. The singing of Mick Jagger completed the legitimisation process. The Rolling Stones' blues influences were deeper than the Beatles' acknowledgement of Chuck Berry. Jagger's singing did not just exhort people to dance (though he was very good at that): he made it possible for the new style to go beyond mere entertainment and address serious subjects. The group's early minor hits were R&B dance numbers but the group's first two LPs revealed an extraordinary ability to assimilate blues idioms and to personalise them in such a way that the songs succeeded on their own terms rather than as pastiche. This was achieved by blurring the line between interpretation and creation. 'Little Red Rooster', described as their most traditional blues recording yet, went straight to Number 1 on its release in November 1964, and is a good example of how completely the Stones had absorbed blues idioms. The song had originally been written for Howlin' Wolf by Willie Dixon, who practically reinvented Chicago blues for the mass market. Wolf's original recording plods along at a steady 70 beats per minute with a one-beat-to-a-bar feel. There is the suggestion of a guitar riff in the background and Wolf howls the lyrics in his eponymous way. The Stones' version rationalises the nascent guitar riff, re-ordering the notes and foregrounding it. It is immediately obvious that Keith Richards is a virtuoso player, unlike Wolf whose playing is only an adjunct to his singing. The youthful Jagger takes Wolf's elliptical style, gliding round the notes, but he does not attempt to mimic Wolf's howling delivery. Jagger was perfectly capable of attempting this (and did on numerous occasions), but rather than make the song a pastiche he really makes the words work, in a subtle and intimate way. He has all of the tension of Wolf but a rhetoric of his own which was new to British popular music at the time. The tempo has been speeded up, partly to make it easier to dance to, and partly, I suspect, because the protagonist is a younger man. The final touch is the addition of a dialogue between harmonica and the bottle-neck guitar as the song fades out. This is not part of the original, but it could have been, and does happen in Howlin' Wolf's 'Smokestack

Lightnin', which the Stones did not record. Interestingly, Howlin' Wolf came to London in 1970 and recorded the song again, with a band consisting largely of English musicians. In the new version he takes exactly the same tempo as the Stones' version. His original riff has been tightened up (though Eric Clapton is tactfully reticent) and the whole is driven along by Charlie Watts and Bill Wyman. Wolf's rhetoric has moved closer to Jagger's: his emphasis on the word 'please' is exactly what Jagger does. This small example is typical of Jagger's treatment of originals by Bo Diddly ('Mona'), Muddy Waters ('I just wanna make love to you') and a host of others.

The Stones' repertoire also included their own material, much of which was a misguided attempt to make their music more commercial, but some of which was so close in character to its blues paradigms that it could have been the original. 'What a Shame', from the second LP, is a typical example. Some of their pieces, like Led Zeppelin's after them, were so immersed in subconscious recollections of blues originals that they could not remember whether they had written them or not. 'The Last Time', for example, is remarkably similar to the Staple Singers' 'This may be the Last Time'. Led Zeppelin had the same problem with 'Whole Lotta Love' and 'The Lemon Song', which call to mind songs by Muddy Waters and Robert Johnson, respectively. Like the Beatles, the Stones also recorded ballads. 'Lady Jane', 'As Tears go by' and others reinforced the dominant position that the new singing could claim: post-Beatles and post-Stones it was possible for any new young singer to sing almost anything without being accused of being unfashionable.

Although the new singing appeared to be 'natural' there were problems of accent for British singers. In the past the question had been obscured by the fact that the lower larynx position used for the old style of singing was related to that used in Received Pronunciation. American accents do not have the same class connotations that British ones have, and America was the source of many of the paradigms used by British singers. The use of pseudo-American accents by non-American singers even when not singing American songs has been a feature of popular-music singing since jazz was first heard in Europe. Jazz was perceived as both quintessentially American, and the first genuinely international popular music. Microphonic singing enabled a speech-like voice production to be used and also meant that considerable socio-musical distance could be put between it and the other international singing style: high-status classical singing (with its laryngeal constraints on accent and tone colour), and (perhaps most importantly) between jazz and its predecessors in variety and dance music.

Peter Trudgill (1984) has drawn attention to the fact that the 'American' accents used by British singers (pseudoAm) are far from accurate: either they involve hyper-correction (the tendency to add features which do not appear in the model, such as a final *r* on words ending in *a*) or they ignore certain normative features. In fact most 'Americanisms' appear in a range of British dialects, though no one dialect contains them all, nor is the British American actually spoken by anybody (unlike RP). There are various related theories which attempt to account both for the existence of British American accents and their relative lack of authenticity. Giles and Smith (1979) pointed to the tendency of individuals to shift speech styles to become more like those with whom they are interacting. There is a negotiative relationship which tends to result in a convergence of styles in which a common set of interpretative procedures is followed, and the speaker is judged by the listener to be 'accommodating' him. While this may often be the case in speech, if it were true in singing one would expect to find a certain transatlantic reciprocity in singing styles as the respective musics influenced each other. Certainly in the twenties American singers such as Gene Austin and 'Whispering' Jack Smith, who described themselves respectively as tenor and baritone, adopted a kind of pseudo-English accent, presumably in a deliberate attempt to distance themselves from jazz and to identify with what they considered to be a higher status. This suggests something more like the group identification theory which Le Page developed in his work on Caribbean languages, and which has been applied by Peter Trudgill to British rock music. Le Page explains linguistic behaviour in terms of the need of particular groups to identify with model groups. Trudgill interprets this as British singers needing to emulate their American peers who are culturally dominant. British singers are, however, often unsuccessful in identifying which Americans they wish to emulate, thus violating one of Le Page's criteria, but hyper-correct in order to compensate for this. Trudgill reinforces the cultural domination theory in an analysis of British pop-song pronunciation with particular emphasis on the Beatles whose pronunciation became less and less American (as the Beatles became, presumably, musically dominant) (Trudgill, 1984). Even after the success of British rock music in the USA British pop singers still have a problem with accent. Since the sixties British rock music has been dominated by middle-class singers who have had to avoid revealing their middle-class origins in order to maintain the myth that rock creators, like their assumed audience, are somehow classless or of 'the people'. Mick Jagger is a good example. Born into a middle-class family in Dartford, he invented an accent which he considered appropriate to his music (Southern black American) and his audience (notionally working-class whites). Here is Bill Wyman on the subject:

His voice changes, for one thing, and he starts talking with that pseudo-Southern accent. And sometimes in private he starts using a very rough Cockney accent, which is also not his real voice. It's actually more like the way Charlie and I talk, dropping the h's and all that. He never talked like that before, because he came from a middle-class family and went to middle-class schools. I've got interviews on tape with him on radio and television from the 60s where he's talking like the queen does . . . He's getting a bit like Peter Sellers; I don't think he knows which is the real Mick Jagger. [1]

Jagger's sung language is in fact a synthesis of his speech and that of his role models. It enables him to command a wide rhetorical style without losing touch with his own roots.

The determinedly working-class enunciation of punk singers in the seventies was also more to do with image and the perception of audiences, than with the class factors which seemed to be implied by the accents used. Although many punk singers were from working-class backgrounds the basic punk concept was dreamed up by Vivienne Westwood and Malcolm McLaren as a set of fashion icons which happened to draw on working-class symbolism (and other, in fashion terms, 'deviant' sources). As Dave Laing (1985) has pointed out, a sizeable minority of punk performers came from outside the working class.

The basic singing technique arrived at by the Beatles and the Stones and their contemporaries has been used by mainstream pop music, known since 'Sgt Pepper' as rock music, ever since. There have been many changes in rhetorical style: R&B evolved into heavy metal, 'progressive' rock gave way to punk, and more recently there has been a great deal of stylistic fragmentation, but all styles use the same speech-related technique. The various singing styles encompassed by world music have had no significant influence on the mainstream technique, which has been dominant since the late sixties, as fewer and fewer old-style singers sold enough records to appear in the charts. The old style did not disappear, but increasingly appealed to those whose taste is more difficult to measure, and who therefore are considered to be outside the mainstream. Old-style singers appear regularly on BBC Radio 2, a channel which is not taken seriously by music journalists and which has an audience made up of older and, in marketing terms, less significant listeners. There are specialist programmes catering for specific aspects of music which use decadent singing styles, principally jazz and country music.

In the late nineties there appears to be no threat to the authority of the 'new' style, although many of the symptoms of decadence are visible in current pop music, but what appears to be happening is a fragmentation of taste markets similar to that which has occurred in classical singing . There has been an enormous upsurge in the sales of classical music CDs, some of which have even registered in the pop charts. This tendency is one aspect of the catch-all phrase 'cross-over', a term often used for anything that cannot, for commecial or musical reasons, easily be categorised as obviously rock or classical. Classical tenors in particular have become the popular celebrities they were in the nineteenth century. Many successful rock musicians have experimented with crossover musics which take them into new fields (Elvis Costello's collaborations with the Brodski Quartet and Fretwork, Jan Garbarek's work with the Hilliard Ensemble, for example). If we assume a continuum of technique between a classical tenor or soprano at one end and a mainstream pop singer such as David Bowie at the other, the options for evolution have to be sought either in an extension of the continuum or in a general shift towards a different sector of it. Extending the continuum towards speech are those varieties of singing, mainly among black musicians, which began as hip hop.

Both the change to jazz-orientated singing and its own metamorphosis into rock'n'roll singing were associated with dance, with urban youth and with a lower social class than that associated with the existing dominant style. The primary characteristic of both changes was a renewed attention to the site at which singing interacts with text. The various styles that rock music has influenced have had their own rhetoric, the cultivated gospel-influenced sound of soul, for example, or the flat, consciously offensive delivery of punk, but none of these sub-styles has involved a significant change in the basic post-sixties rock-singing technique. The exception to this is rap, which fulfils all the criteria outlined above. Rap has the potential to become a new hegemonic style if it could be mediated in such a way that the singing style becomes transferrable to other musics. What it so far lacks is the equivalent of the evolution of rock'n'roll into rock singing (or the change from jazz to dance-band singing), despite rap-influenced styles finding their way into mainstream pop and appearing in more obviously commercial contexts such as television advertisements.

The term 'rapping' had an already-existing meaning as the high form of stylised speech used among urban black youth before it was applied to music (Kochman, 1972). Rap music evolved from the application of this high-style speech to the introductions made by MCs and DJs at street parties, where the MC (Master of Ceremonies, or compère) would introduce the DJ (Disc Jockey) who would create his own performance using two or more turntables to create a new work out of existing ones. These crews, as they are called, were often fiercely competitive, each trying to blast out the other by the power of its portable sound system. Rapping was one of many elements of hip hop, a sub-culture created by New York black musicians and dancers, which included breakdancing (developed from DJs repeating a particular musical 'break' for the benefit of dancers), graffiti, fashion and speech codes which were incomprehensible to white people. It is an interactive form, where the MC and the DJ (both now stylised into performance artists in their own right) exchange sections of text with each other, or with the audience. This has a long history going back through soul singers such as James Brown, the fast rhyming of Cab Calloway, to negro word games such as the dozens.[2] The music of rap singing comes directly from the text itself: the text is not sung to a tune, but follows exaggerated speech inflections, making great play of the rhythms and rhymes in the poem. Performances are often very intense. As Elizabeth Wheeler puts it:

Performers struggle to create their entire being through voice alone . . . Sometimes a rapper's voice seems to be the site of his entire identity, the home of all knowledge and desire.[3]

The poems are highly politicised narratives. There are very few simple love songs, but many specifically about sex. Rap has been perceived as homophobic (Shabba Ranks, the most successful exponent of rap's reggae derivation, ragga, or Buju Banton's hit 'Boom Bye Bye'), anti-women (almost all male rappers at various times), violent, racist, subversive, generally anti-social and dangerous. It has been largely ignored by middle-class white musicologists, especially in Britain (with the notable exception of David Toop), and very few rappers have benefited from major record contracts. Rap is relatively democratic, with its roots still in the streets which formed it, a pyramid of small labels underpinning the few rappers on major labels, despite increasing annexation by television commercials and the mainstream. All this appears to point to a sub-culture that is specifically for young black working-class males. A closer examination of the rap scene suggests that, while it may have begun as such a phenomenon, rap broadened its class base considerably during the eighties and nineties. The racist element of many raps is of an institutional kind similar to that of the anti-Semitism in the Passion settings of Schütz and Bach: the message has lost its potency as performers and listeners convert it to ritual. Images of violence have always been present in pop music. As David Toop (1993) points out, Peetie Wheatstraw's 'Gangster Blues' of 1940 is typical of many blues advocating violence. Ice-T, discussing the parallels between rap and country music, points to Johnny Cash's lines 'I shot a man in Reno just to watch him die.' There are now women rappers, and rappers such as De la Soul who contest the sexism and homophobia of the original paradigms. Katrina Irving (1993) has pointed out the potential for rappers to build new forms of social relations through equivalence-building which cuts across stereoptyped attitudes to gender and race. Perhaps most significantly, there are white rappers, such as Vanilla Ice, who complain about black rappers not being black enough, who claim to be 'blacker' than their black brothers (Batey, 1993). This equation of race and class is the first step in the process of giving rap the wider currency that would move the singing technique into the mainstream. Rap is well established in many countries all over the world, with a potential to link the third world with the industrialised northern hemisphere.[4]

As a form of heightened speech rap is not dissimilar in principle to that used by Classical Greek and Roman dramatists, who were often accused of confusing singing with speech (see chapter 1 above). There is also a historical precedent in more recent classical music for a singing technique based on heightened speech: early baroque recitatives use the pitch contour of speech in a stylised way to produce music directly from the text. This, in principle, is what a rapper does. Like speech, rap has at its disposal the entire rhetorical gamut of language and theatre. At the moment rap texts are still concerned with very specific meanings, allowing the listener little space to personalise a reality that is very different from that of the performer (which is one reason it appeals to children and can make a very effective teaching aid). The potential for carrying multiple meanings is vast and if this can be unlocked, rap-influenced singing style and technique could become much more than simply a facet of hip-hop culture. Like jazz, blues and rock'n'roll earlier in the century, rap-related singing may ultimately be seen to be one of the most significant gifts from black musicians to western musical culture as a whole.

CHAPTER 9

Singing and social processes

The previous chapters have explored how relationships change and evolve between and within vocal styles. The dominance of one style over others is articulated not just on a macro level by stylistic development, however, but is also created by social processes that operate within and between varieties. The way in which singers create meaning, an essential marker of vocal style in any variety, depends on the complex interaction of the many factors that go to make up performance rhetoric. The articulation of language through rhetoric is at the very heart of singing, and this chapter examines in some detail how language works in performance. The channels through which rhetoric is realised include technique, technology, gesture and semiotics, dress codes and the expression of sexuality, and the authority of a particular style is derived in no small degree from the way these extra-musical factors mesh together. The chapter concludes with a brief case study of the phenomenon known as 'cross-over', which illuminates many of the points made in the chapter.

Two striking facts emerge from the study of the literature of music in performance. In the classical field there is almost no performance analysis, apart from journalistic criticism in the form of reviews and the attempts to investigate historical performance practice. Mainstream musicological attention has been focused almost exclusively on the written form of the music. In the field of popular music the reverse is true: there is a great deal of analysis but it, too, tends to objectify performances as works, usually in the form of records. This kind of analysis assumes that quantifiable meanings additional to those intended by the performers reside in the song. The literal, surface meaning is rarely considered: resorting to the simple expedient of asking the performers what they meant would make large tracts of musicology redundant, or reduced to determining the value and truth of performers' statements about their own music. The deconstructionist device of imputing subconscious meanings to rock lyrics, and the classical-music tendency to seek meaning in the actual notes, are both standard practice in the sociology of popular music. Perhaps as a consequence of the need for this branch of socio-musicology to assert itself academically, there is a great deal of conceptual borrowing from other disciplines, especially linguistics, literary criticism, semiotics and film studies, which has resulted in a very eclectic and derivative conceptual vocabulary. As a discipline, popular music sociology is somewhat detached from its subject: most scholars are consumers of popular music but have relatively little experience of the production and performance of the music.

The socio-musicology of current popular music is overwhelmingly orientated towards rock music, to such an extent that a tentative definition of rock (there have been many attempts at this) might define it as that variety of current popular music considered most worthy of the attention of musicologists. This is in contrast to the literature on historical popular song which tends to be monolithic and look at the *genre* as a whole. A possible reason for this is that rock music was a formative influence on the lives of many of the generation of musicologists born in the forties and fifties, and a significant part of the musicological agenda has been to promote the academic study of popular music as an equal to classical music or any other branch of cultural studies. Rock is considered to be both serious musically and important sociologically. Although no figures are available for the numbers of people who listen to rock music (or perform it) as opposed to other varieties, rock has, until recently, been taken as a kind of socio-musical barometer related to significant sections of society as a whole. The performance of classical music, elitist and apparently terminally unsexy, has not generally appealed to scholars wishing to make their mark in the world of socio-musicology.

The tendency to analyse popular music as artefact works up to a point, when the end-product is a video or record, as in the Abba music analysed by Philip Tagg (1982), for example. Its weakness is that it is a methodology of the middle-class academic listener (rather than an 'innocent' listener, or a performer) and is borrowed from 'classical' musicology, which operates on different principles. The associative meanings added by almost all musicologists are mediated by the ideology of the writer. This has been effective in the musicology of classical music, where writer, music and listener share a similar, relatively narrow, ideological background. Almost all classical musicologists have been brought up as listeners to classical compositions, the production of which they have then gone on to study in some depth. One of the functions of classical musicology is to interpret the underlying processes in such a way as to make future manifestations of the music better, to answer questions about how and why the music works. There is a strand of popular music analysis that applies similar criteria to those used in classical music (Wilfrid Mellers' (1973) analyses of Beatles' songs, are a case in point), but such methodology ignores the fact that in popular music the creation of musicology is an entirely different field from the production and consumption of the music. In a music that is not driven by commercial criteria and is, to a large extent, a self-referential system, such a musicology is perfectly adequate on its own terms (whatever else it may or may not be), but when applied to popular music several problems emerge which relate to popular musicology as an academic discipline and popular music as it is articulated in its commercial form. Even those who use a socio-logical/theoretical approach risk objectifying the subject and en-coding it in such a way that its socio-musical function becomes identical to that of classical music. There is, in the application of classical musicological discourse also the implication that it will one day be possible to determine how meaning works in popular songs (if this is not the intention of musicology then the theorising is a purely intellectual activity with no practical outcome). This would carry the risk that music could then be produced on an industrial basis, which would effectively reduce musicology itself to a branch of economics. There is a need for an anti-musicology, which would ideally be a musicology of the performer, but successful performers rarely have the means or inclination to address questions of musicology and those musicologists with performing experience have often reached their present position having given up serious performance at some time in the past.

The closest popular musicology has come to subverting itself is in the work of Antoine Hennion. His article 'The Production of Success: An Anti-Musicology of the Pop Song', demonstrates a position that is probably closer to that which would be taken by a rock musician:

The meaning in question is to be found 'down below', in those areas which carry the public's imagination, its secret desires and hidden passions – one could almost define such areas as socio-sentimental. They include key phrases, sounds, images, attitudes, gestures and signs, infra-linguistic categories which are all the more difficult to pin down insofar as they escape definition by the official language, and are not autonomous but inseparable from the social context within which a given group attributes a special significance to them. At the same time these infra-linguistic categories are ephemeral; as soon as language intervenes, they give up that terrain and re-form elsewhere. Slang, a form of address, a hairstyle, a motorcycle, above all music, that music which 'means' nothing, are all the expressions of that which cannot be put into rational discourse – which is always the discourse of other people . . . These meanings cannot be manufactured, cannot even be decoded. (Hennion, 1983, p. 160)

This position is not a promising one for a musicologist. It does, however, have a kernel of truth that would be recognisable to both fans and performers. There are, as Simon Frith (1982, pp. 142–3) long ago pointed out, very few rock musicians who are also musicologists. A consequence of this is a tendency to marginalise the circumstances in which the music came to be created. Most rock music and jazz is work-in-progress and only reaches what might be called a definitive form in certain circumstances: when a record is pressed (though the master tape remains and can be remixed or remastered at any time) and when the musicians judge that their audience wishes to hear a performance that 'reproduces' the record (a relatively rare event in most rock music despite the presence of technology which allows this to happen). Even if the record of a song is taken to have a particular set of meanings, the listener's response is going to vary according to a multitude of criteria from embedded ideological factors to the immediate context of the act of listening (which itself has a typology of modes from active to passive). There is a tendency among scholars to look for universal meanings, which often amounts to projecting their own subjective meanings onto what is taken to be a definitive performance. Universal meanings could theoretically be deduced by simultaneous analysis of the same material by a representative sample of the entire listening public but this is a practical impossibility. The attributing of universal meanings to pop songs has been partly responsible for the scant regard with which pop musicians hold musicologists. There is a serious problem here: music undoubtedly does produce meanings beyond those immediately obvious to the performer, but in focusing exclusively on these, many analysts effectively reduce the actual performance (and the surface, intended meanings of the performers) to something incidental to the performance itself. Part of the problem is that songs acquire meanings at each stage of the creative process and not all of these are open to analysis. Potential meanings have been acquired by songs long before they reach a listener, and very few songs ever acquire meanings which are universally agreed.

In a recording session the singer's performance is mediated, indeed enabled, by rhetoric. There is little actual emotion expressed within the 'performance' of a song on record, whether it is classical or popular, and the singer can be quite detached from his or her own rhetoric. It is possible for comments on the performance to be exchanged while the song is in progress. A look or a grimace indicating such a comment happens outside the rhetoric so it is generally not perceived by anyone except the performers. In the case of opera and rock stars who present a constructed image which is always to some extent public there may be an additional layer of mediation, in that aspects of the rhetoric will be directed towards anyone who might witness the 'performance' (the orchestra, hangers-on in the control room, for example). It is the rhetorical formula which enables the singer to concentrate on the technical aspects of delivery: accuracy of intonation, management of breath, remembering words (and how to pronounce them if in a foreign language), and so on. Listening to the playback of what one has recorded is a check on the effectiveness of the rhetoric. Singers are not normally moved by their own performances: the aim of a recording is to write the blueprint from which others may construct their own meanings from the rhetorical framework provided by the performers. It is perhaps this dimension that is missing from Hennion's analysis.[1]

The need to produce songs, that point immediately before the blank slate is first scratched, is perhaps where we should seek the basis of meaning generation. Why do people write songs? There is a parallel between the function of singing and that of speech: both share the same mode of delivery and a considerable amount of research has been undertaken into the functions of different aspects of language. Communicative models of language function also have to take into account the degree of intention behind utterances, and to reconcile the balance of activity/ passivity of the transmitter relative to the receiver, just as musicologists should do in seeking meaning in rock. Roman Jakobson's research has yielded conclusions which are helpful to an analysis of why songs are composed and what their function is. Jakobson divided language functions into six numbered categories:

1. Expressive
2. Poetic
3. Conative
4. Phatic
5. Metalinguistic
6. Referential (Jakobson, 1960)

The Expressive function involves the externalising of feelings, communicating them in a general way, while the Poetic adds to that the possibility of structuring those feelings and turning them into 'art'. The Conative function is more directly aimed at the receiver with a specific communicative intent. The fourth category is aimed at keeping the channel of communication open between addresser and addressee; the Metalinguistic function refers to the self-referencing of language, usually in the form of a speech code; the sixth function interprets the message by making clear its context.

If we take singer and audience to be the equivalent of linguistic communities it is easy to see a homologous relationship between Jakobson's language functions and similar categories for singer–listener communication. The Expressive and Poetic functions are clearly recognisable to singers: the ordering of Jakobson's taxonomy gives the primacy to these functions, and self-expression is what most singers (of all varieties) think they do. Self-expression requires in the first instance only one's self as an audience. The Poetic category functions as an elaboration of the first: it, too, does not imply a receiver as a *sine qua non*. The Conative function refers to the political terrain on which songs operate: the transmitter tries to achieve a certain effect, to manipulate his audience. The Metalinguistic and Referential also have their place in a system of singer–listener communication, but it is the Phatic that has most relevance for the creation of songs. While many song writers (Elvis Costello, Bob Dylan, Peter Warlock, Benjamin Britten, the Tin Pan Alley composers) sit down and compose with a particular (Conative) end in view, it is characteristic of a great deal of rock music that at the point of origin the composers will often have no idea of what they are going to write. They need to write songs to maintain or create a repertoire.

This is, of course, mediated ideologically, but the basic need is explainable in terms of Jakobson's Phatic function: they are in the first instance keeping the channel of communication open.

All performances, whether of classical or popular music, have been rehearsed. Rehearsals may seek to create a prototype performance with the aim of reproducing it (or improving on it) during the performance, or they may be much less rigidly structured sessions which explore different possibilities, some or none of which may emerge in the performance. When the style is no longer dynamically evolving (such as current mainstream rock music, or Lieder singing) the former is likely to be the case. When the style is emergent or competing for authority (early punk, 'early' early music) the latter is more likely. These two broad rehearsal strategies are connected to the efficacy of the eventual performance: the decadent mode is a closed one, the meanings received by listeners are fewer and more predictable, the restriction of potential meanings being characteristic of a singing style which has lost its formative relevance. The emergent mode is an open one, still exploring the possibilities of performance. Rehearsals also illustrate significant aspects of the way meaning works in singing. There is no audience: the only listeners are those making the music. Jakobson's first two categories are at work here, rather than the conventional semiotic scheme of transmitter, message and receiver.

Pop songs 'work on ordinary language' (Frith, 1989, p. 121); classical music texts are rarely in ordinary language, and for most English and American people, are often in a foreign language. Many of those with English as their first language will listen to Latin church music, German Lieder and Italian opera with little or no literal understanding of the text. Very often the performers themselves will be singing in a language that is not their own and of which they have only a limited understanding. The singer knows which aspects of the performance or which parts of the piece are likely to move the listener. This will often have nothing to do with the literal meaning of text. How could it, when in some cases neither listener nor performer actually understand the literal meaning of the words, as could be the case, for example, with an Italian tenor singing a Janáček opera in New York? What the Italian tenor understands is the role, and the rhetoric required to make the role work. The point is further made by considering what happens to meaning in a pop song when a singer stops singing and plays an instrument or when different sorts of singing are used in the same performance. Is the meaning of the song changed when Mark Knopfler *plays* a solo as opposed to singing one? There is surely no fundamental difference: the rhetoric continues and listeners continue the process of constructing their personal performance reality.

The dissembling, or dishonesty that is frequently seen to be an aspect of pop music, is just as prevalent in classical music. A substantial part of the early vocal repertoire is sacred (and in Latin); I know of no performer of this repertoire who claims to be religious, and very few with more than a superficial understanding of Latin. For some listeners sacred music is a religious experience even outside its liturgical context. Post-concert meetings between performers and listeners can result in shock to the latter and embarrassment to the former in cases where the meanings contructed by listeners are at variance with those assumed by the performer. 'Dishonesty' in early music can extend to reconstructing liturgies solely in order to recreate the context in which the music was first performed. The role of the singer is to find his or her own, personal meanings in the music, and to present these to the audience, who may perceive them, or may ignore them or misunderstand them in favour of meanings of their own. When a singer arrives at a point where the music has moved listeners on many previous occasions, it is impossible not to be aware of the history of past performances. It is impossible to replicate genuine emotion to order: the consequences would be completely unpredictable for both performer and audience.

No singer ever means the same thing in consecutive performances. All singers' performances are informed by practical considerations which can be extremely banal and have nothing to do with the song that is being sung. When Mick Jagger seems to be pumping out a performance full of energy and meaning, he may actually be worried about whether the sound from the stage monitors bears any relation to what the audience is hearing, or whether a previously rehearsed change will actually happen according to plan. If the show is one that has been repeated many times, he may be singing on 'autopilot', wondering whether the negotiations he began earlier in the day will come to fruition, what he is going to have for dinner after the show, or what time he will have to get up in the morning in order to catch the plane on time. All of these thoughts (known to semioticians as 'noise') will have some effect on his performance, but they will be subsumed into the rhetoric of performance and none of them will be revealed to the audience, most of whom will receive the meanings they expect to receive, having filtered out what they do not perceive as relevant. Miles Davis summed up the feeling of jazz instrumentalists on the subject:

I think people like to hear music and think what they wanna think. When you play like we play, you can think whatever you want.[2]

In the performance of The Who's 'rock opera', *Tommy*, at The Rainbow Theatre in 1975 the chorus of classical session singers gave the work a certain legitimacy and set up certain expectations for some sections of the audience. The choir was part of what made it possible to call the work an 'opera'. The singers themselves (of which I was one) were considered to have performed their task professionally and adequately. The meanings that they made for themselves were strongly influenced by the fact that they were performing with a hugely successful pop group, that the music was very loud (an amplified choir over the amplified London Symphony Orchestra), that some would not call it music at all, but most of all by the fact that the money they would earn seemed out of all proportion to what they were asked to do and that there was a free back-stage bar (something that none of us had experienced before and of which we made more than adequate use). None of this would have been transmitted to the audience, yet had we felt differently about the music and the circumstances of its performance, our performance would have been a different one, but any perceptible difference would have been filtered by the audience to produce the same outcome.

It is rare for either composer or singer to be involved in the composition of the text for a piece of classical music. In classical music the interpretative and creative processes are confused at an early stage in the generation of a song. First the composer searches for a text that appeals to him. Then he 'sets' the text: he interprets it in musical terms. In the context of today's programming ideology the chances are that this stage of the process will have happened anything up to a thousand years before the performance. This whole construct is then passed to the singer who interprets the text through the prescription of the (probably dead) composer. If the work is a large-scale one, such as an opera, the singer's interpretation may be mediated by other 'creative' people (a conductor or a producer, for example); the singer may have been coached by a third party (a process that involves anything from help with the notes to creating an entire role). By the time the singer's definitive (or perhaps not) interpretation arrives at the ears of the listener, it has been through all these processes, all of which also incorporate a 'noise' quotient. Practical considerations ('Am I being upstaged? Is the set going to fall on me? Should I have eaten something which constricts my breath less?') differ in detail, but are probably present to the same degree as in rock music.

The thoughts of a singer at a particularly 'emotional' part of the music are likely to be of the order of 'Is this working? Have I judged the audience correctly? How far can I allow my own feelings to intrude at this point? What do I need to do to capitalise on any effect I might be having?' Even if the singer is recreating an emotional state, the reality for the singer is that he or she is performing. The exhaustion that follows from singing a dramatic and emotional role comes in part from the need to maintain a grip on the performance reality (and its rhetoric), while appearing to live the reality of the drama. The singer dissembles from the moment of first utterance.

The difference between the pop singer and the classical singer at this stage is one of the degree of openness or closedness of meaning. The layers of meaning which accumulate before and during a classical performance are almost always interpretative. To interpret is, by definition, to restrict, to privilege certain meanings over others. The final stage in this process is heavily class-coded in the context of a classical performance (as is demonstrated below) and the end-meanings are located in a very specific framework. The generation of meaning in rock music, by contrast, is an additive process in the sense that the added meanings are creative, rather than interpretative. There is little 'interpretation' as such in rock music. When Rolf Harris and others 'covered' 'Stairway to Heaven' they were not interpreting it, but re-creating it. As I pointed out in chapter 8, one of the revolutionary aspects of rock'n'roll was the fact that the performers produced, or rather, *became* their own songs, unlike the Tin Pan Alley era where the song had a separate existence from its performer/performance. Rock cover versions may not even use the same notes as the song they are using as a model. The Beatles' version of Chuck Berry's 'Roll over Beethoven' uses the same chord sequence as its paradigm and the same text, but the tune is a re-working and there is an added 'middle-eight', complete with extra text. This is re-creation, not interpretation, unlike the thirty or so recorded versions of Schubert's *Winterreise*, which reproduce identical notes and text and differ within a very narrow set of parameters.

The interpretation–creation fracture becomes especially important at moments of stylistic change. It is significant that at each of the historical moments of change in classical singing there has not, until the twentieth century, been significant struggle among possible new potentially dominant varieties. The terrain, interpretation, remains the same, while the intepretative strategy renews itself. What is important is that singers return to a text-orientated mode which satisfies the compositional ideology of the day. When the style is no longer dynamically evolving, meanings lose their focus, and the variety risks becoming marginalised: a return to basic (class) principles is required. In popular music moments of crisis are precipitated when old meanings are no longer relevant: the nature of meaning changes, and it is this which produces the struggle for a new hegemonic style as performers and listeners seek to redefine their requirements.

Changes in potential meanings, or reinforcement of existing ones, occur in specific performance parameters which identify a singer's position in the socio-musical field. These sites of potential meaning fall into a number of broad categories: technical (i.e. aspects of voice production), linguistic, kinesic (non-verbal body language, dress or gestures), technological and sexual. By examining how these markers of meaning operate, it is possible to account for certain areas of meaning creation and to discern specific differences between classical and popular singing.

The cultivated sound of the trained singing voice, its history, physiology and pedagogy, have been considered in earlier chapters above. Popular-music singing generally has little use for pedagogy and the low-larynx technique, although some pop singers, especially those involved in musicals, do have singing lessons, and some singers (Mario Lanza or David Whitfield, for example) have made the charts using a classical technique. The musculature of the human voice is so complex that the chances of any two voices sounding the same are extremely small. Yet the cues given by an individual voice are sufficient to enable many judgements to be made by listeners both in terms of the individual and the set or sets of voices to which he or she may belong. Individual voices may be differentiated by tone colour (or voice quality) and groups of similar sets of voices (opera singers or pop stars, for example) may also be differentiated as groups by perceived differences in voice quality. In practice this means that listeners have no difficulty in distinguishing between classical and pop singers purely on the basis of the sound they make, which is related in some degree to larynx position.

The sound will also contain additional information, which will be used or filtered by the listener. There is an important distinction to be made between anatomical factors, such as the length of the vocal tract, size of tongue, the shape of laryngeal structures, and the use to which these are put. While both contribute to individual differences in auditory colouring, the former are not controllable, whereas the latter 'phonetic settings' are the product of long-term habitual use and muscular constraint, and can be learned. Anatomical features can be a reliable indicator of certain qualities in the speaker such as age, sex and height, all of which will have some bearing on the size, shape and efficiency of the vocal apparatus (Laver and Trudgill, 1979). They serve an informative function for the listener, who may deduce information from them regardless of whether there is communicative intent on the part of the speaker or singer. Voice settings involve both the quasi-permanent muscular adjustments which result in different accents (and language sounds) and also the temporary affective changes in tone of voice (to express anger or to whisper, for example). The long-term settings have been found by many studies to be a useful indicator of social class. If we take the idea of a neutral larynx position for the purpose of comparative analysis, it can be said that many working-class speakers of the British Isles and the USA use a relatively high larynx position for normal speech, whereas middle-class speakers of Received Pronunciation lower the larynx to produce the rounded vowels associated with RP. Because these settings can be learned they can also be used subversively, and the identification of accent purely as a marker of the singer's class may be extremely misleading (as in the case of Mick Jagger or numerous punk singers).

Mainstream classical singing is characterised by the use of vibrato as a defining criterion of its vocal production. Vibrato locates the user within a particular socio-musical field. A rock singer will generally use vibrato only as a cultivated effect because of its association with classical singing. Similarly, singers of more middle-of-the-road pop music will use a greater or lesser amount of vibrato according to which end of the socio-musical spectrum they wish to identify with. The greater use of vibrato in post-war classical singing coincides with its dialectical opposite in the form of rock'n'roll and rock music and serves to differentiate the two extremes. This is in marked contrast to the period between the wars when there was a considerable cross-over between classical and pop songs in the form of light music (John McCormack is a good example) where again the degree of vibrato would be a manifestation of an ideological stance as much as a musical feature. Sinatra and Crosby at the peak of their careers were very much a part of the American establishment and their use of vibrato is an indicator of this.

A further identifying criterion is the efficiency with which the voice is used in terms of the proportion of the airstream used to generate sound. The vocal cords are joined at one end to the thyroid cartilage, and at the other to the arytenoid cartilages. The latter may be closed during phonation, directing all the air through the cords, or they may be open enabling air to by-pass the cords resulting in a mixture of pitched sound and non-pitched sound or noise. This is the husky sound associated with certain sorts of speech and many pop singers. It is not used in standard classical singing, where maximum efficiency is essential to make full use of the resonating potential of the vocal tract. It is to be found in various extended vocal techniques (creak, whispery voice etc.) and is one of the markers that differentiate these techniques from the mainstream. The concepts and practical implications of singing technique open up significant areas of difference between classical and popular singing. A classical technique highlights the class markers of accent and tone colour, mediating the meanings produced by the singer.

Technology has become an important aspect of singing in the twentieth century, enabling the broadcasting, recording and amplification of vocal sounds. Perhaps the most significant long-term effect of the introduction of the microphone is its effect on potential meaning-generation. Classical singing depends on projecting in a specific way in order for it to be heard in modern concert halls. Much of the discipline of singing pedagogy is orientated towards this goal, which for many singers is an end in itself. A great deal of attention is given by both singer and listener to the medium itself, and in focusing on the mode of delivery rather than the message, the breadth of potential meanings is inevitably restricted. The medium is class-coded, and channels its reception into class-coded meanings. Some classical composers have become aware of the potential of the microphone to enable attention to be directed specifically at the text.

Stockhausen, in his opera *Donnerstag* amplifies all the voices (and instruments), which enables him to control personally several important parameters of the singers' performances. Berio, in *Sinfonia* and the *Laborintus* pieces, uses amplified voices in a less autocratic way, especially in *Sinfonia*, where they are supposed to be balanced in such a way that the listener is aware of their presence but cannot distinguish everything they sing or say. Extended vocal techniques often make use of the smaller sounds that would be inaudible without amplification, in what is probably a more democratic use of potential sounds (as in Berio's *A-Ronne*, discussed in chapter 7 above).

None of these functions of the microphone is generally found in popular music. In removing the need for singers to project their voices, microphones also remove the need for singers to insist on specific meanings unless they actually want to. The microphone in pop singing is a democratic device, which enables the singer to leave open the possibility of a large number of additional meanings to be constructed by the listener. The class-coding is far less restrictive, more open-ended. Although mainstream classical singing has made use of microphones (Pavarotti in the Park, or the various stadium operas), this has been strictly for amplification in its literal sense only. Any stylistic implications that might flow from the use of the microphone have always been regarded as a threat by authorities on classical singing. George Baker has a chapter on 'The Voice and the Microphone' in his singing manual published in 1947. He does not consider stage performance at all, confining his remarks to broadcasting and recording except for a swipe at crooners, whom he describes as 'fakers' and 'vocal cheats', with the majority of them not having 'voices, as such'. This attitude is typical of many classical singers today. Ironically, Baker ends his book with the same quotation from St John's Gospel which is so significant in Berio's supremely microphonic work, *A-Ronne*: 'In principio erat verbum'.

The connection between sexuality and music has been the subject of a great deal of debate in the rock music world, less so in the classical field. Sexuality is defined in the *OED* as 'the quality of being sexual', with secondary and tertiary meanings 'possession of sexual powers' and 'recognition or pre-occupation with what is sexual'. None of these suggests an immediate conection with music. If we ignore the purely reproductive implications of sexuality the term becomes an aspect of sensuality, 'that part of the nature of man that is concerned with the senses . . . as distinct from the reason' (*OED*), and it is in this broader sense that a connection between music and sexuality can be drawn. The debate on the role of sexuality in music (or, more precisely, rock music) has tended towards an analysis of the more obvious manifestations of sexuality, and despite the almost obligatory references to Barthes there has been little discussion of the wider issues of music and sexuality: why are the two related, how does the relationship work in different musics, and what socio-historic circumstances actually articulate these relationships.

Barthes 'The Grain of the Voice' (1977b) is something of a lifeline to writers on performance and sexuality, perhaps because it is one of the earliest writings to connect the two. More of a polemic than a rigorous contribution to academic debate, Barthes' essay (which perhaps says as much about its author as it does about his subject) locates the point at which sexuality and sensuality meet, and by identifying this location opens up the possibility of a deeper investigation into singing and sexuality. Singing for Barthes, it should be said, is essentially classical singing (he allows for the possibility that the principles he outlines may be applied to popular music but he did not himself appear to have much taste for it). 'Grain' is specifically 'the very precise space (*genre*) of the encounter between a language and a voice'. It resides in the 'geno-song', that purely aesthetic or poetic area that complements the pheno-song, the more visible (or audible) features which are 'in the service of communication'. Geno-song can produce 'jouissance', a term with no direct English equivalent but meaning enjoyment with further implications of sexual climax. Barthes dismisses the merely technical function of the lungs, 'a stupid organ (lights for cats!)' that 'swells but gets no erection'. He talks (p. 183) of the eroticism of pianists' finger pads, the 'climactic pleasure hoped for', and the erotic nature of his, the listener's, relationship with the performer.

Barthes' essay is problematic for performers (a fact that points to the tremendous conceptual distance between those who perform and those who simply write about it). As a singer, I find it almost impossible to identify the points he makes with the paradigms he chooses (Panzera and Fischer-Dieskau). At best, he appears to have got them the wrong way round. Few singers would wish to have such a physical relationship with their audience as Barthes presumably hopes for: I have not managed to find any examples of people actually achieving sexual climax as a direct result of listening to, or performing, music. Barthes was, however, aware of what many singers are conscious of but are generally unable to put into words, that there is at a fundamental level a connection between singing and sexuality, and which Barthes encapsulates in the concept of geno-song. The roots of geno-song, I would suggest, are extremely ancient. If Ekman's (1977) formulation based on the linguistic theory of Jakobson is valid, then the link between singing and sexuality is older than that between singing and speech. Just as the poetic function of speech/song offers the possibility of articulating otherwise latent behavioural symbolism, so can it articulate elements of sexuality that are also normally hidden. The role of sexuality, the form that the geno-song will take, will be determined by sociocultural forces which will operate on different musics in different ways.

Medieval and Renaissance music are full of references to sex, either directly or through commonly understood conventional symbolism. The Renaissance concept of the 'petit mort' is found throughout Europe. In the seventeenth- and eighteenth-century theatre, composers such as Purcell had no compunction in talking about sex in an explicit way. It was during the nineteenth century that sex and sexuality became taboo subjects, when the increasing separation of the dominant culture from mass culture meant 'the greater the restraint, the linguistic self-supervision and the censorship' (Bourdieu, 1977a, p. 658). It is not until the coming of Futurism and Dada that questions of sexuality in art music arise again, in the period before the First World War.

As far as one can tell, sexual liaisons have always figured in popular music. Broadside ballads from the early sixteenth century and folk poems that may be even older show an age-old concern with sexuality in one form or another. Evidence of the circumstances of the performance of this material is fragmentary. Vic Gammon (1982) gives some eighteenth-century evidence, and it is probable that performances were informal, and to relatively small numbers of people, often in conjunction with the consumption of alcohol. These were perhaps intimate occasions which reflected the direct experience of performers and audience and were not overtly erotic. Although Gammon suggests that the industrial revolution brought with it unprecedented sexual freedom, the wider, more public expression in the form of music hall does not seem to have gone beyond testing the boundaries of decency with sex as humour or 'smut'. Europeans only began to experience the overtly erotic in singers after the arrival on the continent of Afro-American music, which was perceived as heavily sexually orientated. The visit to France of the Revue Négre in 1925 featured Josephine Baker, who was not only black and female, but also prepared to pose in the nude and sing erotic songs in an appropriate manner.

Baker's performances are among the earliest for which film recordings exist, and they suggest something of the expressive power of the original blues singers. Paul Oliver (1962, p. 111) has explained in some detail the question of sexuality and the blues and remarks that it is through the blues that the word 'blue' has come to be associated with pornography, and there is a substantial corpus of blues texts that are frankly pornographic. With nothing else to lose, the inexpressible became expressible in song, together with almost every other detail of post-slavery life. 'Love destroys repression' writes Garon (1979, p. 71), and sexuality, with its admixture of pleasure and violence, reveals 'the dynamic necessity of the poetic destruction of the existing morality and, by implication, the social system that upholds it'. It was with the advent of rock'n'roll in the fifties that the sexuality and aggression of the urban blues found their way into mainstream western dance music. During the following decade the blues, and more especially rhythm and blues, underwent a revival spearheaded by British bands such as John Mayall's Bluesbreakers and the Yardbirds. From these groups, via Cream, there is a direct line to Led Zeppelin, in which the much debated 'cock rock' makes its first acknowledged appearance, and the complex sexuality of the blues enters the geno-song of contemporary rock music.

The first serious contribution to the debate on sexuality was Frith and McRobbie's 1979 article which took as its starting point John Travolta's performance in 'Saturday Night Fever', and looked at 'cock rock' and 'teenybop' (the former being 'an explicit, crude and often aggressive expression of male sexuality' (p. 5), while the latter is associated with young teenage girls). The two authors' analysis of cock rock is generated within a sociological framework and sees the phenomenon in entirely sexist terms. In their insistence that the entire process can be explained as an ideological construct they produce an oversimplified and unnecessarily reductionist account. The obvious symbolism of the macho prominent-genitalled stance with phallic accessory in the form of a guitar has a more elaborate morphology than a purely sexist account would suggest. The wide-legged stance of male guitarists does not in itself suggest sexual imagery, or if it does it is of the most ambiguous kind (and not generally found in gay bands). It recalls the balanced position in which one would wield a weapon, as though the guitar were an emblem of more general violence than simple penetration. If the right-hand gestures on the finger board are taken to be masturbatory, against whom is this putative violence directed and how can it be symbolic of penetration? The ritual phallic displays described by Eibl-Eibesfeldt (1979) act as a spacing function, directed at other males as much as an indication of male dominance. The harsh, rasping tones sometimes employed by the singers accord with the work of Erikson (1968) and the cantometrics research, which suggests that 'rasp' is used to indicate sexual dominance, yet Robert Plant, often held (by Frith and McRobbie among others) to be an original cock rocker, often employs far subtler vocal means. Was Led Zeppelin's association with cock rock then an act? Was cock rock in some measure a creation of promotion departments? The regular throbbing beat of heavy metal music, often taken by feminist commentators to be deeply phallocentric (especially when taken in conjunction with the perceived life-style of many performers) has a common-sense suggestion of reality. Yet this begs the question of what 'sex' actually encompasses in musical terms.[3] Such research as there has been into sexual practices gives little basis for a correlation between regular rhythm, sex and music. There is an assumption that it must be so (and promotion departments and performers certainly exploit the idea), but the connection between, say, dance or military bands and regular rhythm is actually verifiable empirically: that between sex and regular rhythm has only been proved to the satisfaction of certain scholars and the areas of doubt are too strong for a simple theory of male dominance.

The more direct expression of sexuality is potentially a means to greater freedom. It is as an end in itself, rather than as a means, that sexuality becomes problematic. All the sexual manifestations of the blues are surely manifest in cock rock. These encompass aggression, sexism and pleasure but they are born out of repression. This explains the existence of female heavy metal bands, which appear to function in much the same way as their male counterparts. Sexuality in music may be used to serve sexism, but it does not have to do that. Frith and McRobbie (1979, p. 19) ask rhetorically what a non-sexist rock music would be like. It is not difficult to conceive of a music that draws on the non-sexist power of the sexuality inherent in geno-song. It can be found, for example, in the middle period Pink Floyd or Genesis so denigrated by 1990s rock critics.

A weakness of the sexuality debate is the assumption that sexuality is exclusively to do with youth. Because pop music is an industry, it generates statistics whose primary function is market research. It is convenient for sociologists to fall back on these as hard information on which to base their research (Frith, 1979, is a case in point). Until recently, pubescent teenagers constituted the largest slice of the record-buying public and it seemed logical to associate sexuality in music with youth. There certainly is a connection there but it has in the past appeared to blind commentators to any consideration of rock music produced by and for people over the age of twenty five, and specifically to the wider issues of sexuality. Taylor and Laing (1979) rightly assert, in a reply to the Frith and McRobbie article, that the musical expression of sexuality is not confined to rock music and drawing on Barthes, they point to the fact that sexuality is a much more complex phenomenon than the latter suggest. In the early nineties purchasing power was in the hands of the over-forties, as was dramatically shown by the 1993 Brit Awards, which went almost exclusively to artists over the age of forty, who currently provide the mainstay of the industry's wealth. The sexuality debate became noticeably quiet as the industry moved into recession.

Barthes' background as a 'bourgeois' French Marxist led him to apply the geno-song concept to a classical singer (Panzera), but he was almost alone in recognising such a phenomenon in classical music. It is a curious irony that his essay has been used almost exclusively in support of socio-musicological arguments in pop music. Classical singers often use sexual imagery to describe particular ways of singing or a particularly significant sound or chord progression, and the gestures of the recording session may have erotic overtones, but little of this emerges during performance to an audience. John Shepherd (1991), in discussing music and male hegemony, points to what he calls the 'completeness' of classical music timbres which transcend gender relationships through the rationality of post-Renaissance male domination in cultural relations, leading to an implied neutralness or androgyny. Shepherd quotes Barthes in support of this thesis that the timbres of classical music filter out jouissance, rendering social relatedness redundant. This may sometimes be true, but I am fairly sure that most of those singers for whom Shepherd's analysis would have any meaning at all would disagree with him. Shepherd perhaps misconstrues the term 'grain': Barthes was himself writing of classical singing, in which sexuality is bound by strong constraints, but to which he could respond in a sexually mediated way.

It is perhaps this very constraint that has led to a number of composers' interest in the sexuality of the mouth, which they have been able to exploit in the relative freedom of extended vocal technique. Berio's *A-Ronne*, with its agenda of beginnings, middles and ends, has obvious sexual overtones. He talks of 'l'anus' and 'la bouche' and the piece is normally performed with only the singers' mouths lit. The film of the piece made more overtly sexual reference to the mouth. Dieter Schnebel's *Maulwerke* (literally 'mouthworks') is similarly concerned with the expressive qualities of the mouth and includes multi-screen live video filming of mouths in performance. The Nigel Osborne–David Freeman collaboration *Hell's Angels* achieved greater explicitness to almost universal horror on the part of audiences and press alike. The potent combination of religion, pseudo-explicit sex and classical singing so completely subverted the medium that the experiment was rendered meaningless. Because the socio-sexual parameters of classical music are so circumscribed, any attempt to subvert them either fails or becomes something else. In the case of *Hell's Angels* so strong was the sexual coding that it was considered by some as pornographic (and therefore hardly music).

In addition to the deeper implications of geno-song there is the possibility of class relatedness based on sexuality. Bourdieu (1977a), drawing upon the work of Pierre Guiraud, points to the class-related articulatory styles based on the use of the mouth. Two of the formants associated with vowel colour are determined by mouth position, which has a double semiotic function in that it is a determinor of vowel shape (and therefore accent) and has a wider sexually symbolic function. Bourdieu makes a distinction between 'bouche' and 'gueule' (in English the former is translated as 'mouth', while the latter is closer to 'gob'). As a concept 'bouche' represents the bourgeois position, often perceived in a sexually over-determined way by those of the lower classes. The 'closed and pinched mouth, tense and heavily censured' is seen as feminine as opposed to the large, unconstrained masculine 'gueule', which is the working-class means of expression.[4] This distinction is maintained because a lower-class male can adopt bourgeois speech only at some cost to his social and sexual identity. In terms of singing, this can account for the 'sissy' label often applied to classical singing at school and in part for the aggressive symbolism of cock rock and the hyper-corrected working-class accent of the middle-class Mick Jagger. Male/female paralanguage and kinesics are more complex and controversial subjects than Bourdieu is perhaps willing to admit but his linking of mouth, speech and sexuality offers potential insights that may be missed by sociologists and rock critics. Mouth position in classical singing is essentially governed by vocal tract behaviour. The wide position adopted by some sopranos to reach high notes is a direct result of the need to access particular formant frequencies. Though there may be no such communicative intent on the part of the singer the classical singer's mouth position may well be perceived as 'tense and heavily censured' (J. Thompson, 1984, p. 55). This may also explain why there are so few pictures of divas with their mouths open, as any biographical anthology will show (Gattey, 1979, for example).

Music performance very rarely involves physical communication between audience and performers: the sense of touch is absent except for the reaching out that occurs at rock concerts. Peter Gabriel's falling backwards from the stage to be passed round the audience is an extraordinary exception, perhaps indicative of the relatively unconstrained nature of rock music. A classical audience (except, conceivably, at the BBC Promenade concerts where the relationship between performer and audience is unusually informal and unconstrained) would have no use for such a gesture. Perhaps one of the functions of the expression of sexuality in singing is a metaphor for physical contact: an attempt to fuse the two most intimate modes of human communication, the vocal and the sexual.

The constraints placed on classical singing by its class context mean that the expression of sexuality is confined primarily to the singing itself. As an example of the way sexuality functions as a metaphor in classical singing, I propose to examine briefly a notional (present-day) performance of part of a mass movement by the late-fifteenth-century French composer Antoine Brumel. I have not chosen an actual performance since the potential degree of realisation of the points I wish to make will vary from performance to performance. The Agnus Dei is the concluding movement of the five mass 'ordinaries', those movements which remain the same throughout the church's year (as opposed to 'propers' which change

Example 1: Third Agnus Dei from *Missa Victimae Paschali* by Antoine Brumel

daily). It is, in its fifteenth-century realisation, a moment of peace as the mass draws to its close, and has a standardised form of A1-B-A2, with the text 'Lamb of God that takes away the sins of the world have mercy upon us' sung to the first two sections, and 'Lamb of God that takes away the sins of the world give us peace' sung to the last. In fifteenth-century settings the final statement is usually slower and harmonically richer than anything that has gone before.

The *superius* and *bassus* enter together but have to negotiate the tempo, since there is no movement on the second beat. This immediately means that the two singers are in very close aural contact with each other. The *altus* imitates the *superius* half a bar

later, so he has to have been in similarly close contact with the *superius*, who is giving him the music. At the end of bar 1 for a brief instant the three singers sound a G, an A and a B flat simultaneously. It is only a passing moment but it creates a moment of acute pleasure that they may wish to prolong. This may subvert the tempo and the aural communication between them has to be extremely close. The next bar begins with the third voice re-establishing the tempo so that the upper two parts can move in rhythmic unison until they subvert this with a suspension at the end of the bar. The timing of this has to be negotiated, and is ultimately in the hands of the *superius*, who controls the resolution. In controlling the tension and relaxation at this point the *superius* also determines when the *Bassus* finishes his phrase, and when the *tenor* enters with his first note. The *tenor*

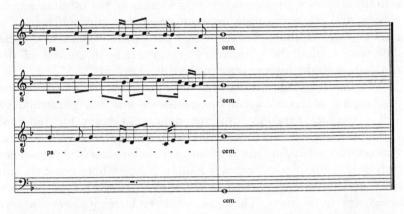

(actually the bass in conventional harmonic terms) has the 'Victimae paschali laudes' plainsong tune on which the mass is based. He sings in long notes, underpinning the sensual weavings that are happening above him. He is particularly conscious of two things: his timing must be absolutely precise and his breath must last the length of several bars without wavering. His timing is not metric, however, because the three singers above him are teasing each other with the tempo, prolonging suspensions, accelerating and slowing, each trying to control the others and give them opportunities to exercise control of their own. There is a high degree of mutual trust as the scales rise and fall, displaced from each other, in the two inner parts between bars 4 and 5, and again between the two upper parts from bar 7 to the end. The part that has any given musical idea first, in effect offers it to the part that will follow him, and then has to be prepared to accept the implications of what he has set up when the following part returns the favour. Throughout, the voices are setting up patterns of tension and relaxation, acutely conscious of each other, both seeking to accommodate each others' desires and to satisfy themselves.

The foregoing description has an obviously sexual metaphorical dimension (an actual sexual encounter would raise questions of gender, which would be to miss the point in this particular example); the principles apply to any music-making by any sort of ensemble. It also suggests that the idea of regular rhythm being a metaphor for sex is perhaps a myth, and that future research could perhaps focus more on the performers' musical relationship with each other as a site of sexual metaphor. Of course, the whole ensemble is also in communication with the audience and many of the mechanisms of tension and release operate between performer and audience in a similar way to those between the performers themselves. The difference is that the performers are generally in control of the situation, with the listeners cast in the role of *voyeurs*.

Whether language pre-dates gesture (as seems likely) or not, the overlapping anthropological disciplines of kinesics, paralanguage and proxemics certainly produce defining criteria for different varieties of singing. Much of the literature is concerned with cultural versus universal arguments. One authority who successfully manages to reconcile the two extremes is Ekman (1977), whose research into body and facial expression has led him to propose four primary categories of gesture. These he calls emblems (context-specific gestures which replace speech often in a conventional way); body manipulators (unconscious actions of one part of the body on another (usually) with no intention to communicate); illustrators (eight categories of broadly descriptive behaviour); and finally emotional expressions (governed by display rules which determine who can say what to whom, when). Emblematic behaviour appears in all types of singing. It governs the framing activity, for example, of bowing and greeting. Firth (1970) points out that bowing is historically a male prerogative. There is a certain irony in the increasing tendency of women singers to use this gesture. It is less a token of male hegemony than recognition of the fact that the curtsey (the only posture in western society to be the object of specific training) reflects sexist attitudes of the nineteenth century and is increasingly considered inappropriate for all but the highest-status (and therefore, usually, most conservative) events. Body manipulators may also occur and in classical singing can account for the redundant hand and head movements caused by nerves or an attempt to contain fear. Emotional expression is extremely hard to recognise and quantify in singing, since it is generally synthesised. The restraint called for in classical singing relegates signs of emotional expression to the face only (except in opera), whereas in rock music the whole body may be used. Ekman's category of illustrators was developed from Efron's original work in the field and consists of the following gestures:

> battons: which accent a particular word
> underliners: which emphasise a phrase or clause
> kinetographs: depicting a bodily or non-human action
> ideographs: sketching a path or direction of thought
> pictographs: which draw the shape of the referent in the air
> rhythmics: depicting the rhythm or pacing of an event
> spatials: depicting a spatial relationship
> deictics: which point to the referent (Ekman, 1977, p. 49)

In concert singing (i.e. not opera) very few of these categories apply. The hand-on-the-piano stance has a spatial function, as does the way the score is held, and an occasional hand may move with an underlining function, but the quasi-religious nature of the performance restricts obvious gestures to the minimum. Rock music finds a use for all Ekman's categories, many of them simultaneously, in an unrestrained semiotic display.

There has, as yet, been no comprehensive semiotic analysis of gestures used by singers (with the exception of the work done on cock rock discussed above). If we imagine a continuum from opera at one end to rock music at the other, the gestural pattern changes from a closed, constrained and formal system to an open and unpredictable one. As a paralinguistic means of communication, gesture cannot exist in a vacuum, but studies have shown that gestural rate decreases markedly if the subject is isolated from normal social interaction: gesture carries general or specific meanings in social contexts.[5] Scotto di Carlo (1973) found during a study over three seasons at the Marseilles opera that singers' gestures were (unsurprisingly) highly integrated into the requirements of operatic production. 70% of singers used a large spread of possible gestures to 'reconcile musical and scenic exigencies' while a further 26% used gestures that were specifically descriptive (the remainder used none at all (1%) or only a few (3%)). This suggests a semiotically closed system in which individual self-expression has little place (perhaps among the 2% included in the 70% who used 'all possible gestures'). Scotto di Carlo's taxonomy includes a fairly comprehensive range of gesture types, and these include many that would fit into Ekman's list of illustrators. Ironically the medium which uses categories of gesture which are also found in rock music, is subject to the greatest degree of gestural constraint, in that almost all of them are specified by the producer. In terms of Ekman's taxonomy, even gestures which outside the theatre would be considered emotional expressions, would presumably be classed as emblems or illustrators.

In the recording studio, away from the conventions of performer– audience relations, classical singers do use gestures (often quite extravagantly), each one appearing to have a personal repertoire which is only used on these occasions. This confirms that the gestural constraint on classical singers is a function of the social context in which they find themselves: with no audience present the singers are much freer in their use of emotionally expressive gestures. In many varieties of pop music the reverse may be the case: gestures are used to enhance a performance. As far as I know, there is no comparative research into the behaviour of musicians in the studio. The limited number of videos of pop singers in the studio are generally for promotional purposes and cannot be considered typical. Ekman suggests that body manipulators (nose picking, crotch scratching etc.) are not normally used consciously except by actors and psychopaths. They may also be a feature of punk and other extrovert rock performances (notably Michael Jackson's), reverting to the redundant form in the studio.

Forms of display rules also govern what is worn by singers during performances. The uniformity of dress in classical concerts is often heavily class coded and reduces individual expression to a minimum. At its most prestigious, the dress consists of the 'white tie and tails' which is an arcane survivor of nineteenth-century evening dress. Dressing for dinner and subsequent evening activities was an aristo- cratic and later bourgeois tradition and implied a particular status to which performers also aspired. At some events the corresponding morning dress is worn, especially in cathedrals. It was the custom for the aristocracy to attend church in the morning, hence the appro- priateness of morning dress in church (evening dress would never have been worn in church since evensong took place earlier than dinner; there is still a reluctance in England to wear evening dress in church). Formal dress remained customary for concerts and recitals despite the more informal eating arrangements of the twentieth century. It has a number of consequences, perhaps the most important of which is the separation of the audience from the performer while containing the event within a specifically bourgeois ambience. It also enhances the formality of the other parameters of the performance. It is essential that the dress is worn correctly, and that the wearer is 'smart'. Excellence in dress and bearing are essential ingredients in the recital aesthetic. Anthropologically, the dress identifies the group, and in its uniformity reinforces a group image and status. The historic tradition symbolises the permanence of classical music. By donning the traditional robes the performer enacts a ritual appropriate to the interpretation of music of the highest spiritual and social significance. This signification may not be intentional but it is a part of the ideological framework within which performer and audience relate to each other.

Not all classical socio-musical locations involve the full rigour of evening dress. There is a hierarchy of dress symbolism, in which decreasing formality may symbolise a greater degree of deviance from the established ideology. Thus, a dinner jacket might be worn on a less formal occasion, reducing to a dark suit, a lighter suit, shirt sleeves with tie, and finally open-necked shirt. For women singers there is a hierarchy of dresses ranging from short black through long black to very grand full coloured. There is now much less general agreement among performers about what should be worn, and when. Not wearing formal dress removes a good deal of the haut-bourgeois symbolism but the less formal alternatives give mixed messages to the audience. Unlike traditional dress they have associations with other functions: the suit is the daily wear of the business or professional man, a tie without a jacket is associated with domestic informality, and so on. Because the music produced on these less formal occasions is more ideologically complex (without the relatively simple semiotic implications of, say, a full-dress performance of Beethoven's *Missa Solemnis*), the reasons for uniformity of dress are called into question. The London Sinfonietta, for example, had an uneasy dress policy during the nineteen eighties, with soloists often dressing formally while the players wore different coloured shirts of similar style, symptomatic perhaps of the ideological problems experienced by an organisation nominally radical but actually very much part of the musical establishment. At the other end of the ideological continuum are the various performers who dispense with uniform in the conventional sense altogether. The instrumentalists of the Kronos Quartet wear stage dress which is often individualistic and provocative. Individuality of dress in the context of classical music removes the traditional bourgeois symbolism altogether, replacing it with subversive images of rock music.

If dress for the classical singer is largely determined by received class norms, that worn by non-classical singers is created specifically for the display of the individual image. As long ago as the 1920s Volosinov was aware of the basic difference between an object and a sign: the former (he gives the example of a hammer) having no ideological significance, unlike the latter (a hammer when combined with a sickle) (Bogatyrev, 1971, pp. 80–5). Classical singers would consider their dress as being 'object', but their very 'objectiveness' is in itself signifying an ideological stance. In rock music dress is invariably sign; its semiotic function has perhaps been put most succinctly by Eco: 'I speak through my clothes' (Hebdige, 1988, p. 100). While there may be some fashion-orientated stylistic unity behind the clothes of particular pop singers, there is a potentially infinite number of costumes that may be worn. These will reflect the singer's (and his audience's) idea of his own socio-musical location. Just as the classical singer's audience will wear appropriate dress, so will that of the pop singer, the essential difference being that the display rules for the former tend towards the closed and formal, though often style-coded, whereas the latter may be semiotically open and informal.

The overall effect of meaning generation within the parameters outlined above is to channel classical singing into a restricted, class-coded mode of expression. This is not to say that all classical singing is equally heavily coded, or that similar coding is not to be found in popular music. The tendency is towards reducing the meanings that may be created in classical singing, with a corresponding openness often present in rock music. The operation of these markers of difference is especially evident in cross-over, where elements of one variety of music are appropriated by another.

Popular music of a certain kind has always had recourse to classical musicians, who are generally to be found at the point where the music demands virtuoso skills acquired through pedagogy of some sort. At its most conventional, this interaction is seen in the person of the arranger, or a session MD. There have also been many successful pop musicians who have studied classical music. This is especially true of keyboard players (Elton John, Rick Wakeman, Keith Emmerson, Tony Banks, Manfred Mann all had respected classical piano teachers). Jazz players (Miles Davis, the Marsalis brothers, for example) have often benefited from a classical technique. During the seventies the legitimation of rock music was probably helped by groups such as Emerson, Lake and Palmer, Sky and Deep Purple, who experimented with classical ideas in the context of rock. More recently, pop musicians have involved themselves in patronage of the elite arts: the Grateful Dead, for example, supporting British avant-garde composers such as Michael Finnissy through its Rex Foundation. The crossing over tends to be in one direction, and in singers this is governed very much by the differences in technique that identify singers as being either popular or classical. Several pop singers have made successful attempts at classical singing (Barbra Streisand singing Lieder, Linda Ronstadt singing Gilbert and Sullivan); others have attempted to fuse their own style and technique with classical idioms (Sting singing Eisler, Elvis Costello performing with the Brodsky Quartet, Ute Lemper singing Michael Nyman). Many opera singers have made albums of popular songs but with the exception of those by Peter Hofmann these have been achieved with very little compromise of their classical technique. What they are perceived to bring to the music is 'quality' and 'excellence', an attempt to redeem popular music for good taste. This process does not work in reverse: those pop singers who attempt classical music are not generally considered to be bringing a desirable element of imperfection to classical music. The debate is always with reference to the excellence implied in classical music.

Nowhere is this demonstrated more clearly than in the duetting between Monserrat Caballé and the late Freddie Mercury. Their collaboration also illustrates the differences between pop singing and classical singing, the constraints that each has relative to the other. An analysis of their work together offers pointers to the future development of a relationship between the styles. The two singers first got together in 1987. Mercury, one of the most extrovert performers in rock, had long been fascinated by opera, and the partnership began as a result of his admiration for Caballé. The two decided to make an album which would be 'a unique combination of rock and opera'.[6] The cover of the ensuing album, *Barcelona*, has the two singers posed as though for a classical publicity shot, Caballé benignly smiling, Mercury wearing black tie but with a waistcoat, snooker-player fashion, instead of a jacket. The cover has something of the contrived restraint of a classical album. The sleeve .1otes contain photographs of the two protagonists in various roles, equating Mercury's various rock creations with Caballé's starring roles. The entire production is in effect an icon which places the collaboration firmly on the terrain of classical music, despite its being marketed as a pop record.

The opening of the eponymous 'Barcelona' begins with the multi-tracked Mercury singing the title, over a widely spaced chord reminiscent of his Queen hits. The bass enters almost immediately this signature has been established, followed by a very nineteenth-century-sounding orchestral passage. More multi-Mercury 'Barce-lonas' come next, ending on a huge dominant seventh 'viva'. There is a drum roll, a cello recitative recalling Beethoven's Ninth Symphony, out of which comes a high note that might be either Caballé or a synthesiser. This is followed by some pseudo-Tchai-kovsky fanfares and a bridge passage leading to a solo piano passage over which the singers begin their duet. The piece thus far has been a series of barely connected pastiche introductory statements that no classical musician would take very seriously, but which align the piece, as far as its intended pop audience is concerned, firmly with high art (mediated by high camp).

Once the singers begin their duet, two things are immediately obvious: firstly, you can hear every word of Mercury's text, whereas it is difficult at times to tell even what language Caballé is singing in much of the time (she sometimes repeats Freddie's English and sometimes sings a Spanish translation); secondly, Caballé's delivery is governed entirely by her technique, from which she cannot depart without risking her *raison d'être* as a singer. She is concerned above all with making beautiful sounds in the conventional singerly way. Mercury's delivery is much more dynamic; he sings with the direct-ness of speech and his performance reflects his personality: he declaims the text in whatever way will make the greatest effect. He does not have the ideological baggage of several hundred years to restrain him. The louder Mercury sings, the more expressive he can become, resorting to something like a controlled shout for the very loudest passages in order to keep the text intelligible. When Caballé crescendos she becomes progressively less intelligible, taking refuge in the powerful vibrato which she can command, to focus the attention on her sound and what it stands for, rather than on the text. Both singers are amplified, but Mercury is able to exploit the microphone to make it an extension of himself in a way that is totally alien to Caballé (although in the gala performance in Barcelona Mercury had to mime to the tape, having lost his voice). Mercury sings in a way that classical singers would describe as musical; he sings in a variety of RP (unlike most other rock singers) and he phrases according to the ebb and flow of the music, with a huge dynamic range.

'Barcelona' is a vivid example of the limitations of classical singing, and the potential of a form of popular singing to supplant it, given a context which can overcome the ideological circumstances of classical music performance. In the current situation of stylistic pluralism there is a possibility that the elite form will eventually lose its authority and be reduced to a stylised art-form enjoyed by an ever-decreasing audience. Traditional Japanese theatre, which still uses the exaggerated court speech of several hundred years ago, is maintained increasingly as a tourist attraction, with only sporadic attempts to make it a living art-form relevant to the everyday lives of the Japanese. A similar fate may be in store for classical singing in the basically nineteenth-century sense that we understand it at the moment. The singing of pop musicians such as Mercury, Sting and Elvis Costello is potentially a much more efficacious vehicle for the articulation of ordinary people's desires. When put into a classical context it becomes capable of redefining what classical music is. This revolution in the singing–taste matrix would be, like all previous revolutions in singing style and technique, a return to singing as carrier of text, a vehicle for the articulation of meanings relevant to a wider section of the population.

CHAPTER 10

Towards a theory of vocal style

I have hinted that it might be possible to derive a theory of vocal style from the analyses of the previous chapters: various patterns of development have emerged in the history of both classical and pop singing, and similar underlying forces seem to be at work in both fields. A theory would need to take account of how a high-status singing variety relates to those that it dominates, as well as how styles evolve within varieties.

I have occasionally used the term 'hegemony' in a very broad way to indicate the authority that one style has over another.[1] Hegemony as formulated by the Italian theorist Antonio Gramsci is a concept which means more than simply 'dominance'. In his *Prison Notebooks* he often uses *direzione* and *egemonia* interchangeably, the former term being derived from *dirigere* meaning to direct, lead or rule. Gramsci's use of these terms embraces two central ideas, those of leading and dominating:

a class is dominant in two ways, i.e. 'leading' and 'dominant'. It leads the classes which are its allies, and dominates those which are its enemies. Therefore, even before attaining power a class can (and must) 'lead'; when it is in power it becomes 'dominant', but continues to 'lead' as well . . . there can and must be a 'political hegemony' even before the attainment of governmental power, and one should not count solely on the power and material force which such a position gives in order to exercise political leadership or hegemony. (Gramsci, 1986, p. 107n)

Central to this formulation is the consent to leadership (and, ultimately, dominance) by those being led (and, ultimately, dominated). Gramsci is talking about political leadership, of course, and the 'material force' to which he refers was a very real threat in the context of fascist Italy. For a peace-time refinement of this idea we can turn to Pierre Bourdieu, whose concept of 'symbolic violence' also assumes the complicity of the dominated. 'Symbolic' violence is that particular 'gentle, invisible' form of coercion by which dominant classes enforce hegemony though the operation of institutions in which people 'collaborate in the destruction of their instruments of expression' (Bourdieu, 1982, p. 34). Beneath the formidable language of these two political commentators (the one a frustrated political activist, the other a noted anthropologist) we can discern a principle that can be applied to singing: by agreeing that classical singing is the highest-status variety all but a very few people consent to their exclusion from its production.

Singing, like any other branch of the expressive arts, does not remain the same for very long, and changes in the hegemonic hierarchy occur at moments of what Gramsci called 'organic crisis', when the dominant party fails to satisfy the desires of those consenting to its hegemonic status, or when intellectuals become active, relegating the ideology of the dominant party to 'historical-political documents of the various phases of past history'. The result is that

At a certain point in their historical lives, social classes become detached from their traditional parties. In other words, the traditional parties in that particular organisational form, with the particular men who constitute, represent and lead them, are no longer recognised by their class (or fraction of a class) as its expression. (Gramsci, 1986, p. 210)

In musical terms, once the currently authoritative style is no longer relevant to the desires and aspirations of those it seeks to dominate, a change in style becomes possible. Symptomatic of this is a pre-occupation with the ideological past.

Classical singing as we know it today is virtually unchanged from a technical point of view since the mid nineteenth century. The low-larynx position, which became the norm for the operas of Verdi and Wagner, enabled an additional resonating formant to be used, by means of which singers can be heard over substantial orchestral forces in large halls. It also created the rounded tone characteristic of modern singing and is supported by a systematised breathing technique. It was these two technical improvements in breathing and tone projection that enabled classical singing to reach such a high point in its development. Classical singing remained on a technical plateau and became ideologically entrenched as the dominant vocal expression. In normal speech, and in folk song, the larynx, while free to move within the vocal tract, tends to maintain a relatively high position. Among other things, this facilitates the comprehensibility of words. The lower larynx position 'darkens' the colour of the voice, but as the base of the tongue is anchored to a bone whose own position is determined by that of the larynx this enriched tone is accompanied by a reduced ability to differentiate vowels. When singing high a singer may need to adopt a wider jaw opening to gain access to additional resonating frequencies, and a lowered jaw facilitates a lower larynx position. The effect of these changes is to generate a special way of 'speaking', one which is not located geographically and which is received as a 'given' in the same way that Received Pronunciation is transmitted. In the depth of its vowel quality, traditional classical singing also shares certain tonal qualities with RP, though this is perhaps less the case than it was. This esoteric way of 'speaking' is underpinned by a unique way of breathing. Breathing in normal speech is taken for granted, although without it life would not exist. Classical singing lays claim to a special use of this life-giving force in order to control its unique language. No other way of 'speaking' (including RP) has such a requirement and it is this ideological base which has been largely responsible for the success of low-larynx technique within the classical field and for the high status of the field itself.

This mode of utterance has its own pedagogy. Bourdieu and Passeron (1990, p. 200) described educational systems as institutions for the exercise of symbolic violence in the imposition of a 'cultural arbitrary'. In other words the legitimacy of education is such that those involved in it have no need to relate what is taught to universal principles since it is accepted as autonomous and self-perpetuating. In this way cultural hierarchies are reproduced and relations of dominance maintained. Classical singing in the nineteenth century gained the benefit of an institutionalised scientifically based pedagogy. Singing in cathedral schools envisaged music as discipline, backed by a moral authority. The increasingly rigorous pedagogy of individual professional singing teaching offered exercises that were an end in themselves. The Music Colleges that were founded to institutionalise this discipline were of the highest status, as is demonstrated by the following report from the *Musical Times* of June 1883, on the occasion of the inauguration of the Royal College of Music:

. . . a mission of a more than usually comprehensive nature; designed ultimately to collect and promote the latent musical talent not only of

London and the home counties, and of the United Kingdom, but of India and the colonies and even of the United States and all the English-speaking countries and nations. (Golby, 1986, p. 229)

The imperialistic ideal applied to the whole of classical music, but it was singing that was uniquely placed to become the ideological flag-bearer of bourgeois music-making. The pedagogy was not only enshrined in state institutions with royal sponsorship, but was increasingly based on what were thought to be scientifically quantifiable principles, themselves of high status in the context of the scientific revolution that was occurring. In contrast to the pre-nineteenth-century tradition of treatises written by singers, 'by the year 1891, almost every new major work [on singing] included sections on anatomy and physiology and various theories of breath, phonatory and resonatory controls. The most important works of the period, it seems, were penned by physicians and scientists' (Monahan, 1978, p. 226). Although there had been a recognisable concept of 'art' music for several centuries (and possibly for millennia), the nineteenth-century developments represent the first time that the stylisation of a singing technique backed by scientific criteria can be identified with a new social class. Teachers who disagreed with (or could not understand) the science could call on a bygone age of excellence to which they claimed unique access, giving rise to the myth of bel canto.

A common thread in the evolution of both classical and popular singing styles is what I should like to call a logocentric articulation of musical style: all changes in style relate in some way to the presentation of text. This is not just a 'common sense' formulation: anthropological research suggests the possibility that singing may have evolved as an expression of territorial markers, with a similar function to that of bird song (Richman, 1980). It is conceivable that singing could have developed without the need for words in such circumstances. There are also aesthetic considerations: in modern classical singing, tone colour (an instrumental or non-verbal parameter) is one of the most significant criteria for evaluating singing. Despite these non-verbal possibilities, at some point in the very remote past singing became associated with text.

I have suggested that in the history of western singing, stylistic development has tended, as far as can be ascertained, to follow a three-stage model of development, decadence and renewal. Each of the three stages of this model has particular characteristics which apply both to popular and classical singing. The development stage is characterised by changes to a performance practice which enable one particular style to achieve a (Gramscian) hegemonic position relative to other competing styles by a new articulation of text. This stage is eventually exhausted when its continued reproduction no longer relates to the social desires and contexts of a significant section of its potential audience. In all historical moments the most significant change to occur is invariably related to the nature of performance rhetoric, the ability of a singer to invest a text with particular meanings. During the decadent phase, which corresponds to Gramsci's 'dominating' but not 'leading', various alternative possibilities emerge. Out of stylistic pluralism, which may be a dynamic phase with many styles struggling to become representative of a wider section of society, a new main variety emerges, possibly fusing several elements of the emergent styles with elements of the old style. This style, newly invested with the potential to carry meanings relevant to a significant listenership, can be expected to achieve hegemony over the alternatives as the process renews itself. We currently live at a time of stylistic pluralism in both classical and popular singing. It is probable that singing in the present always appears to be more pluralistic than it will later appear to historians (who will rationalise events according to their own ideological agendas). From this pluralistic position it is not possible to locate the present at an exact point in a cycle of stylistic development. It is possible, however, by examining how meaning works in singing, to come closer to an understanding of the relationship between varieties, and of their possible future development.

The exhaustion of a certain formulation of the creative force and its replacement or re-articulation in a different artistic form is a phenomenon which occurs throughout western music and art. Gramsci talks of the 'crisis of authority' which can occur when traditional forms are no longer recognised as adequate by their own adherents. Roland Barthes made a similar formulation:

One immunizes the contents of the collective imagination by means of a small inoculation of acknowledged evil; one thus protects it against the risk of a generalised subversion. (Barthes, 1984, p. 150)

Even outside materialist accounts, analogous perspectives can be found, as in Gerald Abraham, for example:

Artistic styles are like political empires, nurturing always within them the forces which are to bring about their decay, and never more strongly than when they themselves appear to be at the height of their power. (Abraham, 1985, p. xxii)

This corresponds closely to Gramsci's concept of passive revolution, in which a revolution from within incorporates elements of the new. It is a regenerative feature of all vocal styles. Gramsci's concept derives from Marx's *Critique of Political Economy* in which he states that

No social order ever perishes before all the productive forces for which there is room in it have developed; and new, higher relations of production never appear before the material conditions of their existence have matured in the womb of the old society itself. (Marx, 1971, preface)

Thus it is that Schoenberg's 'Sprechgesang', which, as an attempt to translate actual speech into music, might have been considered a threat to the hegemony of classical singing, was incorporated into the repertoire of classical techniques, not as real speech but as stylised, rhetorical speech which could be judged on criteria of excellence. It emerged generations later as a foundation for extended vocal techniques, themselves speech-related but distanced by context and rhetoric from ordinary speech. The same principle can be applied to all changes in popular style: no style is ever completely new or completely revolutionary; it always contains elements of that style which it seeks to supplant. More recently, there have been signs of classical music seeking to retain its dominance in the face of a Gramscian crisis of authority which has resulted from the legitimation of many kinds of popular music. At such a moment of crisis renewal may be achieved by incorporating elements of the new into the old ideology, thus preserving the existing hegemonic structure by means of passive revolution. This process may underlie the various manifestations of crossover, when one type of music may seek to incorporate elements from another in order to maintain its existing dominance. It can be seen in opera at Wembley Stadium, or Kiri te Kanawa singing Gershwin, where classical singing seeks to extend its authority; in Elvis Costello singing with the Brodski Quartet, where he attempts to align pop singing with the intellectual concerns and idioms of classical music; and in the duetting between Freddie Mercury and Montserrat Caballé, who each hope that by incorporating elements of each other's style into their own they will widen their respective markets.

In an extrapolation from Gramsci Richard Middleton demonstrates three points of major organic crisis, or 'moments of radical situational change' at which the formation of musical-ideological fields can be clearly identified. The three periods identified by Middleton are those of the bourgeois revolutions between the end of the eighteenth century and the middle of the nineteenth, the period of 'mass culture' from the late nineteenth century to about 1930, and the period of 'pop culture' which begins after 1945 (Middleton, 1985, pp. 5–43). It is during these three 'moments' that it is particularly easy to point to the articulation of musical events by cultural and ideological phenomena. Both the time-periods suggested by Middleton and the idea of 'crisis' in its Gramscian sense can be related to developments in vocal style and technique. In vocal terms the 'moments' are characterised by the emergence of a style or technique that attempts to return to a logocentric view of vocal performance. This is followed by relatively rapid development and then a period of what I should like to call decadence, which corresponds to the 'relative situational stability' of the Middleton/ Gramsci analysis, a period where no further significant stylistic developments are likely to occur. It is also possible to make a case for other historical 'moments'. The radical change from the polyphony of the late Renaissance to the vertically orientated monody of the early baroque around 1600 can be clearly shown to be articulated by the intellectual and economic developments that were occurring during the period. There is also a case to be made for a similar process taking place over a more extended time-scale in the transformation from scholastic to humanist thought during the three hundred years or so which preceded it. This 'moment' is more problematic because of the uneven survival of the necessary vocal evidence. Going back further still, though we are reduced to speculation because of the almost total lack of suitable evidence, it is possible to suggest a further 'moment' when the classical period merged into feudalism, when singing became the prerogative of free men (especially in the embryonic Christian church) as opposed to the unfree activity that it had been throughout much of the ancient world.

The three-stage model of stylistic development can be most clearly seen from the baroque period onwards. There is an obvious 'moment of change' when the fifteenth-century division school is reined in by Caccini and his successors: virtuosity for its own sake is replaced by a new attention to text. This evolves until, perhaps towards the end of the seventeenth century, it gradually becomes decadent. By this I mean that the text is no longer the prime consideration, and that vocal display has become an end in itself. I would argue that this period of decadence lasted until the early nineteenth century, around the time of Middleton's first period, where a clear contrast can be seen between the singing required for Rossini (virtuosic in what was essentially a Handelian, or, conceivably, even a fifteenth-century manner) and that needed for the dramatic singing of Verdi. Verdi's correspondence confirms that the overriding criterion of good singing was the dramatic presentation of text. A new vocal technique was developed in connection with this logocentric return to first principles, the first time in history that a real technical change can be observed. This early-nineteenth-century technique, with its focus on tone colour and control, is the basis for most modern classical singing.

Popular music is subject to the same basic principles. The pre-jazz singing of minstrelsy and variety theatres seems to have aped aspects of classical singing. It is with Armstrong and Crosby that a new style emerges (during Middleton's period of 'mass culture'), based on speech-like declamation which makes the text absolutely clear. This in its turn became accepted into the mainstream where it degenerated into crooning, awaiting a logocentric revolution in the shape of Elvis Presley and 'pop culture'. A speech-like delivery similar to that of Presley continues to be used by singers of every variety of rock music today.

From a technical point of view there have been relatively few changes in conventional classical singing this century, although early recordings reveal surprisingly wide variations in such parameters as vibrato and tone colour. The history of classical singing on record, especially from the LP onwards, is about a certain standardisation, a more common definition of what singing is. Particularly successful singers have had imitators who have developed certain stylistic traits: the singing of Robert Tear, for example, owed a great deal to that of his teacher, Peter Pears. Pears himself was always careful to ensure the primacy of the text, as was Dietrich Fischer-Dieskau, whose records of Webern in the sixties demonstrated a commitment to texual meanings rather than beauty of sound. In early music Emma

Kirkby became a paradigm for aspiring sopranos. Vibrato is used more, both in early and mainstream singing. The vast pedagogical literature has continued to expand and the workings of the voice are now more clearly understood.[2] There have been many singers who have been recognised as 'great' but who have in fact merely maintained the existing hegemony of the style. If one of the indicators of a state of decadence in the hegemonic style is the emergence of possible alternatives, then it may be that classical singing has been decadent from the early years of the century, following a relatively short period of development. If this is so, according to the three-stage stylistic model we could eventually expect to see the occurrence of Gramscian crises of authority, and, in the ensuing struggle, the emergence of a new hegemonic form. What has actually occurred is rather more subtle, although future research may reveal that the nuances observable at relatively close quarters, historically speaking, have parallels in earlier periods. The elite form has continued to maintain its authority, at least in part because western governments continue to subsidise opera houses for reasons of cultural prestige. Various alternative 'singings' have arisen, however, as different sections of society have felt alienated by the elite form. As the theory would predict, these alternatives are concerned with attempts to redefine singing in terms of its logo-centric function, a return to the exploration of the voice as a carrier of word and idea rather than a kind of human wind instrument which produces beautiful sounds. In the early part of the century, Dada and Futurism experimented with spoken declamation, and Schoenberg (the self-appointed guardian of the classical tradition) attempted to apply the speech-song of melodrama and cabaret to his own compositions. Since the Second World War, the most promising alternatives, which have developed hegemonic structures of their own, are to be found in early music and extended vocal techniques. Both styles raise important questions about language, legitimacy and class. It is not inconceivable that this fragmentation into stylistic pluralism will eventually see mainstream classical singing reduced to one variety among many in competing taste markets.

The voice is, as Meredith Monk (1976, p. 13) put it, 'a direct line to the emotions': it is the first, and possibly the oldest means of human expression. From childhood we are socialised into the acceptance of various ideologies of singing discussed in this study, with the result that for most 'some natural and spontaneous part of our human inheritance is squeezed out of us' (Armstrong, 1985, p. 22) This is an inevitable result of accepting the authoritative status of an elite variety. The process of marginalising a truly democratic and 'natural' singing has occurred since ancient times, as singing became at a certain level a means of articulating social power. During the nineteenth century, the new and dynamic middle class appropriated 'classical' singing, which became an institutionalised style legitimised by science, myth and and a morality expressed through discipline. For technical reasons classical singing could lay claim to a unique way of breathing and 'speaking', which reinforced the idea, still regarded by many people as a given, that classical singing is inherently superior to all other possible varieties. The efficacy of this style, and therefore its hegemonic position relative to all others, may now be in doubt as society enters what might be a post-bourgeois stage. The loosening hold that rock music has on its old hegemonic status in popular music, is contributing to the stylistic pluralism of the present. The struggle among different vocal styles, each the site of collective and individual desires, may yield yet another set of relations which produce a new hegemonic style. It is also possible that changing social relations may result in a more general stylistic pluralism, though singers are still likely to be judged on how well they conform to an accepted norm rather than as individuals. This would not be Frankie Armstrong's 'natural and spontaneous' style, but it would be more representative of more people, enabling a wider section of society to 'find its voice' (Armstrong, 1985, p. 20).

Notes

I CLASSICAL IDEOLOGY AND THE PRE-HISTORY OF SINGING

1 The term 'classical' is used specifically of Greek or Latin antiquity, and pre-Romantic music associated with the Viennese school of Haydn and Mozart. It also has a more general meaning, intended here, referring to music which is characterised by 'formal discipline' and 'generic excellence' (Heartz (1980)).

2 These date from around 1250–1200 BC and consist of fragmentary hymns and instructions for tuning a lyre. See West (1994) for a current interpretation of the fragments.

3 Livingstone (1973) and Richman (1980) have sought to explain the origins of speech in territorial markers similar to bird song, and the massed 'singing' of certain types of ape, respectively. Sachs (1943) and Wellesz (1957) are now rather dated summative works on the musicology of the ancient world.

4 The British Museum has an important collection; see, for example, BM89359 which dates from the second millennium BC.

5 See, for example, Shepherd et al. (1977), especially Wishart's contribution; also the latter's On Sonic Art (1985).

6 As an example of crude bias it is worth quoting Sachs (1943): 'But whoever attends Coptic services . . . must be struck by the discouraging vagueness of all notes inside a fourth or a fifth, and, as a consequence, will prefer to refrain from modal analysis.'

7 Hucbald, De harmonica institutione, quoted in Treitler (1984).

8 VAT 9307 held in the Vorderasiatische Abteilung of the Berlin State Museum.

9 See Spector (1965) and Katz (1974).

10 On Homer and oral poetry see Parry (1987) and Lord (1981). Lord explains how substantial amounts of information can be transmitted orally over time by the use of formulaic structures, by applying the analyses of Milman Parry in what he calls the 'living laboratory of Jugoslav epic' (p. 143) to the works of Homer. There is a considerable literature on oral poetry which uses the earlier work of Parry and Lord as its starting point.

11 Athenaeus, *Deipnosophistae* (second century AD, but his sources are several hundred years earlier). Unless otherwise specified all classical quotations are from Barker (1987) to which the general historical background in this section is indebted. There is a useful summary of music in ancient Greece, together with a bibliography, in *The New Grove Dictionary of Music and Musicians*. The surviving examples of ancient Greek notation are contained in an important new study by M. L. West (1994).

12 'Free man' is used here to mean anyone not a slave. In medieval Europe the term is applied specifically to people not tied to the land by serfdom.

13 Pseudo-Plutarch contrasts 'manly and inspired music' with 'effeminate twitterings' (*De musica 15*), an epithet which he himself found in many of his sources. The undesirability of effeminacy in music re-surfaced in medieval Europe and is still with us today.

2 THE MEDIEVAL PERIOD: RELIGION, LITERACY AND CONTROL

1 There is a review of the literature in Browning (1988).

2 *Sybilline Oracles* quoted in McKinnon (1986).

3 See McKinnon (1986) for a lucid account of Christianity's liturgical debt to Judaism.

4 *Etymologiarum* (*c.* 622–33) quoted in Strunk (1981). Giulio Cattin (1984) suggests it may have taken ten years to gain a working knowledge of the repertoire. Odo of Cluny, in his *Enchiridion musices* (*c.* 935, quoted in Strunk, 1981) complains that fifty years may not be long enough. Treitler (1974) examines the application of modern research on memory to formula learning.

5 See McKinnon (1990) pp. 102ff. on the argument for Gregory II as the eponymous chant codifier.

6 *Prologus antiphonarii sui* quoted in Strunk (1981).

7 For the economics of book production see Febvre and Martin (1984).

8 Allen (1969), p. 20. An unbroken tradition of Latin literacy survived in the area of St Gall, whose monastic foundation was to play a significant role in the creation of chant. See McKitterick (1989).

9 Johannes de Grochieo lists a Saracen guitar among the vielles, psalteries, lyres and other instruments in his treatise *De musica* (Page, 1993a, p. 30).

10 *Commentary on the Epistle of Paul to the Ephesians* quoted in Strunk (1981), p. 72. Jerome's exhortation is also full of implication for the survival of classical rhetorical (secular) performance.

11 In Dyer (1980). See also Page (1991) for a similarly conservative source accompanied by an invaluable commentary.

12 In Dyer (1978).

13 C. Wright (1990) gives a list of all surviving references to the singing of *organum*.

14 See Petrovic (1965). Many non-European societies have an epic tradition. See Araki (1978) for a Japanese variety, for example.

3 THE ITALIAN BAROQUE REVOLUTION

1 See Reynolds and Wilson (1991).
2 The early chapters of Stephens (1979) make this point, as does C. Wright (1990, pp. 317–18).
3 There is an overview of Italian improvising traditions in Haar (1986).
4 For iconographical examples see Bowles (1983). The question of instruments used in the songs of the troubadours and trouvères is the subject of Page (1987).
5 Translated by Charles Singleton (1959).
6 Ganassi and other sources of the period are discussed at length in Brown (1984).
7 From the translation by Hitchcock (1970).
8 See Pirotta (1982).
9 See Rosselli (1984).
10 See Duey (1980) and Heriot (1975).
11 There is a discussion of these sources in Uberti (1981).
12 Quoted in Brown (1978).
13 Tosi (1743/1967), which is a facsimile of the English edition of 1743.
14 See Baskerville (1929).
15 Burney, *A General History of Music* quoted in Walter White (1983a).

4 THE DEVELOPMENT OF THE MODERN VOICE

1 Berlioz (1862). There is a translation of a relevant extract in MacClintock (1994), pp. 420–32.
2 For an analysis of the requirements of Mozart's singers see N. Baker (1989). There are examples of Rossini's expected ornamentation in Garcia (1841/1872).
3 This description of the workings of the voice is based on Sundberg (1977) and Howard (1992).
4 See Uberti (1981) for an overview of what pre-Garcian singing may have been like.
5 See the entries by Elizabeth Forbes and Julian Budden in *The New Grove*.
6 See M. Scott (1977) and its accompanying discs, which together form the most comprehensive history of classical singing so far available.
7 See Durant (1984), chapter 5, for a case study of the Elizabethan madrigal in terms of the 'Golden Age' syndrome.

5 CONCERTS, CHOIRS AND MUSIC HALLS

1 Middleton (1990) deals comprehensively with the problem of definition. See also *Popular Music* 1 (1981), Russell (1987), Hamm (1983), and Middleton (1991).
2 For comprehensive details for the history of the halls see Bailey (1986)

and Bratton (1986). The recent historiography of music hall is dealt with in Pennybacker (1987).

3 Both D. Scott (1989) and Temperley (1991) draw attention to the significance of the nineteenth-century Christmas carol.

4 See Jackson (1933/1965) and Wicks (1989).

5 See the entry on Day by Miriam Miller in *The New Grove Dictionary of Music and Musicians*.

6 See the table in Gammon (1981), p. 65. See also Temperley (1983) for the wider history of church music in this context. Both Temperley and Gammon draw on the earlier work of MacDermott (1948).

7 In his entry on Popular Music in *The New Grove Dictionary of Music and Musicians* Andrew Lamb refers to 'the tonic sol-fa system invented by John Hullah' (vol. xv, p. 88). This is incorrect on two counts.

6 ARMSTRONG TO SINATRA: SWING AND SUB-TEXT

1 France in 1848, the USA 1862–5, the Netherlands 1863–9, Portugal 1858–78 and Brazil 1871–88.

2 Tempo is used throughout this section in a qualitative sense. Among jazz musicians (and a small number of classical musicians) there is an unspoken but commonly agreed definition of the term that implies more than simply speed. It is possible to talk of a good tempo, meaning one in which all the significance which flows from rhythmic considerations has room for expression. This is as much to do with what players call 'feel' as speed.

3 For a description of the invention of the drum kit, see Danny Baker in Shapiro and Hentoff (1992), pp. 20–1.

4 Taylor (1978) also makes the point that 'to be negro was to be two-faced' in his chapter on jazz.

5 Quoted at the head of Gates (1988).

6 See Leonard (1964, p. 71) for a description of Ellington's band playing the Cotton Club.

7 McClary (1991) chapter 7. For a different perspective see Potter (1994).

8 See Southern (1979).

7 EARLY MUSIC AND THE AVANT-GARDE: TWENTIETH-CENTURY FRAGMENTATION

1 Doctrinal and political factors had led to a steady decline in the quality of English cathedral and college choirs during the eighteenth and early nineteenth centuries. This began to reverse itself later in the nineteenth century. See Gatens (1986) and Routley (1968) for accounts of pre-Ord choirs.

2 Falsetto is produced as a result of the arytenoid cartilages coming together in such a way that the vibrating length of the cords is reduced

by approximately one third (see P. Giles, 1982). In many European choirs the alto lines are sung by boys rather than adult falsettists.

3 See Potter (1992) for a more detailed consideration of the extent to which 'lost' voices can be re-discovered.

4 See Page (1993b) for an overview of the English early music singing scene in the mid-nineties.

5 See, for example, Alison Wray's contribution to Knighton and Fallows (1992).

6 I am grateful to my son Edward for pointing this out in connection with Jason Kay of Jamiroquai and Thom Yorke of Radiohead among many others.

7 See Anhalt (1984) for a summary of speech-related vocal activity in the early part of the twentieth century.

8 See Pardo (1982) and Coghlan (1979).

9 See the interview with Berio in Varga (1985, p. 141).

8 ELVIS PRESLEY TO RAP: MOMENTS OF CHANGE SINCE THE FORTIES

1 Wyman (1987). I am grateful to John Butt for pointing out a parallel between Jagger and the violinist Nigel Kennedy.

2 The literature on rap is increasing rapidly, especially from black scholars. For an introduction to the subject see Toop (1991).

3 Wheeler (1992). Wheeler's theory of rap is based on Bakhtin.

4 See Bernard (1992) and other articles in the *New York Times* survey of rap, which look at the music in Brazil, Mexico, the Caribbean, Australia, Russia, China, Japan, Afric, Eastern Europe, Britain and France.

9 SINGING AND SOCIAL PROCESSES

1 Like Hennion's, my observations are based on experience in the studio (and in live performance), although as a performer rather than an independent observer. The views expressed here are based on participation in the recording of over one hundred classical albums and a smaller number of pop albums by Emmerson, Lake and Palmer, Manfred Mann, Vangelis, Mike Oldfield, Swingle II and many others.

2 From the video *Miles Davis in Paris* (Warner, 1990).

3 See Potter (1994) for a more detailed discussion of sexuality in connection with Madonna and k d lang.

4 Frith (1979, p. 59) quotes Paul Johnson describing the 'open, sagging mouths' of TV pop audiences, which recalls the open-mouthed display discussed in Eibl-Eibesfeldt (1979).

5 'One cannot not communicate' (Watzlawick *et al.*, 1967, p. 51). See Ekman (1977, p. 69) for case studies. Other commentators (notably

Bakhtin) also require an audience before expression can be said to have taken place. The definition of self-expression would have to include the self as potential audience.

6 See the sleeve notes to the album *Barcelona* (Polydor INT 837277–2).

10 TOWARDS A THEORY OF VOCAL STYLE

1 I am grateful to Alan Durant for suggesting the term 'vocal authority' to mean the dominance of one style by another.

2 The history of the pedagogical literature of the twentieth century is broadly one of differing emphasis on the same recurring ideas, with occasional excursions into fantasy, such as the works of Ernest White on the subject of sinus tone production (E. White, 1927; 1938). For a detailed analysis of the literature see Monahan (1978) for the period to 1927, Fields (1979) for 1928–42, and Burgin (1973) for 1943–71. The best socio-musical documents of what it meant to be an aspiring or successful classical singer in England during the seventies and eighties are to be found in Faulkner (1983).

References

Abraham, G. (ed.). 1985. *The New Oxford History of Music*, vol. IV: *The Age of Humanism* (London).

Addison, J. *The Spectator* 21 April 1711 (repr. 1749, vol. I, pp. 76–9).

Allen, P. 1969. *The Romanesque Lyric* (New York).

Allen, W., Garrison, L. and Ware, C. (eds.). 1867/repr. 1965. *Slave Songs of the United States* (New York).

Anderson, P. 1987. *Lineages of the Absolutist State* (London).

  1988. *Passages from Antiquity to Feudalism* (London).

Anhalt, I. 1984. *Alternative Voices* (Toronto).

Araki, J. 1978. *The Ballad Drama of Medieval Japan* (Tokyo).

Armstrong, F. 1985. 'Finding Our Voices', in N. Jackowska (ed.), *Voices* (London).

Arnold, D. and Fortune, N. 1985. *The New Monteverdi Companion* (London).

Aristotle. *Politics*, in Barker (1987), pp. 171–82.

Atheneus. *Deipnosophistae*, in Barker (1987), pp. 258–303.

Augustine. *Enarrationes in Psalmos*, in McKinnon (1987), pp. 155–60.

Bailey, P. (ed.). 1986. *Music Hall: The Business of Pleasure* (Milton Keynes).

Baker, G. 1947. *This Singing Business* (London).

Baker, H. 1987. *Modernism and the Harlem Renaissance* (Chicago).

  1991. 'Hybridity, the Rap Race, and Pedagogy for the 1990s', *Black Music Research Journal* 2/2.

Baker, N. 1989. 'Concerning the Performance of Mozart's Concert Arias K294 and K528', *Performance Practice Review* 2/2, pp. 133–43.

Banfield, S. 1985. *Sensibility and English Song* (Cambridge).

Baraka, A. 1963. *Blues People: Negro Music in White America* (New York).

Barker, A. 1987. *Greek Musical Writings* (Cambridge).

Barthes, R. 1977a. 'Musica Practica', in Barthes (1993).

  1977b. 'The Grain of the Voice', in Barthes (1993).

  1984. *Mythologies* (London).

  1993. *Image Music Text* (London).

Baskerville, C. 1929. *The English Jig and Related Song Drama* (Chicago).

Batey, A. 1993. 'Bring me the Head of Charlton Heston: An Interview with Ice-T', *New Musical Express*, 13 March 1993, pp. 28–30.

Baym, N. 1988. 'The Rise of the Woman Author', in Elliott (1988).

Beare, W. 1950. *The Roman Stage* (London).

Beecher Stowe, H. 1981. *Uncle Tom's Cabin* (New York).

Berio, L. 1976. Sleeve notes to *A-Ronne* (Decca 425620–2).

Berlioz, H. 1862. *A travers chants* (Paris).

Bernard, J. 1992. 'Abroad, Rap Speaks Up', *New York Times*, 23 August 1992, pp. 1ff.

Bianconi, L. 1989. *Music in the Seventeenth Century* (Cambridge).

Bidgood, Z. 1980. 'The Significance of Thomas Ravenscroft', *Folk Music Journal* 1/4 , pp. 24–34.

Blacking, J. 1977. 'Towards an Anthropology of the Body', in Blacking (ed.), *The Anthropology of the Body* (London).

Bloomfield, J. (ed.). 1979. *Class, Hegemony and Party* (London).

Boethius. *De institutiones musicae*, in Strunk, vol. 1 (1981), pp. 79–86.

Bogatyrev, P. 1971. 'Costume as a Sign', in *The Functions of Folk Costume in Moravian Slovakia* (The Hague), pp. 80–5.

Bourdieu, P. 1977a. 'The Economics of Linguistic Exchanges', *Social Science Information* 16/6, pp. 645–68.

1977b. *Outline of a Theory of Practice* (Cambridge).

1982. *Ce que parler veut dire* (Paris).

1986. *Distinction* (London).

Bourdieu, P. and Passeron, J. 1990. *Reproduction in Education, Society and Culture* (London).

Bower, C. (trans.). 1989. *Fundamentals of Music* (New Haven).

Bowles, E. 1983. *La Pratique musicale au Moyen Age* (Paris).

Brackett, D. 1992. 'James Brown's "Superbad" and the Double-voiced Utterance', *Popular Music* 11/3, pp. 309–24.

Bramley, H. and Stainer, J. 1871. *Christmas Carols Old and New* (London).

Branscombe, P. 1980. 'Melodrama', in *The New Grove Dictionary of Music and Musicians*, vol. XII (London), pp. 116–18.

Bratton, J. 1986. *Music Hall: Performance and Style* (Milton Keynes).

Brooks, W. 1982. Sleeve notes to *Madrigals* (Wergo WER 60094).

Brown, H. M. 1978. 'Choral Music in the Renaissance', *Early Music* 6/2, pp. 164–9.

1984. *Embellishing Sixteenth Century Music* (Oxford).

1990. 'Pedantry or Liberation? A Sketch of the Historical Performance Movement', in Kenyon (1990), pp. 27–56.

Browning, R. 1988. 'Early Christianity', *New Left Review* 168, pp. 122–8.

Budden, J. 1980. 'Rubini', in *The New Grove Dictionary of Music and Musicians*, vol. XVI (London), pp. 295–6.

Burgin, J. 1973. *Teaching Singing* (New Jersey).

Burney, C. 1770/repr. 1969. *Music, Men and Manners* (London).

1776. *A General History of Music* (London).

1988. *Memoirs of Dr Charles Burney*, ed. Klima *et al.* (Nebraska).

Cage, J. 1969. *Notations* (New York).

Cairns, C. (ed.). 1969. *The Memoirs of Hector Berlioz* (London).

Cardew, C. (ed.). 1972. *Scratch Music* (London).

Caruso, E. and Tetrazzini, L. 1909/repr. 1975. *Caruso and Tetrazzini on the Art of Singing* (New York).

Castiglione, B. 1959. *The Book of the Courtier* (New York).

Cattin, G. 1984. *Music of the Middle Ages 1* (Cambridge).

Celetti, R. 1991. A *History of Bel Canto* (Oxford).

Chorley, H. 1862/repr. 1972. *Thirty Years' Musical Recollections* (London).

Clayson, A. 1993. 'Ringo Starr: the Country Connection', *Country Music* 24/4, pp. 39–41.

Coghlan, B. 1979. *Roy Hart Theatre* (Thoiras).

Cranach, M. von. 1979. *Human Ethology* (Cambridge).

Dahl, L. 1989. *Stormy Weather: The Music and Lives of a Century of Jazz Women* (New York).

Davis, M. (with Troupe, Q.) 1990. *Miles: The Autobiography* (London).

Davis, T. 1991. 'The Moral Sense of the Majorities: Indecency and Vigilance in Late-Victorian Music Halls', *Popular Music* 10/1, pp. 39–52.

Dibdin, C. 1800. *A Complete History of the English Stage* (London).

Dixon, W. (with Snowden, D). 1989. *I am the Blues* (London).

Dobson, E. 1968. *English Pronunciation 1500–1700* (Oxford).

Douglass, F. 1845/repr. 1990. *Narrative of the Life of Frederick Douglass, an American Slave* (New York).

Duey, P. 1980. *Bel Canto in its Golden Age* (New York).

Durant, A. 1984. *Conditions of Music* (London).

Dyer, J. 1978. 'Singing with Proper Refinement', *Early Music* 6/2, pp. 207–27.

  1980. 'A Thirteenth Century Choirmaster', *The Musical Quarterly* 66, pp. 83–111.

Eco, U. 1979. *A Theory of Semiotics* (Indiana).

Eibl-Eibesfeld, I. 1979. 'Ritual and Ritualisation from a Biological Perspective', in M. von Cranach (1979), pp. 3–55.

Ehrlich, C. 1988. *The Music Profession in Britain Since the Eighteenth Century* (Oxford).

Ekman, P. 1977. 'Biological and Cultural Contributions to Body and Facial Movement', in Blacking (1977), pp. 39–84.

Elam, K. 1980. *The Semiotics of Theatre and Drama* (London).

Elliott, E. (ed.). 1988. *Columbia Literary History of the United States* (New York).

Erikson, E. 1968. 'Self-assertion, Sex-role and Vocal Rasp', in Lomax (1968), pp. 204–10 (New Jersey).

Faulkner, K. (ed.). 1983. *Voice* (London).

Febvre, L. and Martin, H. 1984. *The Coming of the Book* (London).

Fellowes, E. 1948/repr. 1972 (2nd edn). *The English Madrigal Composers* (Oxford).

Fenlon, I. 1984. 'Monteverdi's Mantuan *Orfeo*', *Early Music* 12/2, pp. 163–72.

Fields, V. 1979. *Training the Singing Voice* (New York).

Firth, R. 1970. 'Postures and Gestures of Respect', in J. Pouillon and P. Maranda (eds.), *Exchanges et Communications* (The Hague), pp. 188–209.

Floyd, S. 1991. 'Ring Shout! Literary Studies, Historical Studies and Black Music Inquiry', *Black Music Research Journal* 11/2, pp. 265–87.

Forbes, E. 1980a. 'Tamberlik', in *The New Grove Dictionary of Music and Musicians*, vol. xviii, pp. 550–1.

1980b. 'Varesi', in *The New Grove Dictionary of Music and Musicians*, vol. xix, p. 534.

Foucault, M. 1977. *Discipline and Punish* (London).

Friedwald, W. 1989. Sleeve notes to *Radio Classics of the 50s* (cbs 434822).

1991. *Jazz Singing* (London).

Frith, S. 1979. *The Sociology of Rock* (London).

1982. 'The Sociology of Rock – Notes from Britain', in *Popular Music Perspectives* (Göteborg), pp. 142–54.

Frith, S. (ed.). 1989. 'Why do Songs have Words?', in *Music for Pleasure* (Cambridge), pp. 105–28.

Frith, S. and McRobbie, A. 1979. 'Rock and Sexuality', *Screen Education* 29, pp. 3–19.

Gal, H. (ed.). 1965. *Letters of the Great Composers* (London).

Gallo, F. 1985. *The Middle Ages II* (Cambridge).

Gammon, V. 1981. 'Babylonian Performances: The Rise and Suppression of Popular Church Music 1660–1870', in Yeo (1981), pp. 62–88.

1982. 'Song, Sex and Society in England 1600–1850', *Folk Music Journal* 4/3, pp. 208–45.

Garcia, M. 1841/1872. *A Complete Treatise on the Art of Singing* (L'Art du chant'), trans. Paschke 1975 and 1984 (New York).

Garon, P. 1979. *Blues and the Poetic Spirit* (New York).

Gatens, W. 1986. *Victorian Cathedral Music in Theory and Practice* (Cambridge).

Gates, H. L. 1988. *The Signifying Monkey* (Oxford).

Gattey, C. 1979. *Queens of Song* (London).

Giles, H. and Smith, P. 1979. 'Accommodation Theory: Optimal Levels of Convergence', in H. Giles and R. St Clair, *Language and Social Psychology* (Oxford).

Giles, P. 1982. *The Counter Tenor* (London).

Glover, S. 1835. *Scheme to Render Psalmody Congregational* (Norwich).

Golby, J. (ed.). 1986. *Culture and Society in Britain: a Source Book* (Oxford).

Goodman, B. and Kolodin, I. 1939. *The Kingdom of Swing* (New York).

Gordon, R. (trans.) 1976. *Anglo-Saxon Poetry* (London).

Gramsci, A. 1985. *Selections from Cultural Writings* (London).

1986. *Selections from Prison Notebooks* (London).

Gray, R. 1979. 'Bourgeois Hegemony in Victorian Britain', in Bloomfield (ed.) 1979, pp. 73–94.

Guido of Arezzo. 'Epistola de Ignoto Canto', in Strunk (1981), pp. 121–5.

Haar, J. 1986. *Italian Poetry and Music in the Renaissance* (Berkeley).

Hamm, C. 1983. *Yesterdays* (New York).

Hansen, C. 1960. 'Social Influences on Jazz Styles: Chicago 1929–30', *American Quarterly* 12, pp. 493–507.

Hatch, D. and Millward, S. 1987. *From Blues to Rock* (Manchester).

Haweis, H. 1871. *Music and Morals* (London).

Hay, D. 1964. *The Medieval Centuries* (London).

Heartz, D. 1980. 'Classical', in *The New Grove Dictionary of Music and Musicians*, vol. IV (London), pp. 44–50.

Hebdige, D. 1988 *Subculture and the Meaning of Style* (London).

Henderson, W. 1938. *The Art of Singing* (New York).

Hennion, A. 1983 'The Production of Success: An Anti-musicology of the Pop Song', *Popular Music* 3, pp. 159–93.

Heriot, A. 1975. *The Castrati in Opera* (London).

Heslam, D. (ed.). 1992. *NME Rock'n'Roll Years* (London).

Hewitt, R. 1983. 'Black through White: Hoagy Carmichael and the Cultural Reproduction of Racism', *Popular Music* 3, pp. 33–50.

Hitchcock, H. W. (ed.). 1970. *Le nuove musiche* (Madison).

Hoppin, R. 1978. *Medieval Music* (New York).

Howard, D. 1992. 'Quantifiable Aspects of Different Singing Styles: A Case Study', *Voice* 1, pp. 47–62.

Hucbald. *De harmonica institutione*, in Palisca (1979).

Hucke, H. 1980. 'Towards a New Historical View of Gregorian Chant', *Journal of the American Musicological Society* 33, pp. 437–67.

Hullah, J. 1842 repr. 1983. *Wilhelm's Method of Teaching Singing* (London/ Kilkenny).

Hyde, D. 1991. *New Found Voices: Women in Nineteenth-Century English Music* (Ash).

Irving, K. 1993. ' "I Wanna Lay my Hands on you": Building Equivalences through Rap', *Popular Music* 12/2.

Isidore of Seville. *Etymologiarum*, in Strunk (1981), pp. 93–100.

Jackson, J. 1933/repr. 1965. *White Spirituals in the Southern Uplands: The Story of the Fasola Folk, their Songs, Singing and 'Buckwheat' Notes* (Chapel Hill/New York).

Jakobson, R. 1960. 'Linguistics and Poetics', in Sebeok (1960), pp. 350–77.

Jerome. *Commentary on the Epistle of Paul to the Ephesians*, in Strunk (1981), pp. 71–2.

Joyce, J. 1981. *The Monodies of Sigismondo d'India* (Ann Arbor).

Katz, R. 1974. 'On "Nonsense" Syllables as Oral Group Notation', *Music Quarterly* (July 1974), pp. 187–94.

Kelly, M. 1826/repr. 1965. *Reminiscences* (London).

Kenyon, N. (ed.). 1990. *Authenticity and Early Music* (Oxford).

Kimbell, D. 1981. *Verdi in the Age of Italian Romanticism* (Cambridge).

Kirby, M. 1971. *Futurist Performance* (New York).

Klein, H. 1923. *An Essay on the Bel Canto* (Oxford).

Knighton, T. and Fallows, D. (eds.). 1992. *Companion to Medieval and Renaissance Music* (London).

Kochman, T. (ed.). 1972. *Rappin' and Stylin' Out: Communication in Urban Black America* (Urbana).

Kristeva, J. 1973. 'The Semiotic Activity', *Screen* 14/1–2.

Laing, D. 1985. *One Chord Wonders: Power and Meaning in Punk Rock* (Milton Keynes).

Laver, J. 1980. *The Phonetic Description of Voice Quality* (Cambridge).

Laver, J. and Trudgill, P. 1979. 'Phonetic and Linguistic Markers in Speech', in Scherer and Giles (1979), pp. 1–32.

Leonard, N. 1964. *Jazz and the White Americans* (Chicago).

Leppert, R. and Lipsitz, G. 1990. ' "Everybody's Lonesome for Somebody": Age, the Body and Experience in the Music of Hank Williams', *Popular Music* 9/3, pp. 259–74.

Leppert, R. and McClary, S. 1987. *Music and Society: The Politics of Composition, Performance and Reception* (Cambridge).

Ley, H. and Davies, W. (eds.). 1933 (15th impression 1966). *The Church Anthem Book* (Oxford).

Livingstone, F. 1973. 'Did the Australopithecines Sing?', *Current Anthropolgy* 14/1–2, pp. 25–9.

Lloyd, A. 1975. *Folksong in England* (London).

Lord, A. 1981. *The Singer of Tales* (Harvard).

Lomax, A. 1968. *Folksong Style and Culture* (New Jersey).

MacClintock, C. 1994. *Readings in the History of Music in Performance* (Milton Keynes).

MacDermott, K. 1948. *The Old Church Gallery Minstrels* (London).

Manen, L. 1987. *Bel Canto: The Teaching of the Classical Italian Song-Schools* (Oxford).

Maniates, M. 1979. *Mannerism in Italian Music and Culture* (Manchester).

Maróthy, J. 1974. *Music of the Bourgeois / Music of the Proletariat* (Budapest).

　1981. 'A Music of your Own', *Popular Music* 1, pp. 15–25.

Marx. K. 1971. *Critique of Political Economy* (London).

McClary, S. 1991. *Feminine Endings: Music, Gender and Sexuality* (Minnesota).

McKitterick, R. 1989. *The Carolingians and the Written Word* (Cambridge).

McKinnon, J. 1986. 'On the Question of Psalmody in the Ancient Synagogue', *Early Music History* 6, pp. 159–91.

　1987. *Music in Early Christian Literature* (Cambridge).

　1990. 'The Emergence of Gregorian Chant', in McKinnon (ed.), *Antiquity and the Middle Ages* (London).

Mellers, W. 1973. *Twilight of the Gods: The Beatles in Retrospect* (London).

Mezzrow, M. and Wolfe, B. 1946. *Really the Blues* (New York).

Middleton, R. 1972. *Pop Music and the Blues* (London).

　1985. 'Articulating Meaning/Re-constructing Musical History/ Locating the "Popular" ', *Popular Music* 5, pp. 5–43.

　1990. *Studying Popular Music* (Milton Keynes).

1991. 'Popular Music of the Lower Classes', in Temperley (1991), pp. 63–91.

Mitchell, T. (ed.). 1980. *Music and Civilisation* (London).

Monahan, B. 1978. *The Art of Singing* (New Jersey).

Monk, M. 1976. 'Notes on the Voice', *The Painted Bride Quarterly* 3/2 (Spring 1976).

Moore, A. 1993. *Rock: The Primary Text* (Milton Keynes).

Mount Edgcumbe, R. 1824, 4th edn 1834. *Musical Reminiscences, Containing an Account of the Italian Opera in England from 1773* (London).

Newman, E. 1961. *The Life of Richard Wagner* (New York).

O'Connor, P. 1986. 'Josephine', *The Observer*, 19. January 1986, pp. 20–9.

Odo of Cluny. *Enchiridion musices*, in Strunk (1981), pp. 103–16.

Ogren, J. 1992. *The Jazz Revolution* (Oxford).

Oliver, P. 1962. *Blues Fell this Morning* (London).

  1984. *Songsters and Saints* (Cambridge).

Page, C. 1987. *Voices and Instruments of the Middle Ages* (London).

  1991. *Summa Musice: A Thirteenth Century Manual for Singers* (Cambridge).

  1992. 'A Treatise on Musicians from ?c.1400: The *Tractatulus de differentiis et gradibus cantorum* by Arnulf de St Ghislain', *Journal of the American Musicological Society* 117, pp. 1–21.

  1993a. 'Johannes de Grocheio on Secular Music: A Corrected Text and a New Translation', *Plainsong and Medieval Music* 2/1, pp. 17–41.

  1993b. 'The English a cappella Renaissance', *Early Music* 21/3 pp. 452–71.

Palisca, C. (ed.). 1979. *Hucbald, Guido, and John on Music: Three Medieval Treatises* (New Haven).

Pardo, E. 1982. 'The Work of the Roy Hart Theatre', in *Project Voice: An Introduction* (Cardiff).

Parry, M. 1987. *The Making of Homeric Verse: The Collected Works of Milman Parry* (Oxford).

Pearsall, R. 1973. *Victorian Popular Music* (Newton Abbot).

Pennybacker, S. 1987. 'It was not what she said but the way in which she said it', in Bailey (1986), pp. 118–39.

Pestelli, G. 1987. *The Age of Mozart and Beethoven* (Cambridge).

Petrovic, R. 1965. 'The Oldest Notation of Folk Tunes in Jugoslavia', *Studia Musicologica* 7/1–4, pp. 109–14.

Phillipps, K. 1985. *Language and Class in Victorian England* (Oxford).

Pirotta, N. 1982. *Music and Theatre from Poliziano to Monteverdi* (Cambridge).

Plato. *Republic*, in Barker (1987), pp. 127–40.

  Ion, in Barker (1987), pp. 125–7.

Potter, J. 1992. 'Reconstructing Lost Voices', in Knighton and Fallows (1992), pp. 311–16.

  1994. 'The Singer, not the Song: Women Singers as Composer-poets', *Popular Music* 12/2, pp. 191–9.

Price, C. 1979. *Music in the Restoration Theatre* (Ann Arbor).

Pseudo-Aristotle. *Problems*, in McKinnon (1987), pp. 190–204.

Pseudo-Plutarch. *De musica*, in McKinnon (1987), pp. 205–49.

Quintilian. *Institutio oratoria*, trans. H. Butler (London, 1922).

Rainbow, B. 1982. *English Psalmody Prefaces* (Kilkenny).

Rankin, S. 1984. 'From Memory to Record: Musical Notations in Manuscripts from Exeter', *Anglo-Saxon England* 13, pp. 97–112.

Rees, D., Lazel, B. and Osborne, R. 1992. *40 Years of the NME Charts* (London).

Renwick, R. 1980. *English Folk Poetry* (London).

Reynolds, L. and Wilson, N. 1991. *Scribes and Scholars: A Guide to the Transmission of Greek and Latin Literature* (Oxford).

Richman, B. 1980. 'Did Human Speech Originate in Co-ordinated Vocal Music?', *Semiotica* 32/3–4, pp. 232–44.

Richter, H. 1978. *Dada: Art and Anti-Art* (London).

Rosselli, J. 1984. *The Opera Industry in Northern Italy from Cimarosa to Verdi* (Cambridge).

Routley, E. 1968. *The Musical Wesleys* (London).

Rushmore, R. 1984. *The Singing Voice* (New York).

Russell, D. 1987. *Popular Music in England 1840–1914* (Manchester).

Sachs, C. 1943. *The Rise of Music in the Ancient World* (New York).

Santley, C. 1893. *Student and Singer* (London).

Scherer. K. and Giles, H. (eds.). 1979. *Social Markers in Speech* (Cambridge).

Scholes, P. 1924. *Crotchets* (London).

Schuller, G. 1968. *Early Jazz* (Oxford).

    1989. *The Swing Era* (Oxford).

Scott, D. 1989. *The Singing Bourgeois* (Milton Keynes).

Scott, M. 1977. *The Record of Singing to 1914* (London).

Scotto di Carlo, N. 1973. 'Analyse sémiologique des gestes et mimiques des chanteurs d'opéra', *Semiotica* 9/4, pp. 289–317.

Seashore, C. (ed.). 1936a. 'The Vibrato', *University of Iowa Studies in the Psychology of Music*, vol. I.

    1936b. 'Psychology of the Vibrato in Voices and Instruments', *University of Iowa Studies in the Psychology of Music* vol. III.

Sebeok, T. (ed.). 1960. *Style in Language* (Cambridge, Mass.).

Shapiro, N. and Hentoff, N. 1992. *Hear me Talkin' to Ya* (New York).

Shephard, L. 1978. *The Broadside Ballad* (Wakefield).

Shepherd, J. 1987. 'Music and Male Hegemony', in Leppert and McClary (1987), pp. 151–72.

    1991. *Music as Social Text* (Cambridge).

Shepherd, J., Virden, P., Vulliamy, G. and Wishart, T. 1977. *Whose Music?* (London).

Singleton, C. (ed.). 1959. *The Book of the Courtier* (New York).

Smart, B. 1836. *Walker Remodelled: A New Critical Pronouncing Dictionary of the English Language* (London).

Smith, J. and Guttridge, L. 1960. *Jack Teagarden* (London).

Southern, E. 1979. 'Conversation with Billy Eckstine', *Black Perspectives in Music*, vol. 7 (pp. 182–98) and vol. 8 (pp. 54–64).

 1983. *Music of the Black Americans* (New York).

Spector, J. 1965. 'The Significance of Samaritan Neumes and Contemporary Practice', *Studia Musicologica* 7, pp. 141–53.

Stevens, J. 1979. *Music and Poetry in the Early Tudor Court* (Cambridge).

 1986. *Words and Music in the Middle Ages: Song, Narrative, Dance and Drama 1050–1350* (Cambridge).

Strunk, O. 1981. *Source Readings in Music History* (London).

Summerfield, P. 1981. 'The Effingham Arms and the Empire: Deliberate Selection in the Evolution of the Music Hall in London', in Yeo (1981), pp. 209–40.

Sundberg, J. 1977. 'The Acoustics of the Singing Voice', *Scientific American*, March 1977.

 1988. *The Science of the Singing Voice* (Dekalb).

Tagg, P. 1982. 'Analysing Popular Music: Theory, Method, Practice', *Popular Music* 2, pp. 37–67.

 1989 'Open Letter', *Popular Music* 8/3, pp. 285–98.

Taylor, R. 1978. *Art an Enemy of the People* (Hassocks).

Taylor, J. and Laing, D. 1979. 'Disco-Pleasure-Discourse: on 'Rock and Sexuality', *Screen Education* 31, pp. 43–8.

Temperley, N. 1983. *The Music of the English Parish Church* (Cambridge).

 1991. The Romantic Age (The Blackwell History of Music in Britain) (Oxford).

Thompson, C. 1975. *Bing – the Authorised Biography* (London).

Thompson, J. 1984. *Studies in the Theory of Ideology* (Cambridge).

Tomlinson, G. 1986. Introduction to *Italian Secular Song 1606–1636* (New York).

Toop, D. 1991. *Rap Attack 2* (London).

 1993. 'Looking for a Reason in Rhyme' *The Times*, 12 March 1993, p. 39.

Tosi, P. 1743 repr. 1967. *Observations on the Florid Song* (London).

Treitler, L. 1974. 'Homer and Gregory: The Transmission of Epic Poetry and Plainchant', *Musical Quarterly* 60, pp. 333–71.

 1981. 'Oral, Written and Literate Process', *Speculum* 56, pp. 471–91.

 1984. 'Reading and Singing: On the Genesis of Occidental Music-writing', *Early Music History* 4, pp. 135–208.

Trudgill, P. 1984. *On Dialect: Social and Geographical Perspectives* (Cambridge).

Turner, J. 1833/repr. 1983. *Manual of Instruction in Vocal Music* (London/Kilkenny).

Uberti, L. 1981. 'Vocal Techniques in Italy in the Second Half of the Sixteenth Century', *Early Music* 9/4, pp. 486–95.

Varga, B. 1985. *Berio: Two Interviews* (London).

Waddell, H. 1968. *The Wandering Scholars* (London).

Wagner, P. 1911–21. *Einführung in die gregorischen Melodien* (Leipzig).

Walter White, E. 1983a. *A History of English Opera* (London).

1983b. *A Register of First Performances of English Opera* (London).

Watzlawick, P., Beavin, J. and Jackson, D. 1967. *Pragmatics of Human Communication* (New York).

Weber, W. 1975. *Music and the Middle Class* (London).

1992. *The Rise of Musical Classics in Eighteenth Century England* (Oxford).

Wellesz, E. (ed.). 1957. *Ancient and Oriental Music* (London).

1971. *Arnold Schoenberg, the Formative Years* (London).

Wells, J. 1982. *Accents of English* (Cambridge, 1982).

West, M. 1992. *Ancient Greek Music* (Oxford).

1994. 'The Babylonian Musical Notation and the Hurrian Mode Texts', *Music and Letters* 75/2, pp. 167–79.

Wheeler, E. 1992. 'Most of my Heroes don't appear on no Stamps': The Dialogics of Rap Music', *Black Music Research Journal* 2/2.

White, C. 1984. Sleeve notes to *Look out! . . . it's Louis Jordan and the Tympany Five* (Charly CRB 1048).

White, E. 1927. *The Voice Beautiful* (London).

1938. *Sinus Tone Production* (London).

Wicks, S. 1989. 'A Belated Salute to the Old Way of Snaking the Voice on its (ca) 345th Birthday', *Popular Music* 8/1, pp. 59–96.

Wishart, T. 1980. *Book of Lost Voices* (York).

1985. *On Sonic Art* (York).

Worsthorne, S. 1968. *Venetian Opera in the Seventeenth Century* (Oxford).

Wright, C. 1990. *Music and Ceremony at Notre Dame of Paris 500–1550* (Cambridge).

Wright, R. 1937 repr. 1989. *Black Boy* (New York).

Wroth, W. 1896 repr. 1979. *The London Pleasure Gardens of the Eighteenth Century* (London).

Wulstan, D. 1985. *Tudor Music* (London).

Wyman, B. 1987. 'Mick Jagger', *Musician* (February 1987), pp. 13–15.

Yeo, E. and S. (eds.). 1981. *Popular Culture and Class Conflict* (Brighton).

Young, F. 1911. *More Mastersingers* (London).

Index